AN INTRODUCTION TO KASENA SOCIETY AND CULTURE THROUGH THEIR PROVERBS

A. K. Awedoba

University Press of America,® Inc.
Lanham • New York • Oxford

Copyright 2000 by
University Press of America,® Inc.
4720 Boston Way
Lanham, Maryland 20706

12 Hid's Copse Rd.
Cumnor Hill, Oxford OX2 9JJ

Library of Congress Cataloging-in-Publication Data

Awedoba, A. K.
An introduction to Kasena society and culture through their proverbs /
A. K. Awedoba.
p.   cm.
.Includes bibliographical references and index.
1.   Proverbs, Kasem. 2. Kasem (African people)—Social life
and customs.   I. Title.
PN6519.K29 A95   1999   398.9'9635—dc21   99-052244 CIP

ISBN 0-7618-1542-2 (cloth: alk. ppr.)

♾™ The paper used in this publication meets the minimum
requirements of American National Standard for Information
Sciences—Permanence of Paper for Printed Library Materials,
ANSI Z39.48—1984

CONTENTS

ACKNOWLEDGEMENTS

My thanks go to the Kasena people whose collective wisdom is enshrined in these pages. This is not a creative work. My task has been to note proverb utterances and their usage, to document and to apply anthropological insight to the interpretation of these wise sayings.

Secondly, I wish to acknowledge the contribution of several generations of students of the School of Ghana Languages (1973-1991) which used to be located at Ajumako, the Kasem unit of the Dept of Ghanaian languages at the University College of Education of Winneba and the series of tutors who have generously sacrificed their time to teach in these institutions. I wish to name here Messrs Atipaga, Ayiwah, Danti and Logoje who have been at one time or the other students and/ or tutors of the Kasem language. As I revised this work prior to carrying out the typesetting, I have benefitted from the able assistance Mr Alexis Danti who has advised on the interpretation of some of the convoluted proverbs. I appreciate the interest of all the above gentlemen and ladies in the Kasem language and I am grateful for the opportunity they have given me over the years to be the external examiner of the subject.

My acknowledgments will not be complete without the mention of the late Mr John Cosore whose tragic death is a great loss to the Kasena people and lovers of Ghanaian languages. I record with profound gratitude the assistance of the late John Cosore who was himself interested in Kasena proverbs and had made available to me several years ago a modest private collection recorded by him from Kasena communities in Southern Burkina Faso. I regret that I have not been able to include most of those proverbs a resolution to whose interpretation is still pending.

I am especially grateful to Prof Mary Esther Dakubu of the Institute of African Studies for her continued interest in my academic development. At a time when colleagues are too busy to be of assistance, Prof Dakubu not only consented to help, she actually created time from her very busy schedule to assist with the proofreading. Many were the typographical, grammatical and other errors from which this manuscript was rescued through her advice.

Finally I should be ungrateful if I failed to record my gratitude to the Takemi Program in International Health of the Harvard School of Public Health where I was one of several Takemi fellows in International Health for the 1997-98 year. While I struggled to make sense of my data on onchocerciasis and to complete a book on the subject, I varied by routine my the occasional trip to the Tozzer Library at the Cambridge campus of Harvard where I researched further on proverb scholarship.

In conclusion, I thank my Kasena friends (too many to be mentioned here) who have been my informants, albeit sometimes unknowingly.

PREFACE

The Kasena are an ethnic group found in both Upper Eastern Ghana and Burkina Faso. Their language is one of the ten or so languages sponsored by the Ghana government. It has been one of the officially sponsored languages since the 1950s. It has been a school subject, taught formerly in the elementary schools in the Kasena-Nankani District. Now it is taught not only in some of the junior and senior secondary schools in the Upper-East Region, it is taken up to the first degree level in some of the Ghanaian universities. Ghanaian language education at all levels comprises a number of sub-disciplines and proverb scholarship is an important feature.

To my knowledge the traditional oral literature of the peoples of the Upper East Region of Ghana, unlike their languages, is still to receive the scholarly attention it deserves. In the case of the Kasena-Nankana people, very little of their rich literature has been studied systematically. The same, in fact, seems to be true of their cultures, since the pioneer work of Fortes on Tallensi social structure in the colonial era . Though Fortes' work will remain anthropological classics for the Voltaic cultural zone, it has to be accepted that not only has society changed tremendously since the 1930s when Fortes engaged in research there, the societies of the areas similar as they may seem, have no uniform culture. There is thus the pressing need to study the institutions and practices of people like the Kasena and to document their culture for the present as well as for the future generations. What the Kasena stand in danger of losing most is their literature, given the deleterious effects of the inroads that the electronic media (radio and TV) make into the society and its projection of non-Kasena-Nankana norms and outlooks.

The aim of this book is to analyse and interpret the traditional Kasena proverb and sayings so as to shed light on their culture and society. That the African proverb has this potential is strongly suggested by the repeated use of proverbs by researchers and students of African culture to illustrate and shed light on the many facets of African life. For societies lacking written documentary records, the proverb serves as valuable evidence. Societies like the Kasena consider their proverbs as statements that are backed by the force of tradition and the authority of their ancestors whose wisdom they are believed to enshrine. The Proverb is thus a worthy subject to engage the attention of the scholar interested in the insider perspective on a society and its culture.

The objective of the book is achieved by a method of analysis that considers the literal meanings of the proverb statements and other sayings as well as their deeper and underlying meanings and significance. The position taken here is that for most proverbs and even more so the other sayings a background knowledge of the society that fashions these statements is essential to their appreciation. Statements are given surface interpretations which show their relevance in the context of the wider cultural background. Then the underlying meanings of these statements are discussed and finally, their potential applications.

The book is organised as follows. Before the main chapters of the book, there is introductory information on Kasem orthography to assist the reader gain an appreciation of the conventions used in the writing of Kasem generally and in particular the Kasem texts in this book.

Chapter One: An introduction. It gives an overview of Kasena history and oral traditions, the geographical and physical features of the area and comments on their language and its dialects, and their social structure (on kinship, marriage and affinity, religious beliefs, the traditional economy, and political institutions).

Chapter Two examines the etymology of terms, the meanings of the Kasena proverb for the Kasena, its place in their society and culture. The linguistic structure and literary features of the proverb and the sayings are described and discussed.

Chapter Three presents 267 proverb texts which are introduced in the form in which they are normally cited followed by translations into English and a commentary on symbols and their imagery. Chapter Four discusses a number of sayings (*senseiri*) collected in the Navrongo chiefdom.

LIST OF ABBREVIATIONS

/../	Markers of phrase boundary in sentence analysis or Phonemic representation of a word
//..//	Markers of clause boundary in sentence analysis
[..]	Phonetic representation
[..]	In grammatical analysis this represents rankshifting of a higher or comparable grammatical unit or embedding in the structure of a lower or comparable unit
::	Clauselet boundary in a serial sentence structure
A	Adjunct element in clause analysis
C	Complement or Object element in clause analysis
P	Predicator (verb)
S	Subject element in clause analysis
V	Verb element in clause analysis
∝-	Minor sentence, one without a verb
∝!	Imperative sentence
det	Determiner
Ex	Example
lit	Literal or literally
no.	Journal Number
pl	Place
pp	Pages

vol	Volume in which an article is found
#	Number of an item
Unpubl	Unpublished manuscript
ed.	editor
eds	Editors
publ	Publications
O.U.P	Oxford University Press
Inst of Ed	Institute of Education
Univ Coll	University College
IAI	International African Institute
mss	Manuscript
Diss	Dissertation
Amer Anthr	American Anthropology
BGL	Bureau of Ghana Languages

Remarks on Kasem Orthography And Writing

The Kasem Alphabet

Since the Kasem language began to be written in the first decade of the twentieth century various groups of writers and interest groups have represented Kasem utterances differently. These representations have unfortunately exhibited many inconsistencies with the result that spellings for the same word can at times vary within the same document and sometimes even in the same page. The writers have themselves been aware of these problems. A committee set up by the Bureau of Ghana Languages was given the opportunity to meet and deliberate on these differences and the inconsistencies in spellings and come up with suggestions for the writing of the language. Its deliberations and the set of rules that were agreed and subsequently endorsed by the Kasem Language Committee have been the basis for the orthographic conventions used in this publication. The suggestions are being outlined below for the benefit of the user of this book, especially as the Bureau of Ghana Languages has still to publish the set of rules approved for the writing of the language.

Consonant Symbols: b, ch, d, f, g, j, k, l, m, n, (ɲ)ny, ŋ, p, r, s, t, v, w, y, z, (h) (twenty-one)

Vowel Symbols: a, e, i, o, u, ɔ, ɛ, (seven)

Note 1. Symbols like the following which were at one time in use are no longer accepted: "ng", "dʒ", "tʃ", "ɣ", "gh"

Note 2. Where necessary, any of the consonant symbols except "r" may form digraphs with "w". Thus it will be possible to have "bw", "chw", "dw", "gw", "jw", "kw", "lw", "nw" "ŋw" "sw", "tw", "vw", "yw", "zw", "fw", "nyw", "mw", "pw".

Kasem orthography requires these digraphs if its words are to be represented in the least ambiguous manner possible.

Representation of Vowel Sounds

Whereas Kasem uses only 7 vowel symbols, the language has at least TEN (10) vowel sounds. We cannot therefore hope to achieve a one-to-one representation between distinct vowel sounds (phonemes) and vowel orthographic symbols. For this reason accommodations are called for. Note that Kasem is not alone in this regard. Most languages including the Akan languages have had to make the necessary adjustments. These are in many respects similar to the adjustments that we have sought to introduce in this document for vowel representations.

1. /a/ is represented by   "a" as in **ba** "neck", **da** "to follow", **pa** "to give"
2. /ɛ/ by   "ɛ" as in **bɛ** "bangles", **dɛ** "day" **pɛ** "chief".
3. /i/ by   "i" as in **bi** "hundred", **di** "to eat", **li** "to cover".
4. /u/ by   "u" as in **bu** "child", **du** "to sow" **lu** "to dip into"
5. /ɔ/ by   "ɔ" as in t**ɔ** "which", d**ɔ** "which", l**ɔ** "to break"

These representations are straight forward and no difficulty is envisaged in the writing of the vowel sounds in question. In addition, the following vowel sound representations are adopted in line with the approved New Orthography.

6. /ɪ/ to be represented by "e" as in **be** " to mature, "**de**" to drop", **pe** "yam", **yere** "name", **tete** "night", **teene** "towns".

Note that this vowel is not the same as /i/. As a matter of fact, /ɪ/ and /i/ contrast in some respects as in the words [bi], spelt as **bi**, ' to rejuvenate' and [bɪ] 'to ripen, to mature' as spelt above.

7. /ʊ/ to be represented by "o" as in **do** "to distill", **bobo** "to start", **lo** "to give birth", **to** "corpse", **tooro** "honey", **go** "to kill"

Now that we have exhausted the vowel orthographic symbols by using all the seven symbols a decision had to be taken on what to do about the remaining vowel sounds in Kasem: These are /e/, /o/, and /ɜ/ or /ə/. It is here that accommodations are called for if the same spelt is not to represent several words. This happens a lot of the time in the previous conventions that had hitherto been in use. Awedoba's study of the development of Kasem orthographic conventions illustrate this.

8. /e/ should be represented by "ei", as in the following: **bei** "beams" **pei** "sheep", **dwei** "to prepare a fire", **lei** "songs" or "greetings - thanks", **yei** "to know".

Note that what we are suggesting here does not amount to an

innovation: we have found this vowel sound to be so represented in some writings including B.G.L. texts and GILLBT books and it is now suggested that this be adopted as the accepted representation of /e/ in all cases. We do not wish to introduce complications and ambiguity by writing the sound /e/ as "e" since this vowel symbol now stands for sound /ɪ/.

9. /o/ is represented by "wo" as in **bwo** "to hawk goods", **dwo** "when", **lwo** "to pour", **swo** "to marry", **ywo** "here", **chwo** "to be mad".

Note that the word /ko/ "father" has always been spelt as **kwo** in Kasem. Now we are suggesting that in all other words where the /o/ sound occurs it should be spelt as "wo" unless of course there are two of such identical sounds in the same word. Where this is the case only the first occurrence of the /o/ sound will be written as "wo".

10. /ɜ/ or [ə] should be represented as follows:
i) when it occurs in single syllable words with CV shape write it as "ei" i.e. /bɜ/ as **bei** "to whip", /lɜ/ as **lei** "to hang", /tɜ/ as **tei** "to eat **gole** without sauce".

You will observe that words like these are few in the language. Therefore the fact that the vowels /ə/ and /e/ and now being represented by the same orthographic symbol does not cause too much harm to the writing of the language.

ii) when /ɜ/ occurs in monosyllable (one syllable) words in which the consonant is labialised, write it as "oa", Thus /kwɜ/ will be spelt as **kwoa** "fathers", /swɜ/ "guinea chicks" as **swoa** /dwɜ/ "soup" as **"dwoa"**, /ywɜ/ "wooden pillars" as **ywoa**, /twɜ/ "fruits of baobab" as **twoa** etc.

iii) when /ɜ/ occurs in the initial syllable of a two syllable word write it as "ei" as in /kɜli/ "cheek", /yɜli/ "tooth", /tɜri/ "pig", /bɜri/ "to faint" etc. Write these words as **keili**, **yeili**, **teiri**, **beiri**, respectively.

iv) when /ɜ/ occurs in the final syllable of a word containing two or more syllables write it as "a". Thus /kɜlɜ/ "cheeks" /bɜllɜ/ will be written as **keila** (cheeks) and **beilla** (Mossiman) respectively.

CHAPTER ONE

KASENA AND THEIR SOCIETY

Introduction:

As many researchers on the proverb have had reason to remark proverbs are not coined in a vacuum but derived from the culture of the society in which they are current. It behoves therefore that a discussion like this should begin by an outline discussion of the Kasena as a people, their country, the language and the social institutions. This is particularly necessary in view of the fact that although the Kasem language has received some scholarly attention their society and its institutions and social structures have not benefitted to the same extent. This is not to belittle the work of German and French scholars such as Zwernemann (1964) and (1990) on divinatory processes and ritual fertility respectively, Dittmer (1961) on sacred chieftaincy among the Kasena, Liberski(1984) on time and the traditional Kasena calendar, Liberski (1991) on the cult of the earth among the Kasena, Liberski (1994) and Liberski-Bagnoud (1996) on funerary rituals and practices of the Kasena of Burkina Faso. Many of these accounts have been in French and German publications and not easily accessible to English speaking students. In English we have the recent work of Alison Howell (1994) which gives an account of Kasena history and their social and religious institutions dwelling at considerable length on their exposure to the influence of Christianity.

Kasena Country

Since proverbs are social and cultural artifacts which cannot be fully understood without taking into consideration their societal and cultural backgrounds we need to know about the Kasena and their society. A few remarks about the Kasena and their society are provided here by way of introduction. Proverbs are not of course peculiar in this respect. What is true for proverbs is equally true for other oral or verbal genres.

The Kasena people are found straddling the international boundary in both Ghana and Burkina Faso. Though they call themselves by the ethnonym, Kasena, which seems not to have any etymological meaning to my knowledge, their neighbours call them by several sobriquets such as yulsi (used by the Frafra speaking people), Awuna (which means, "I say"), Achilong (My friend) etc. Their country falls within the Sudan savannah vegetation zone. This is a grassland interspersed with short trees such the acacias (acacia albida is very common), the gigantic baobab, shea nut trees to mention some of the popular woody plants.

The rainfall is moderate, with an annual average of about 48 inches. Much of this falls in the short wet season which lasts from about May to October with a peak in August. The early part of the dry season, November to February is cool due to the influence of the dry dusty Harmattan wind that blows from the Sahara at this time of year however, the latter part of the dry season is characterised by high diurnal temperatures which can reach over 100° Fahrenheit in the shade in March April. Water is critical at this time of year. This is mitigated by the provision of potable water and water from boreholes. The construction of small earth dam since the colonial days has alleviated the situation in some parts. Today the construction of large dams like the Tono Irrigation Scheme makes it possible to grow food and cash crops in the dry seasons well.

Who are the Kasena?

The Kasena are a collection of people speaking Kasem, a Gur language of the Grusi sub-branch, and also sometimes Nankani, another Gur language belonging to the Oti-Volta sub-branch. They live in savanna chiefdoms which in former times maintained some form of rivalry between themselves occasionally resulting in armed conflict. This seemed to have been the case at least at the time of colonial penetration in the beginning of the 20th Century. In the southern parts of Kasenaland Nankani and Kasena identities seem to merge as personal names there illustrate. This is true for the chiefdom of Navrongo, in particular. There a person may have a Nankana name but speak Kasem as first language. The reverse is equally true. A number of people are in fact bilingual in these languages in the southern parts of Kasenaland or rather Kasena-Nankanaland.

Zwernemann (1963:191) distinguishes three subgroups of Kasena: the western (kasəm occidental exemplified by Koumbili in Burkina Faso), eastern (kasəm oriental exemplified by Tiebele and Kampala in Burkina Faso) and southern Kasena (kasəm meridional exemplified by Navrongo), a distinction that goes back to Tauxier (1912) who divided the Kasena in the French possessions into "Fra" and "Boura". Zwernemann takes the main Pô-Ouagadougou road to be the dividing line between the eastern and western sub-groups while the Ghanaian Kasena are the southern group. These distinctions do not appear to be based on any single criterion.

Kasena have as their neighbours the Frafra (Gurene) speaking peoples whose territories lie to the east and south, the Bulsa who are to be found to the southwest, then the Sisala to the west and the Fra-Kasena who speak a dialect of Kasem are sandwiched between Sisala and Kasena proper. Their territories extend beyond the international boundary into Burkina Faso. To the north are Kasena related peoples like the Nuna or Nounouma and Lyele speakers of Burkina Faso, as well as others like the Moshie and the Kaparsi whose languages differ from Kasem.

Kasena and, to a large extent the Nankana, exhibit a more or less uniform culture which is enshrined in their institutions. Although there is no single legend that suggests that these people had a common origin they have nevertheless similar legends explaining how they came to be where they are today. They never saw themselves as one people sprung from a common apical ancestor as other African peoples like the Tiv of Nigeria (see Bohannan 1970) or the Somalis of Somalia (Lewis 1975) did. The views of colonial authorities like Eyre-Smith (1933) which suggest that the Kasena once lived in Kasena near Zamfara can only be taken as baseless conjecture. In the absence of other evidence, it would be misguided to depend on place names found on ancient maps alone to arrive at a people's source of origin. This is not to say that linguistic evidence has no place in the historical studies.

Groups of Kasena sometimes identify themselves by different ethnonyms such as Awuna, Achilon, Jogobu, etc. It is customary for them, when talking to others, to refer to themselves as Grunshie when they find themselves outside the Kasena homeland but they do not use such a designation when talking about themselves as an ethnic group in their own language. Outside Kasenaland, they are generally known as Grunshie but this is a term with negative connotations. The Frafra call them Yulsi, a term that is related to the dialect term yula mentioned and exemplified in Koelle's (1854) **Polyglotta Africana** and suspected by Zwernemann (1963) to be Kàsəm occidental. Kasena call their country *kaseɲo*, their language and culture is *kasene* or *Kasem* and the people are *Kasena* to themselves. The variety of legends that Kasena clans recount usually trace their origins to diffusion centres located further north in what is today Burkina Faso. The hunter features prominently in these legends. He is depicted as having quarrelled with his siblings who either did not respect his rights to personal property, such as his dog, or to the chiefship of his community, which he should have succeeded to. Rather than engage his kin in internecine war he chose to leave home. In his wanderings he eventually arrived at the homes of people who by all accounts were troglodytes living in subterranean homes. He was welcomed as he came with good news of slain game. He taught the locals to build houses above the ground and more importantly he introduced chiefship to these people who had hitherto no knowledge of that institution. He thus became their first chief, acknowledged priest of the *kwara* or chieftaincy shrine and was respected as such especially as his *kwara* was projected as a fetish shrine that could bring prosperity to the local community.

What languages the migrants and the autochthonous people spoke on first contact is not always clearly defined. In the case of the chiefdom of Navrongo, the migrants who hailed from Zeko in present day Burkina Faso spoke Nankani. Whether the autochthonous people spoke Kasem or Nankani is not clear. One of these immigrants from further north is acknowledged as the founder of Navrongo in legends collected by St John Parsons (1956)[1]. The list of earthpriests collected from Telania, a section of Navrongo which is regarded as autochthonous features both Kasena names as well as some Nankani sounding names. Today these people speak Kasem. Pendaa, lying to the northwest of Paga, which is another settlement believed to have predated the coming of the migrants, has been Kasem-speaking for as long as anybody can remember but Biu lying several miles south of Navrongo town, another autochthonous division is predominantly Nankani-speaking.

The Social Structure in Outline:

Kinship is the bedrock, so to speak of the society and this is reflected in the subject matter of Kasena proverbs. The social structure of the Kasena-Nankana people is based on a patrilineal mode of reckoning descent. Right to hold traditional office, where this is application, inheritance and community membership rights are all determined by filiation ties traced through the father.

The lineage comprises a number of agnatic kin who trace their descent to a common apical ancestor. It constitutes a residential unit within the clan-settlement which is an association of agnatic lineages and attached or accessory lineages occupying a parish. Lineage headship is determined by seniority in age and generation with the latter criteria taking precedence. Ultimo-geniture (succession by the most junior son), though an interim measure obtains and lasts till the celebration of the final funeral rites of the previous incumbent. A Kasena lineage is a ritual congregation which occasionally meets to make sacrifice to the lineage ancestors. The headship of the clan-settlement is usually vested in one of the 'authentic' lineages tracing direct descent to the apical ancestors or founders of the groups. Clan-settlements bear a name which may combine a personal name (often the name of its founder or the apical ancestor of the core lineage) and suffix -nia which can be translated as "people of" or -bia, "children of". Examples are Korania, Nogesenia, and Yibanabia. Clan-settlements themselves maintain clanship ties with other clans in the chiefdom. These are described in the idiom of siblingship and a joking tie may obtain between such clan-settlements. A chiefdom is an association of clan-settlements.

Kinship (nubiu) traceable bilaterally is acknowledged where the evidence exists but is not emphasised while maternal connections remain even today important in the fabrication of personal ties that cross-cut patrilineal jural links. Within a clan-settlement individuals whose mothers come from a common village or clan-settlement regard each other as kin and are expected to lend each other support in times of need. Funeral occasions provide a context for the acknowledgement and demonstration of such ties among village mates. The bereaved person expects to receive from his nubia within his clan-settlement material assistance to support the performance of the final funeral rites.

True nubia (literally, mother's children among the Kasena or mabiisi among the Nankani-speaking segments) are matrilineal kin, individuals whose mothers are uterine sisters. Such kin though they may not be agnates or live in the same clan-settlement are believed to share the same witchcraft propensities and capabilities. When one person from the nubia group is accused the rest by implication stand accused. Thus Kasena practice treats individuals who are half-siblings on the paternal side but share a common maternal grandmother as full siblings. Sororal polygyny is practiced, though less common in contemporary times due to the reluctance of young girls to accept older men. If my mother brought over her brother's daughter as a maid helper and latter decided to marry her to my father, her children would be counted as my full siblings.

Complementary filiation ties are an important asset to individuals and through them privileges and resources can be accessed. Referring to the importance of the mother's people, Zwernemann (1990) remarks as follows: "Everybody receives efficient support from his mother's family and lineage. In case of problems children and young people often address their mother's brother, who will help them." It is for this reason that Kasena have a saying that "one does not use the left hand to point to the mother's village" (*Nɔɔno ba mae jagwia o bere o nabɔŋɔ*). We find a similar injunction against the use of the left hand to point to the father's village among the Akan who are matrilineal. Witchcraft is however believed to be transmitted matrilineally among the Kasena.

Marriage

Marriage is an exogamous union between two persons from different clans. There should not be any demonstrable kinship relationship between the couple prior to the birth of their children and where there is a kinship tie it can only be a very remote one, if the marriage is to receive any encouragement and some recognition. Paradoxically, Kasena have a saying that "you marry a kin to ensure that she will serve your immediate needs, food wise" (*N swo n nakɔ se o ke dwoa n kabeila ne*). Marriage between patrilineal kin, no matter the distance, is absolutely forbidden. The mother's patrilineage are also forbidden to a person for marriage purposes. Affines, strictly, are not forbidden although taking an agnate's in-law's wife brings about bad feelings between lineages and can result in the withdrawal of the agnate's wife. Sororal polygyny is practised as it is not forbidden for female siblings to be married to the same man; even a form of the sororate occurs; this is the practice whereby a dead woman's junior sister is given in marriage to a widower to serve as a replacement for his deceased wife. It is not common these days.

Women on marriage leave their natal home settlements for those of their husbands, where they are expected to live for the rest of their lives. As compensation for lost of a married daughter's contributions (in productive and reproductive domains) to the viability and prosperity of her natal lineage, bridewealth is received which enables her male relatives to settle bridewealth obligations. Marriage does not however alienate the daughter as far as her lineage is concerned.

A man may take as many wives as he is capable but in reality only chiefs and the wealthy can afford several wives. The high divorce rate, especially at the initial stages of marriage life when the marriage has not fully concretised, appears to furnish a justification for men who wish to have several wives. A fair number of wives do not remain with their husbands for life. The period between the day the bride was taken home and the day the formal marriage rites of *gwoŋna* are performed is to all intents and purposes a period of trial marriage since the bride is technically at liberty to return to her family and remarry. In real life the situation is more complicated than that as the perspectives of the various players have to be taken into consideration.

The dividing line between divorce and separation is however hard to establish, especially if the couple have lived together for several years and children have been born to them[2]. We could say that a former husband and his lineage retain an interest in an estranged wife for life. So longer as she has had children by her estranged husband the latter and his lineage continue to hope that she would return to them some day, perhaps in her old age.

Technically, from the point of view of the husband's lineage and clan-settlement, marriage to a woman is acknowledged once the woman has been brought home and the most basic of marriage rites, *wula*, the ululation that announces marriage, has been made by proclamation performed by the women of the household. From the day of the ululation henceforth nobody from the groom's village or any of the villages allied to it by clanship and extra-clanship ties may court or marry such a woman if she left her husband. However, without the performance of *gwoŋna* her family can give her hand out in marriage to another suitor. There have in fact been cases where a woman lived for a number of years with her husband but on her death, her family had claimed her mortal remains on the grounds that the *gwoŋna* rites had not been performed by her husband.

Patrilineal norms tie a person to his father's descent group and his clan-settlement. However, marriage enables him or her to establish affinal ties with others who fall outside the patrilineal group. The wife's father's village and lineage or the daughter's husband's village and lineage are important in a person's life. Social and ritual exchanges bind affines.

Political Structure:

Proverbs made repeated reference to the political structure, to chiefs and elders. These references suggest the ideal conceptualisation of socio-political life of the Kasena.

Societies like those exemplified by the Kasena were not acephalous in the exact sense (i.e. lacking a political or administrative head), although they may not have exhibited the centralising features commonly associated with statal governmental systems by Fortes and Evans-Pritchard (1940). Kasena have recognised chiefs since time immemorial. This is evidenced by the existence of an indigenous term for chief, *pɛ* or *peɔ* and *paare*, chieftaincy. These are not words that can be considered as loans from neighbouring languages spoken by those groups known to have had chiefship institutions and to have attempted in the past to colonise the acephalous peoples in their hinterlands, such as the Mamprusi, Moshi and the Dagomba. The Kasem term for chief bears no resemblances whatsoever with terms like *naaba* (Frafra or Gurenne) *na* or *naa* (Mamprusi or Dagomba), and *nab* (Buli and Kusaal) which are common in Oti-Volta languages and this is in spite of the fact that Kasem has many words that it may have borrowed from neighbouring languages. However, if there was one person whose authority was widely acknowledged, that was the chief.

These remarks are made against the background of traditions indicating that chieftaincy in the southern Kasena zone, at least, was introduced by immigrants who came from population centres where Nankani, a Moore-Dagbani or Oti-Volta language, was spoken. Though the evidence of the foreign origins of chiefship in Navrongo, Paga, Chiana, Kayoro etc is overwhelming the institution was not unknown and it may have undergone changes since it was institutionalised there. In the case of Paga, their chieftaincy was introduced, according to the legends of Nave, the hunter, from Kampala in northern Kasenaland which is today in Po province of southern Burkina Faso.

The chief's powers were however, very limited until colonial times. He was perceived more as a ritual specialist or priest figure who sacrificed to the *kwara* shrine on behalf of the community than as a law giver, judge or ruler. So important was his duty it was thought that the community's existence would be threatened if the chief did not perform his sacerdotal duties. The chief was the only functionary whose ritual jurisdiction extended over a number of clan-settlements in a named parish which evolved into a chiefdom. That position was in no way due to conquest. Kasena traditions, which portray chieftaincy as an institution brought in by migrants, insist that the acceptance of that institution was based on consent and a realisation that the community stood to gain by incorporation of the chiefly institution in the politico-religious structure.

Kasena chiefs have traditionally been pacific, unlike their Mamprusi-Dagomba-Moshi counterparts. They maintained no armies or even bodyguards except for their reliance, like any other Kasena patriarch, on the support of their dependent kin. They are ritually forbidden to exercise personal violence and although Navrongo and Paga have gone down in history as having fought each other, it seemed that kin acted as the means for mobilisation.

The chief did not extort a surplus from his subjects, and it seemed he depended on his own resources to met ritual requirements that entailed expenditures. He was however, assisted by his people to cultivate his farms, since rituals prohibited his engaging in active labour. In times of need he requested section heads to make a contribution for the good of the community. His wealth springs from the gifts that are made to him by individuals seeking his services or those of the *kwara* shrine. The chiefship as an institution seems to have mediated in the resolution of internal conflicts between lineages and individuals. The expression "*zo Aŋwe peɔ*" (seek refuge from another) continues to remind us that traditionally fugitives could seek refuge with the chief.

Thus, in many respects, the Kasena chief was unlike his Moore-Dagbomba counterpart. On the other hand the balanced opposition between earthpriest and chief which has become a classic in anthropological studies of political relations did not exist among the Kasena. Without doubting the existence of earthpriests among Kasena, it seems that today this office has a rather low profile in their communities. The few individuals who hold the title of *tegatu* are also holders of the office of *nakwe* of the clan-settlement. The clan-settlement elder plays a critical role in the ritual and mundane administration of the clan-settlement which he also represents in external relations. It seemed that in pre-colonial times even the chief could not ignore the clan-elder and deal directly with an individual. This functionary's permission was necessary for settlement in the area under his jurisdiction and under certain circumstances, he was ritually empowered to banish a member of the clan-settlement. Thus the Kasena chief's office articulates with that of the various clan-settlement elders who seem to embody the duties of earthpriest. Elders just as the clan-settlements themselves are however, not deemed equivalent in the chiefdom as some are definitely more important that others and have a greater say in the affairs of the community. It seems that clans that were first to arrive in the area are ritually more important in that they originally gave land to others for settlement.

Succession:

A person's self earned property is shared among his children after the performance of the final funeral rites. This applies to farms, cattle and items of clothing or jewelry. This is a system in which a son cannot be disowned and written out of the will by a father. The most important items of property, the shrines and gods that the deceased once possessed, go to his eldest son but prior to the celebration of his funeral, his youngest son administers the estate on his behalf. Widows may, if they so choose enter into leviratic marriages with the younger siblings (including classificatory siblings) of the deceased. Office is however treated as lineage or collective property and its transmission is therefore regulated by a different set of principles.

The office of chief shares attributes with that of the clan-settlement eldership but they differs in some respects, for example in the mode of transmission of office. The eldership is based on genealogical and chronological seniority. The oldest person within the most senior generation succeeds to that office even if he happens to be younger than some of his agnates. Eldership is not necessarily bequeathed to the previous incumbent's son although it may be vested in a lineage or segment of the clan. This is notwithstanding the fact that until the final funeral obsequies of the last incumbent have been held his last born should act. In the succession to the elderships merit and achievement are not taken into account. These principles apply in the transmission of all lineage derived office.

Chiefship is vested in a lineage but within that lineage eligibility to contest for the office rests on the rule that only those whose fathers have in their time contested for the office may enter the competition. This is in contrast to the Moore-Dagomba blueprint which restricts claims to paramount chiefship titles to those whose fathers have ever held that title. In that scheme a man may not rise above his father.

Kasena Religion:

The religion of the Kasena peoples was oriented towards the ancestors who in loco parentis were entitled to receive some veneration from the living kin. This can take several forms. The recent dead continue to receive their nourishment of food as it is believed that their ghosts still visit the home. The living owe them the duty to perform their funerals to pave the way for their entry into the land of the ancestors. They are given "water" from time to time. They are informed of events in the family as well as consulted at crisis points through the rites of divination. They were expected to reciprocate by ensuring that the living descendants enjoyed prosperity and well-being since their enhanced position places them close to the local gods with whom they are in communion, the Earth and God. If the living violated any of the norms sanctioned by the ancestors they were punished by illness or misfortune. An elder who abuses the trust reposed in him might be "called over" to be queried in much the same way as a father summons his recalcitrant child for rebuke.

Man himself or herself, comprising a body and a soul, is both material and spiritual. Human life is believed to pre-exist on another plane, the divine or *Wɛ Sɔŋɔ* (God's compound) from which a person descends to the world of mortals. The decision derives from the individual who also informs God on a chosen path or destiny on earth. All this is enshrined in the concept of *o jaane o nwoŋi o Wɛ Sɔŋɔ* (bringing over from God's compound) or *o na tage o Wɛ Sɔŋɔ tei* (how he or she said it in God's compound). What has been so determined is immutable. However, events that happen outside this can be influenced and changed for the better. The gods (*tangɔna*), fetishes and shrines (*jwona*) and the ancestors as well as other humans (especially witches) can intervene for better or worse in a person's life.

Kasena believe that some people acquire at birth the ability to "see"; that is to say, they can see spirits and people's souls and be able to harm others by snatching their souls which they can eat or destroy in some other way. Such are the *chera* or witches. They are believed to have acquired the propensity from their mothers and the concept of *ka fo da yia* (to deny one another's eyes) confirms this. It is an axiom that within the full sibling group, if one is proved to be a witch then the other full siblings are also witches since the propensities inheres in the matriline. It is also believed that a mother who is a witch will not fail to feed the witchcraft substance to her children. The *chera* or witches are believed to be more powerful that ordinary people but that power compares in no way with the greater power of the ancestors (*chira*) and the local gods or *tangɔna*. This is evidenced by the tendency to call upon the gods to deal with the witches. One rule observed by witches is not to transgress lineage boundaries. A witch can only prey on his or her lineage members. Parents may catch their children or present them to the other witches in the clan-settlement in settlement of witchcraft debts. Marriage severs the right of a woman's lineage to catch her or use her or her children in settlement of witchcraft obligations. To do this would provoke the anger of the ancestors. On the other hand after marriage a woman witch becomes eligible for recruitment to the coven of witches in her husband's clan-settlement.

The *tangɔna*, what might be referred to as lesser gods, also play an important role in the life of the Kasena. They are lodged in rivers, rocks, forest groves etc. They are powerful and can benefit or harm man. They might move about at night when men and woman are asleep. Each locality has its *tangɔna*. They play a protective role and people, especially those in their ritual congregations, appeal to them for assistance. Sometimes a contract may be "signed" with the deity promising it a reward if it granted the wishes of the supplicant. This is not always a wise thing to do, as far as Kasena are concerned because the *tangɔna* are exacting and merciless in claiming what is their due. The saying *Kukula jene ba di* says it all (the divinity Kukula does not have mercy for those who incur its debt). Nevertheless those who are desperate do enter into contractual relations with the gods. Kasena dealt with the *tangɔna* through sacrificial offerings and a meticulous adherence to their taboos and edicts. There seems to be some confusion between the *tangɔne* and the earthshrine or *tega*.

The earth was seen as a spiritual force regulating agriculture and other activities based on it. This meant every human activity from birth to death. God Wɛ, the author of human destiny worked through the ancestors and the other gods. As the Kasena say, *Wɛ ná wo go tega baa di* (Before the earth will consume God must have killed). The importance of God explains the recurrence of God in proverbs. In fact, the Kasem proverb can be seen as a useful introduction to their religion.

In addition to the lesser gods Kasena recognise the existence of *liri*, magical objects some of which might be of foreign origin. People acquire such medicines for healing and protective purposes but they might as well acquire them for nefarious purpose such as harming their enemies. A *lira* would usually have its ritual pot over which sacrificial offerings would be performed from time to time. Most of these *lira* would have their 'dos' and 'donts', as well as taboos that the agent must keep. A person may on his death bequeath the magical objects to one of his children. The magical object might also impose itself on one of the deceased person's immediate kin. This might take the form of spirit possession evidenced by illness that resists treatment. Eventually, the soothsayers will confirm the sources of the illness and prescribe the modes of dealing with it.

Individuals, such as the soothsayers, might be possessed by some spirit entity because of something they have done, wittingly or unwillingly such killing a hyena, cutting a tree or disturbing a rock that habours the spirit.

In Kasena belief, the origin of man is in Wɛ Sɔŋɔ or God's house. A person's destiny is mapped out there before birth. The individual tells God what his destiny would be and God acquiesces. On death he or she goes to the land of the ancestors, *churu*, which is in the bosom of the earth where he continues to live as he or she once lived, though at a higher plane of existence. The dead may return to the world of the living in spirit form or in material form. They do not remain aloof but participate actively in the affairs of the living as arbiters.

Human beings are perceived as unequal spiritually. Some are witches (*chera*), with the ability to see and commune with the invisible. The witch cannot only see the invisible, he or she may be capable of flight and might or might not have a propensity to indulge in the "eating" of other human beings. Witches kill their kin rather than others. They do so out of envy, ill-will or in response to the demands of other witches to whom a human debt is owed. Essentially a person is believed to have born witch or non-witch. Witches may linger on after death in a waif-like existence (*kwogo*) and continue to be a danger to others. For this reason known witches are subjected to special burial procedures that would make it impossible for them to resurrect as *kwogo*. The waif of the witch dies eventually when it comes into contact with ashes or the flakes of burnt grass, perhaps an additional reason for the annual setting of fire to the bushes.

Kasena do not believe that everything born of woman is human. They acknowledge that certain births are bush spirits masquerading in human guise with the ultimate objective of subverting man. Such births are indicated by evidence of congenital deformities in the neonate and characterised by a host of beliefs centering on the unusual prowess of the neonate. In the past, such neonates when detected and proved to be non-human or *chuchuru*, were got rid of as soon as possible in the perceived interest of the family. A specialist was invited in and paid to do a job which was believed to endanger the life of the specialist.

Aspects of Kasena Economy:

In terms of their traditional economy, the Kasena can be described as cultivators who specialised in millet and other grains and legumes and kept livestock and poultry. Grain crops include early millet or pennisetum typhideum (*chaara* in Kasem), late millet or pennisetum spicatum (*minpwoona* in Kasem), guinea corn or sorghum vulgare (*yara* in Kasem). These may well predate European introduced crops. Legumes include groundnuts or arachis hypogea, (*sunuga* or *sinuga* in Kasem) which may have been a crop of South American origin introduced into West Africa by the middle of the nineteenth century, if Bovill (1968: 250) is to be believed[3]. Cow peas (*sia*) are alsocultivated although on a small scale as well as beans. The hibiscus varieties of canabinus and sabdariffa are cultivated more for their leaves which are an important vegetable and okra occupy a special place in the traditional domestic economy. They are best when fresh but can be sun-dried and stored against the dry seasons. In addition to these vegetables may be mentioned *nangene* or *kalena,*, gynandropsis pentaphylla, which grows so well between late May, the beginning of the sowing season, and late June, the flowering of the early millet. In lean seasons some poor families in the past depended almost exclusively on this vegetable to tide them over the lean season. The ubiquitous cassava crop does not grow here but sweet and coleus potatoes are cultivated for consumption in the wet season. Most crops can be preserved and stored for use in the dry season.

In recent years, beginning in the 1970s, improved varieties of sorghum, maize and rice have assumed greater importance in the traditional economy. Unlike the neighbouring Frafra people of the Bolgatanga District, Kasena did not grow the varieties of early maturing sorghum. Rice, scathingly referred to as *ga-bia* (weed seed), and maize were not very popular. Today maize and the fast yielding varieties of sorghum occupy a considerable portion of the compound farms. The transformation is due in no small part to a realisation that weather changes no longer make the cultivation of the traditional varieties sustainable.

Dry season gardening gained popularity since the first decades of Twentieth Century due to the encouragement given by the early White Fathers. The mango (valued for its fruit), guava (for its fruits and medicinal leaves), nim (for timber and medicinal leaves), kapok (for fruit and cotton) and the teak (for timber) have all become popular trees thanks to dry season gardening, while tomato has since the damming of some streams in the 1960s achieved importance as a cash crop. The Tono Irrigation Scheme began in the mid 1970s has boosted the tomato industry even further.

The livestock and poultry served as a store of value. The main types of livestock are cattle, sheep and goats. A family may keep a dog or two and a cat. Donkeys which are kept by a few people have never been popular. Perhaps because donkey meat has never been valued as food, the animal is not usually sacrificed and its use is mainly as a beast of burden, not that there has been much that it carries. Proverbs affirm this. Horses are rare. For poultry, chickens are kept together with the semi-domesticated guinea fowl. In recent times, pigs, and ducks have been reared. Today a family sells its fowls or livestock to generate cash for essential expenses. In former times, (Awedoba 1985) livestock might be exchanged for traditional staples in a crisis moment. Ritual sacrifices relied very much on availability of poultry and livestock.

The food for their subsistence requirements was produced on the main farm which is usually close by and surrounds the compound in which they dwell. It is under permanent cultivation and requires the compound's manure derived from cattle droppings and household refuse to restore its fertility. In the pre-colonial era production was for domestic consumption with whatever surplus resulting from a good year destined for use in the celebration of ancestral funeral rites and festivals such as *faao*. More often than not yields were meagre and famine occurred at least one in three years. The poverty of the top soil compounded by low seasonal rainfall and crop pests like locust and worms accounted for this low yield. Food security and other forms of insecurity were of great concern to the Kasena at the turn of the 20th Century and we see these concerns reflected abundantly in their proverbs.

Kasena kept a few cattle and herds of goats and sheep. These were looked after by young boys and sometimes girls who herded the livestock out into the meadows to feed in the open. This was to ensure that domestic livestock did not do any damage to crops. In the dry season the animals were free to rove about. Livestock are important traditionally because they were the store of value, had a ritual purpose and more importantly, were the medium in which bridewealth was settled. Today animal husbandry is being marginalised due to modernisation. Not only are there fewer meadows for the livestock to graze, children have to go to school. Poultry was and is still kept by individuals. Like livestock the chickens are not confined to hen coops but are allowed to roam free. Guinea fowls (a semi-domesticated fowl of the francolin species) and hens are valued for several reasons. They are commonly slaughtered in ancestral rituals and often serve as the medium in which diviners, medicine men and healers are paid for their services. As personal property no permission or consultation is necessary before they are sold or used as gifts to friends. As the response to a Kasena riddle states, *veiru ná tu chibweɔ lwia* (when a guest arrives the cockerel trembles).

People would also hunt for game and trap fish. These are seasonal activities which take place in the dry season when there is less farmwork. Their contribution to the domestic fare is meagre. The traditional hunting tools were simple and hardly effective against big game and the same can be said for the fishing gear, since cross-nets, casting nets and even metal hooks were uncommon.

People eked out a living in a bad year by exploiting the wild resources in the bushlands. A number of trees were of critical importance in this respect and they included the shea butter tree (butyrospermum parkii), the locust bean tree (parkia filicoidea), the baobab (adansonia digitata) to mention a few. They fruited towards the end of the dry season when food reserves were depleted.

We notice in Kasena proverbs abundant reference made to the precariousness of life at the turn of the nineteenth century. Towards the end of the 19th century the area was devastated by foreign slave raiders (known as Gwala) acting with the collaboration of some Fra-Kasena from what is now the Tumu District of the Upper West who captured whoever they could lay hands on for sale in the slave markets of Salaga and Ashanti. The annual tribute in slaves imposed on the Dagomba and the Gonja kingdoms by Ashanti precipitated these raids although the Zamberma slavers who were directly responsible later acted independently of their Dagomba hosts. See Holden (1965) and Tamakloe (1931) for a description of the slave raids of the Moshi-Dagomba hinterland. The advent of the colonial powers put an end to the work of the slavers. Even before the arrival of the Zamberma the Moshi appeared to have raided Kasena and other acephalous peoples nearby for slaves. In later times when Moshi, also known to the Kasena as Gwala, began to send caravans to the Salaga market, the Kasena did not fail to pay them back in their own coin by mounting attacks on the caravans and extracting booty, as did other acephalous peoples in the area, like the Tallensi, as

Goody (1977) and Keith Hart (1978) point out.

Kasem Language:

The language as we have mentioned above is a Gur language belonging in the Grusi branch together with languages like Sisala, Vagala, Tampulma, Chakali, Mo or Deg etc. These languages which are spoken in Ghana are more closely related to each other than to Kasem. There are quasi-kinship and joking ties that Kasena share with Sisala whom they call their paternal cousins. They have traditions which suggest that they once shared community ties until they quarrelled and each went their individual ways. The legends that Sisala and Vagala, Tampulma etc say account for their separation and dispersal from a common home land are not extended to the Kasena. Kasem, the most northernly of the Ghanaian Grusi languages, has its closest cousins in central Burkina Faso in languages like Nuni, Lyele and Pana. Fra-Kasem is certainly a dialect of Kasem although the degree of mutual intelligibility is not as high as one could have expected. Certainly, lack of close contiguity and the fact that the Fra are classified in the Upper West while the central dialects of Kasem are in the Upper East Region of Ghana and in Southern Burkina Faso may explain the reduced level of mutual intelligibility.

Kasem has several dialects which can be distinguished on chiefdom basis even within the Navrongo and Paga Districts. There the more northern dialects are perceived as more correct while the western dialects enjoy less prestige. It would certainly seem that the northern dialects contain more archaic words and expressions. This is however more a hypothesis than a factually verifiable conclusion.

CHAPTER TWO

The Meaning and Structure of the Kasena Proverb and Saying (*Sinseira*)

Situations and circumstances suggest to Kasena users whether to apply and what proverb to play. This is probably true of most cases of proverb usage. Proverbs, as researchers on the Akan proverb generally agree, reflect situational parameters. Obeng's (1996) listing of the rules governing the use of proverbs takes into account sensitivity to audience and other players, place and time of use, occasion and contextual features as well as the mode of proverb presentation. It is in this connection that he elaborates on the mitigating qualities of Akan proverbs and their potential to protect and save face in certain encounters. The situational characteristic of proverbs makes it difficult to elicit them from informants for research purposes, all the more reason why Christaller's collection of over 3600 Twi proverbs must remain an incomparable feat.

The reader will find here a collection of proverbs made over a period of time. They are not limited to particular dialect areas but come from all over the Kasem-speaking areas, including those communities located on the Burkina Faso side of the international boundary from which a small sample was obtained. As proverbs are projected as the edicts of the sages of old and sometimes incorporate structures that are not current in contemporary speech forms of the communities from which they were collected, it becomes difficult to distinguish between dialectal variations, aesthetic embellishment of language and archaic structures.

This collection discussed is by no means a comprehensive compendium of Kasena proverbs; on the contrary, it would not surprise this writer to find that the list omits some very common proverbs. The majority of the proverbs discussed here were collected from the Navrongo chiefdom.

This is because the researcher has a better knowledge of this area and has interacted with people from this area all his life.

The researcher is indebted to several individuals, users of proverbs who might not necessarily have been made aware that their proverb was being memorised and added to a collection. The approach used is typically one of participant observation. No attempt was made to gather freelists of proverbs, precisely because the respondents would have been at a lost to recollect proverbs out of context. Experience with freelists carried out among Bulsa women shows that respondents were not usually at ease with freelisting procedures and individual's lists generated consequently were short.

My task is to attempt to provide the cultural background to the proverbs that are included here. To achieve this objective, I have drawn upon my own experiences as an insider and anthropologist. My procedure has been to pick a particular proverb and interpret it in terms of Kasena social institutions and practices without losing sight of the etymology and derivational history of the expression. Each is explained in such a way that it should become clear how Kasena craft their proverbs using as their base material their cultural experiences and the wealth of language resources. We cannot fully appreciate a proverb until we have some insight into the society and culture of the people and the institutions, norms and practices that underpin these proverbs. Working from the surface interpretations we arrive at the general message of each proverb and its application.

Insight into Kasena society and culture cannot be taken for granted even by those who were born and bred in the Kasena society. Not only has social change affected many of the traditional institutions, the traditional modes of enculturation have also been affected. While in former times children spent their childhood and adulthood in the local community and learned from their parents and kin through participation and observation as well as by instruction, these days most children spend more time in the classroom where their teacher may not even be a local or have adequate knowledge of Kasena ways. Competence in proverbs has been affected noticeably. While in former times children sat by their parents and listened to their manner of speech, the best means of hearing and acquiring proverbs, today few have these opportunities. This makes it all the more urgent that a work such as this one be provided as assistance to those Kasena (young and old alike) who wish to learn about the proverbial wisdom of their forebears.

In this chapter we shall attempt a general introduction to the Kasena proverb as a social artifact and as an aesthetic product. We examine therefore the etymological bases of the Kasem term for proverb, the structural characteristics of Kasena proverbs and other features that could distinguish it from other Kasem oral or verbal literature genres, such as the *sinseira* or saying.

The Meaning of the Term Proverb in Kasena Thought:

The proverb is defined variously as a short well known saying, an epigramme, a short pithy utterance more or less fixed in expression whose features include the allegorical, Dalfovo (1991:49). Some scholars consider the proverb as prose, see Finnegan (1970) but this is disputed by others on grounds that the African proverb at least exhibits the qualities of poetry, qualities like metaphorical and figurative language, alliteration, assonance, word play, rhythm and so on, see Nwachukwu (1994). These are not issues that engage my attention here. The dividing line between poetry and prose must remain a moot point and this discussion does not intend to joint that debate.

There have also been arguments about whether the proverb qualifies as indigenous African philosophy or not. Gyekye (1995) does not doubt that proverbs, in whatever language or culture qualify as philosophy. He maintains that even as products of individual wise persons, they are perforce influenced by ideas and beliefs in the community. Brookman-Amissah writing on Akan proverbs also refers to the individual source of the proverb and remarks as follows:

> What has gained common currency and acceptance might have originated from individual efforts. But as time goes on it passes into the store of accumulated knowledge of the group and becomes part and parcel of the conventional wisdom (Brookman-Amissah 1989:84)

Moreover, Brookman-Amissah (op cit: 75) holds that among other things proverbs encode the philosophical outlook of the community.

The rootedness of the proverb in the culture of the society in which it is current has been remarked upon by several scholars. Dalfovo remarks that "A Lugbara proverb is experiential in the sense that it originates from experience" and that experience is derived, in his opinion, from Lugbara society, particularly the traditional Lugbara society, Dalfovo (1991:45).

To understand the meaning of the Kasena proverb we need to consider how the Kasena themselves make sense of the institution of proverb in the context of their language. Kasena call the proverb *memaŋe* which is an abbreviation for the phrase *faŋa tu memaŋe*. The word *memaŋe* is derived from the verb *maŋe* which, like most Kasem words is polysemous. It can mean, among other things, 'to measure', as in marketing idiom where commodities like grain are measured out in standard measuring units. The word also means 'to be suitable or fitting' as in the utterance *garebwora kam maɲe bu wom* (the smock fits the child). The verb *maɲe* also means to compare things, ideas, or persons. Finally, the verb means to recount or narrate. The following utterance illustrates this: *ba na maɲe se amo ni to..* ("according to what I have heard recounted"). It is this last meaning that comes closest to the meaning of proverb. The nominal derived from this verb, *memaɲe*, is polysemous as it can mean on the one hand a story or an account of an event that may or may not have actually occurred or on the other, a proverb. To avoid the ambiguity or the possibility of confusion between any account and the proverb, since it is not every account or narrative that qualifies to be a proverb, the phrase *faɲa tu memaɲe* has become a more precise description of proverb in Kasem.

The etymology of the term *faɲa tu memaɲa* (translatable as "the ancient man's utterances") throws light on the Kasena concept of the proverb. The first question to ask is why proverb should be identified with *faɲa tu*, the ancient man, and secondly who that personality might be. The answer lies in what the time markers *diim* 'yesterday' and *zem* 'today' imply as concepts in Kasena thought. These are dyads in terms of which Global time is perceived. Past generations are classified as *diim* and the present as *zem*. The world of today or the contemporary world, *zem*, is opposed to the remote past, *diim*, in Kasena dialectics of social change. In the views of traditional Kasena the golden age, *diim*, was in the remote past or in their dream time, in the days of their forebears. Their representations, as manifested in their prose and poetic accounts, depict the people of those bygone days in close association with divinity. The people of those days were wise though not other worldly; they are said to have been righteous in their ways.

The world of the bygone era, *diim*, was better in all respects, according to Kasena representations. People were stronger and more capable physically. They were successful in their day to day activities such as farming, hunting etc. Nature yielded its abundance and people did not have to worry much. There was also harmony in their universe. For example, it rained in season and in adequate amounts. Their lives were simple and uncomplicated. This then is an ideal epoch for which there is nostalgia as is evidenced by Kasena references to it in everyday discourse. For example, we hear comments such the following: '*X ye diim tiina nɔɔno mo*' or "so and so is a leaf from a bygone age" made in reference to a person who is believed to still exhibit the behaviour, beliefs and attitudes of the denizens of the old world. The men and women of those days were also close to nature; they had not only a better perspective on the physical and material environment but also the spiritual world. They observed and understood birds and animal behaviour as well as plants and vegetables. This enabled them to order their lives and cope with the problems of life without complex technology. Although positive moral values are identified with that golden era, Kasena do not necessarily think that the simple-mindedness of the bygone era is always desirable.

It should also be remarked that the world of *diim* is not one that is situated in a particular century, traditional Kasena do not think in terms of centuries. What is however clear is that their dream world came before the colonial era. We know this to be so because everywhere modern money economy the introduction of which is linked to colonialism is blamed for the erosion of moral values. The world of *diim* encompasses the period before the arrival of the Zegna who are credited with the introduction of chieftaincy[4]. This was the era when the society was more egalitarian. Siblings did not fight for chiefships but were willing to step aside in favour of needy siblings[5]. Chiefs, earth priests and elders performed their rituals to improve the lot of the world without exercising repressive authority. As the world of *zem*, the contemporary epoch, gradually came into being mankind depreciated and as life became more complicated from generation to generation morality underwent a transformation for the worse as greed and covetousness became the order of the world that the Kasena live in.

The conclusion we draw from the assertions of Kasena suggests that the replacement of the world of *diim* by the world of *zem* was not a punctilineal event but one that took place by gradual evolution. For example, the great grandparents of today think and assert that life and morality were better in their youth than now and that the morality prevailing in their own generation was inferior by comparison with that of their grandparents' generation. Many a Kasena septuagenarian without the benefit of formal education can still be heard reminiscing about how it used not to fail to rain on the eve of Easter and how Catholics would skip sowing to attend Easter mass while non-Christians got on with their farm work[6]. Beliefs such these which have characterised Kasena people's utterances enable us to understand their attachment to ancestors and the ancestor complex and the ideal of the good old days.

Kasena believe that the culture of the *diim* world and its wisdom have been transmitted to the succeeding generations and that the proverb genre encapsulates that wisdom more than any other medium. This explains the designation of the proverb as statements that encapsulate wisdom handed down by their wise and incomparable ancestors. The Kasena like most African peoples (the Vai of Liberia, Bamum and Bafut of Cameroon and a few others would be possible exceptions) did not invent an indigenous system of writing or recording events graphologically. They educated their off-spring through an oral medium and by encouraging them to participate in daily activities and to learn more or less on the job.

As the world of *diim* is projected as morally superior to the present world, its culture is by this logic rated superior and can thus serve as a paradigm for proper behaviour. This fact, in the opinion of Kasena, has not only imbued the proverb with its moral force but inoculates it against criticism. The truth of the proverb is thus of an order that cannot be challenged. Kasena seem by their attitudes to accept tacitly that it is unseemly to call into question the proverb or its tenets. To do so would appear to amount to a challenging of the wise ancestors, an exercise not only in arrogance, but in itself a sacrilege. While individual ancestors are not above criticism, as a collective category they surely are above it, in the views of the Kasena[7]. Abraham (1972:122) makes the same point when he remarks the impersonalisation of the proverb: "This impersonalization is achieved not only by the casting of the description in witty and traditional terms, but by using what seems to be an objective frame of reference". This is in spite of the fact that Kasena proverbs, like most other African proverbs, do contradict. This does not however, seem to matter to Kasena. It is unlikely that Kasena proverb users would exhibit any overt interest in contradictions between proverbs, make a comparison between proverbs that are perceived to contradict or attempt to 'fight with proverbs" as is reported in cultures where proverbs are cited in traditional law courts. Even in those cases where proverbs have what Yankah (1986:288) calls a meta-judicial function " .. draw [ing] the attention of other jury members to a judicial norm or procedure" as happens in Ashanti courts, contradictory proverbs might not surprise users. After all, Dalfovo (op cit) rightly remarks, experience embodies contradictory situations.

The Authorship of the Proverb:

It goes without saying that a true proverb is always attributed to the ancestors as a collective category. The acknowledgment usually comes in the phrase entitling the proverb. Though the acknowledgment of collective authorship is optional in the statement of the proverb overt acknowledgment in some form serves as one of the important markers of the proverb utterance in Kasem. This feature enables us to distinguish between the proverb and other similar genres such as the *Sinseira*, popular saying. The author of a *sinseira* is usually a known individual; the context of authorship might also be known. What is more, these details may be incorporated in the statement of the *sinseira*. In fact, it is the context and the situation that contribute to the meaning and significance of a *sinseira*.

When people cite a proverb like *zem mo zem nabara wiiru* ("today is today, like the hyena and the stream") the audience and the player of the *sinseira* are recalling an utterance once made by an individual who had found himself in a fix and who had felt that his situation was comparable to that of the hyena whose greed took it to the human settlements to catch smaller livestock, whose greed furthermore led to overstaying in the precincts of human settlements and thus on its way back to its bush habit found that the stream which divides settlement from bush and which hitherto was empty had subsequently overflowed its banks.

With the proverb we are never told which ancestor authored it, when, where and what motivated the author to create it. The *sinseira* and the proverb are however, so similar that Wedjong (1969) chose not to differentiate between them. He refers to them collectively as *sinseiri*. We can imagine the possibility of a *sinseira* becoming transformed into a proverb or vice versa.

The perceived lack of individual or specific authorship or the ascription of such authorship to the ancestors should not imply that the stock of proverbs remains static to be handed down wholesale and unchanged from generation to generation. It is obvious that innovation goes on as new samples of proverbs enter the culture through borrowing or by individual invention. The existence of versions of the same proverb would suggest that different authors have at different times been instrumental in the creation of proverbs or, in any case, in their modification. It seems that any wise saying which accords with the proverb blue print might pass for such.

The Function of Proverbs

Proverbs are rarely told for the sake of telling them. They occur in discourse, any discourse but particularly in serious discussions and arguments. In these contexts it is not unusual to select appropriate proverbs to serve as clinchers for an argument or as means of illustrating the logic of a statement. We would normally expect to hear more proverbial language in use in chiefs' courts or where elders are gathered, for example at funerals and burials. The latter would seem particularly appropriate occasions as they remind the living of the close proximity of the ancestors just as the choice of communication medium is made to reflect the contemporary linguistic realities and the linguistic history of the clan-settlement where these events are taking place.

Proverb use is to some extent a function of age and status among the Kasena. Agalic (1983) seems to make the same point when he remarks that among the Bulsa, neighbours of the Kasena, proverbs are common in the speech of the chief's elders and clan leaders. It is even possible that gender differences are a factor in proverb use although this is a matter for systematic research. Youth have less need or the desire to use proverbs which, as we have seen above, are associated not only with antiquity but also with the wisdom of maturity which traditionally comes through experience which was a function of age in this gerontocratic type of society. A young man who is fond of proverbs earns the accolade, *nan-kwebu*, "young old man" which is ambiguous as it suggests wisdom as well as arrogance or a pre-mature attempt at usurping the status normally conferred on the aged.

Status elevation may therefore be associated with elaborate or profuse use of proverbs. We can well imagine scenarios where a person who is anxious to project himself uses proverbs often in his conversations with others. In the same way, those who do not wish to be identified with old age, since the old are generally believed to be knowledgeable in proverbs, or with the traditional culture of their people, might use them less or not use them at all. This will remain a hypothesis which may not be easily tested here in the absence of more detailed research and data. An illustration of these remarks can be found in the behaviour of some young persons born and bred in Kasenaland who upon getting out of the Kasena-Nankana District for the first time begin to speak Kasem with an affected accent as a means of distancing herself and suggesting to her Kasena audience that she might have been born outside the traditional area[8]. It is a minority that we can accuse of this but the fact that the accusation sticks as far as some young girls' behaviours show goes to confirm the point that loyalty to the ethnic unit, and even more so to its traditional ways can be questioned.

The Kasena folktale illustrates the use of proverbs to underline a point, almost in the literal sense. It is the expected practice in the narration of Kasena folktales to conclude the tale by citing an appropriate proverb. The standard formula is the end with the phrase: "*Konto ŋwaane mo ba we* .... " (that is why they say .....) followed by the text of a proverb which illustrates the wisdom in the folktale. Alternatively, the narrator may provide a comment in his or her own words which illustrates the wisdom and advice that follow from the folktale. It is remarkable that these could be some of the occasions on which individuals invent proverbs that eventually enter the stock of proverbs circulating in the community. Allowance is given to the narrator; he or she could either cite a proverb or provide words of wisdom that would clinch the moral of the folktale much in the way that proverbs do. As Brookman-Amissah (1986:84) remarked, "What has gained common currency and acceptance might have originated from individual efforts. But as time goes on it passes into the store of accumulated knowledge of the group and becomes part and parcel of the conventionable wisdom".

Proverbs are often allegorical or metaphorical statements but their teleological and consequentialist functions are only too obvious. They are symbols whose specific meanings emerge as they find use on a particular occasion and in a particular situation which is being assimilated to the picture presented in the imagery of the proverb statements. However, some Kasena proverbs are almost literal. For example some issue direct warnings to the audience telling them what should or should not be done. A proverb says "You don't elect a short man to lead the way and then complain about his pace" *Ba ba yage kukula yiga ne ye be daa gwooni ka veiŋa.* Dalfovo regards them as having some ethical functions among the Lugbara of Uganda. The above proverb maintains that if you put a short man in the lead you will not cover the same distance that would be covered were a taller person to set the pace. It seems to maintain that there is nothing intrinsically wrong with asking a shorter person to lead the way and once such a person takes the lead speed would be sacrifice. Another proverb in fact explains some of the circumstances under which a shorter person might be requested to lead: namely a visit to his mother's village where he obvious takes the place of honour or when he leads the delegation to his wife's village, where again he should take centre stage because of his greatest interest in the visit.

In some cases, proverbs are used to comment on negative behaviour and events. The proverb that quotes the cry of the dove does exactly this: "Unwillingness to heed advice accounts for the pile of plucked feathers" or "It is foolhardiness that accounts for the pile of plucked feathers" (*Beregeɔ koro mom tigi tento puu, konkwonpwongo de ko keira*). There is a price for foolhardiness or unwillingness to accept advice.

There are also proverbs that give advice such as the council given to the sex maniac: he should not leave his wife at home when he journeys abroad: *Manjɔro-gɔgɔ vei de ko kaane mo.* It is advised that the way in is the way out for the arrow that has pierced the body: *Chene na dɛ mɛ de zo to de wó da kojeira mo de nwoŋi.* This proverb advises that the solution to a problem lies in the problem itself; its diagnosis. It is probably also reminding people of the traditional norms associated with warfare. When a person is hit by a poisoned arrow, painful as it may be that arrow has to be extracted, if the victim is to live. This was done by cutting the area that was pierced and taking out the arrow. That is to say one must understand a problem and investigate its origin and causes in order to arrive at the solution to the problem.

These proverbs at the literal or surface level therefore provide useful advice that can guide people but the proverbs can also have general applications that transcend the particular. For example, just as a sex maniac is advised to take along his wife on his errands so is anybody who has a special craving, disability or weakness advised to take advanced precautions against eventualities.

There are some proverbs that are limited to certain contexts and situations. We find for example proverbs that occur predominantly at greetings. The following two proverbs are examples:

Faŋa tu mo nɛ ye o ta o we ko ná tera n ni ne ko wo n tampɔgɔ ne
(It has been said since the days of the ancestors that if it is not in your mouth it must be in your bag)

Veiru zoore de dam mo se o ba nwoŋi de dam
(A visitor forces his way in but does not force his way out)

These are not proverbs that we are likely to hear except in the context of greetings. The guest utters the first proverb to signal that a visit is never meaningless. The visitor must have a purpose if he or she has left his or her village and taken so much trouble to visit another village. After, this comment the guest would then state the purpose of his or her visit. This procedure is probably the opposite of the Ghanaian Akan practice where the host entitles the guest by asking the visitor what his mission is, or what had brought him or her over.

In the case of the second proverb above, the host would use this to detain a visitor who seems anxious to take leave by reminding the guest to wait until permission is given; i.e. after the women had prepared a meal or some form of reception for the guest.

Death is another context that leads to the use of special proverbs such as the proverb that states that "rot takes place in the earth's bowels and not above ground". (*Ko pɔe tega ne mo se ko ba pɔe wɛ ne*). This is a consolation for the bereaved who is told that death is not the end of life and one should be consoled that the deceased has left behind kin. Take also this other one: *Te se n daare mo toom lira*, "The antidote to death is having living off-spring".

These are just a sample of uses to which proverbs can be put in Kasena society. Additional functions would include the use of proverbs to widen and amplify discourse, to instruct and educate, as well as to satirize, see Nwachukwu (1994), and in the case of Yankah's (1986) account, they could be used also to corroborate or denounce a cause, ratify a verdict or to draw attention to procedural issues in court cases. Even if we are not in a position to illustrate all of these functions from the Kasena corpus, the functional power of Kasena proverbs cannot be underestimated. Obeng (1996:523) summaries the point quite well when he concludes his study of the communicative functions of proverbs and their role in safeguarding face by remarking that "they thus provide strategies for dealing with a variety of communicative situations".

Transmission of Proverbs

Proverbs, like other aspects of African traditional culture, are transmitted through the processes of enculturation. However, the mode of their transmission differs from that of other genres like, for example, folktales and riddles. With the latter, older kin perform for their own entertainment and for audiences which invariably include the younger generations. As children listen to these they come to acquire the knowledge and necessary expertise in the genre. Children also have the opportunities to practice story telling and riddling among themselves alone or under the watchful eye of their seniors. Proverbs are not learnt in this way. They are not regarded as material for entertainment, although a good proverb does not fail to receive acknowledgement. There are therefore no performance sessions for proverbs. They are utterances that are functional in adult discourse and in this context they are used to illustrate an argument or to clinch a point, as Yankah (1986) remarked for Akan proverbs. The transmission of proverbs is not therefore through formal instructional processes. However, as children audit the conversations of their elders they get the opportunity to hear and note proverb usages and the situations under which a particular proverb might be used. Children are not told the meanings of proverbs, except in cases where a child has requested for the explanation of a particular proverb; but as they hear them used repeatedly in varied contexts and situations children come to acquire an understanding of the proverbs of their culture. With time and cognitive maturation they too become adept at proverb usage.

As children attain adulthood they begin to use simple proverbs in the peer group. It is considered as out of character for a child, even a teenager, to use proverbs in a conversation with his or her elders. Even among adults, it is considered presumptuous for juniors to be seen to over indulge in proverbs. As a person ages he or she is however expected to exhibit greater expertise in proverb idiom. That expertise appears to be a function of regular attendance at serious sessions where the use of complex proverbs is called for.

It must be lamented that these days as expertise in proverb usage declines more and more the ability to recall and use proverbs is seen as an index of a person's home background. It is becoming customary these days for literate Kasena to describe as *nɔn-kwea sɔŋɔ bu* (child of an old man's compound) the individual who exhibits considerable knowledgeable of proverbs and their usage. The Kasena of Navrongo certainly admire the ability of a local priest to cite proverbs at church sermons in a way that indicates the wisdom of that is enshrined in the traditional culture.

Given the traditional role of kin and family in the transmission of oral genres, it does not come as a surprise that as modern socio-cultural change overtakes families, often leading to a temporary separation of the family members, the opportunities for learning and using genres like proverbs should decline. More and more it now falls to schools to assume the roles of transmitters of the cultural heritage and while schools have attempted to do this for genres like folktales, riddles and play tunes they have not been effective at teaching proverb culture because, as we have suggested above, it is the situation that evokes its own proverb. Moreover teachers themselves no longer are conversant in the traditional proverbs.

Attachment to an aged parent or relation, rightly or wrongly, is believed to explain proverb expertise acquired by a modern day Kasena person of middle age or one who is younger. Yet we must also not rule out personal interest in the acquisition of proverbs; those for whom the proverb is another manifestation of obsolete traditional culture, whatever their educational background, never exhibit any reasonable knowledge of the proverbs of their culture.

Variation in Proverb Idiom

The proverb statement is not a fixed unchanging formula. In describing the Lugbara proverb as "fixed linguistic expressions" Dalfovo (op cit: 53) is careful to define fixity in this regard in terms of its template. An examination of Kasena proverbs shows that variations of several kinds are allowed. These include the following:

1. The application or omission of entitling phrase. This has been described in the section below.

2. The choice of pronoun subject. The third person plural pronoun **ba** and the second person singular pronoun **n** are the pronouns we find more often in subject place in the pronoun statement. Though they are by no means always mutually substitutable there are nevertheless proverbs in which substitution is possible without resulting in substantial meaning change. The substitution is not however reciprocal; the second person

pronoun may be substituted for the third person pronoun but it does not usually work in the reverse direction. The example below shows how this can be achieved.

Ba gane bu mo ba tore jeŋa o tampɔgɔ ne "It is by persuasion that one gains access to the child's bag" can be paraphrased as *N wó gane bu mo n tore jeŋa o tampɔgɔ ne.* (You will have to persuade the child to allow you to do so if you are to access its bag)

Note here that a future marker *wó* has also been introduced in the process and the statement which was initially in the imperfective aspect communicating a fact now gets transformed into the future.

Observe also that the proverb *N ná yeiri leiŋa ka pa-m chuchwooru* (If you do not know a song it makes you mad) cannot be replaced with **Ba ná yeiri leiŋa ka pa-ba chuchwooru* (which will mean 'if they do not know a song it maddens them'). The latter though grammatically and lexically correct it is not a proverb. It is a simple factual remark.

3. The second person singular pronoun can be replaced with *nɔɔno* "person" but the result is usually a form that sounds more prosaic. For example, it is possible to replace *N ná lage doa ka ne n nawara ne* (If you long for rain it will fall on your parapet walls) with *Nɔɔno ná lage doa ka wó ne o nawara ne mo* (If a person prays for the rain it will fall on his/her parapet wall). The latter version is more or less an explanation of the proverb. Note the addition of *wó* the future marker and *mo*, the emphatic particle.

4. The linguistic skills of the person who performs the proverb and the dialect background may also be factors shaping the output utterance. The adjustments that may be made in this respect defy description. They may range from change of word or clause order, substitution of dialectal variants and archaic expressions to introduction of emphasizers and use of ellipsis etc. For example while it sounds more like a proverb to say *"ba lwom dwoŋ seɔ mo se ba ba lwom dwoŋ kio"* (while we may copy a style of dancing, we do not ape people's ways), it is also possible to express the same proverb in more prosaic form as *"ba lwoni dwoŋ sam mo se ba ba lwom dwoŋ keim"*. In this example *seɔ* "dance" is a more archaic word which occurs in quoted expressions like *"zem mo seɔ"*, "today is the dance day" or less literally, "today is the d-day". The noun *kio* does not exist as a free form except in this usage where the stem morpheme in the

word *kikio*, "action" has been extracted and made an independent form.

5. Finally, the same proverb idea may be expressed in two different ways. *Naao ba ke bwolo lei* (The cow does not thank the valley) and *Chworo ba ke kazɔgɔ lei* (The fowl does not thank the mortar) are the same proverb, essentially. The difference lies in the choice of subject markers and their associations. The cow feeds in the valley and the hen feeds from the mortar where grain is pounded and winnowed. If these two seem different, consider the following: *Ba ba mae yi ba laɲe yɛ dwoa* (The eye does not taste soup to ascertain the amount of salt in it) and *Ba ba mae yi ba lɔre yɛ dwoa* (The eye does not determine the salt content of soup). These two differ with respect to the lexemes *laɲe* (to taste) and *lɔre* (to know), words that compare the eye in the former case with the tongue and in the latter with the cognitive functions of the brain.

6. The need to avoid or to indulge in obscenities appears to account for certain proverbs like the following having two forms or versions:

Lelala peina ba zoora (the penis that is inserted hurriedly does not enter the vagina fully) is obscene but *Lelala bu ba lora* (that child whose birth is hurried is still-born) is not. We are dealing with the same proverb here; the difference is that one is obscene while the other has no obscenity. Not that adult Kasena whom I have heard use the former feel any qualms on the issue. There are certainly occasions when it would be inappropriate to use an obscene proverb, such as before one's mother-in-law or before children.

Style and Artistry in the Proverb

The proverb is usually regarded as a piece of prose, a position espoused by Finnegan (1960) yet the Kasem proverb can be seen to contain stylistic features that are not usually found in the language of everyday conversation. We see in it various kinds of linguistic elaborations that can be said to have been used for their own sake in an attempt to add colour to the proverb rather than to achieve communication efficiency or effectiveness. Some of these features include the following:

1. Introduction of archaic expressions and words as well as neologisms:

We find in the proverb, *Kenkaa jɔgɔ ba twogi zore* (The cockroach's pants do not solve the problem of the naked pauper), the verb *twogi* (not translatable) is otherwise rare in Kasem. This author has not encountered this word in any other context. We can only regard it as either a dialectal variant (it does not exist in the central dialect of Kasem associated with Navrongo) or as an archaic expression. In the proverb *N ná jege wiiru bukɔ n daa ba kua kua?* (It does not imply that if you are married to hyena's daughter you are not allowed to taste a bone), the verb *kua* is again unusual in that it is rarely met with in ordinary language. It is probably a neologism derived from the word *kua* (bone) and meant "what is done to a bone either to extract the juice or remove the flesh stuck to it". Here it has the same meaning as *kwooni* (to use the teeth to remove bits of flesh on a bone). The verb *kwooni* has several other meanings in addition to these.

2. Replication of words and Structural Patterns:

The following proverb, *Adidaane de adidaane mo di daane* which illustrates replication of words and structures is also ambiguous at the surface level. We see *daane* repeated threefold, and the syllables *di, de daa* also occur. It can mean literally, *Adidaane de Adidaane mo di daane* (Mr. I-eat-with-others and Mr. I-eat-with-others eat together) or (Those who are predisposed to share associate fruitfully). The phrase *di daane* also refers to groups that can intermarry. Whichever interpretation is taken the proverb illustrates several layers of such replications, not to mention the tongue twisting that is evident. It is almost as though we were being introduced to a riddle whose objective is to confuse and mask the identity of the riddle query by playing on words and thus puzzling the audience or diverting attention from the solution to the riddle.

3. The use of hyperbole and exaggeration

Hyperbole and exaggeration are other features found with Kasem proverbs, as is exemplified by the following proverb utterance: *Kanvwogili mo lore tuu* (It is the puny frog that begets the elephant) or *Nabiina nia goe chana* (The human mouth kills the moon) i.e., the words that issue from the human mouth are capable of killing the moon. *Nabiinu faro mo o dono* (A man's sympathiser is also his enemies). These are statements that embody paradox and extreme exaggeration. Proverbs like these differ from the more literal ones such as *N ná ba jege bu se ba jwa bwoɲi n yere ko buga* (If you do not have a child to ensure that your name will be remembered in future, then dig a well). It is to the imagination of most Kasena an impossibility for one species of animal such as a frog to beget another species of animal such as the elephant, not even in the folktale do we encounter this kind of exaggeration. This is not to doubt that Kasena genuinely believe that some humans like the witches can transform themselves into were-cats and other animals, and the divinities which are physically represented by trees can take on the guise of humans. In the same way they are certainly aware that the phases of the moon is not something that humans can influence in anyway. There are of course certain atmospheric phenomena that Kasena believe can be controlled by men with the special powers to do this. Rain is an example here. Kasena consider rain makers to be equipped with ritual powers that enable them to control the rain and manipulate it.

4. Metaphorical Associations:

There are also unusual associations or the attribution of characteristics to things that could not by any stretch of the Kasena imagination have had such attributes. For example the sleeping mat is said in one proverb to be a soothsayer, poverty is represented as building its nest, and there is a proverb statement that courtesy does not induce nausea. What we see here is the application of metaphor and imagery as ingredients in proverb making. When the sleeping mat is described as a soothsayer, what is implied is that the mat is in some respects like the soothsayer: for example, as you sleep in it you ponder over issues, you even dream about your problems and through this you discover the solutions to your problems. We find also in the Kasena proverbs animals and birds that are personified and endowed not only with the ability to speak but with morals and ethical sentiments. The hen says it would state its own case but it could not speak for its chick or egg and the dove cries out a lament at the sight of the pool of plucked feathers: "Behold the reward for failure to heed maternal advice!".

5. Unusual Syntax:

We find also an unusual ordering of the elements of clause structure in some proverbs. Proverb idiom prefers to include the object within the verb, where the verb is negative. For example, *Zula ba bam bwora* [lit. courtesy the heart does not puke] or (Courtesy does not cause nausea) in which the complement is enclosed in the verb, is preferable to *Zula ba bwora bam* [lit. courtesy does not puke the heart] in which the complement follows the verb as in more normal sentences. There is no substantial change in meaning either way. This type of sentence structure can also be found in folksongs which exhibit verbal artistry. Below we take a further look at the structural or syntactic features of the proverb utterance.

Finally, the answer to the question about the literary status of the proverb in Kasem, i.e whether we are dealing with prose or poetry, must take into account the fact that there cannot always be a strict dichotomy between prose and poetry. The proverb seems to illustrate this; it straddles the two.

The Structure of the Proverb Statement

The Kasena proverb usually takes the form of a statement, a declarative sentence that we can consider as a form of prose. Nevertheless we find features like rhythm, repetition of syllabic patterns, a deliberate play on words and sounds or even a replication of a structural pattern effected in such a way that it begins to look as though the aim was to complement or restore structural balance to the proverb utterance. As language that is projected as having been handed down from the ancestors, it is not surprising that we should find these unusual archaic expressions and features. These can be considered as devices aimed at achieving make-belief, an attempt at suggesting the verbal contribution of the ancestors to their formulation.

The proverb utterance or sentence may be a simple clause or a more complex utterance. As a simple statement, the proverb usually has elements such as subject (S), verb or predicator (V), complement or object (C) and adjuncts or adverbials (A). The presence of the Subject and Verb elements are crucial in that they are usually found in the structure. The complement and the adverbial or adjunct may or may not be present. In this respect, the simple proverb is not too different from the typically simple one clause sentence in Kasem. We can represent the structure of the simple clause proverb by a formula such as the following: SV(C)(A). Elements between brackets are optional to the definition of the simple proverb structure. Below are examples:

Ex1: **Namɔra/ ba mɔne /na-tuntwogo//**:SVC
    Calf   does not mock   horn-less cow
"The calf does not poke fun at the horn-less cow (on account of its handicap)"

Ex2: **Anɛcham bu/ sage/ de chwoŋa//**: SVA
    Son of Anecham rests with arms close by
"When the son of I-have-experienced-trouble takes his rest his weapons are on hand"

Ex3: **Lelala bu/ ba lora//:SV**
      A hurried baby   does not get born
"The baby delivered hurriedly does not get born"

One type of simple structure contains an equation of ideas or things made possible by the introduction of an equative verbal such as *mo* or *ye* (positive equative or existential), *dae* (negative equative) and *gare* (evaluative comparison). See examples below.

Ex 4a: **Chega jei/ ye / ŋɔne mo//:SVC**
        Truth place is sore
"The truth is like a sore, it is painful"

Ex 4b: **Kanyambwoga nam/ mo / ka kweeim//:SVC**
"Sighting the tortoise is its capture"

There is another structure that seems complex yet nevertheless is basically a case of a simple sentence complicated by subordination (or what in systemic grammar is known as rankshifting) of what could in other contexts possibly have been independent sentences.

Ex5: **Ko ywona mo/ tei /   fɔ-n daŋe da//:SVC**
      It   sweet   emph takes care of   cut you place on there
"It is amity that accounts for generosity"

In the above the structure is analysable as "X control Y" yet from another perspective *ko ywona* and *fɔ-n daŋe da* are themselves autonomous sentences; the former a declarative and the latter an imperative structure exhibiting serialisation.

Relative clause structures are also in evidence. In Kasem the subordinated relative clause is marked by the discontinuous marker *na ..to*, as in the example below:

Ex6: **[Wolo na lage kukuri-kokɔra nɔna to] mo twi /mim: o ke ka kuri ne//**
      Whoever   likes dog- mangy meat   Emph feeds fire he do it bottom
"He who is interested in the meat of mangy dog must be prepared to feed the fire that will cook it".

More complex proverb structures can involve two or more clauses one or more of which may be a principal or independent clause on which the rest depend. It is also possible to have compound sentences where two or more principal or independent clauses are linked overtly or covertly. One favourite clause structure is the conditional which exhibits the marker *ná* in the dependent clause that usually precedes, as in the example below:

Ex7: **Buga ywona ná puli// ya di daane mo//**
     River fish   if increase, they eat each other emph
"When the fish population in a river explodes fish will prey on their own kind"

Usually, sentences with this type of structure can be paraphrased by introducing the future tense marker in the major clause, as follows:

Ex7a: **Buga ywona ná puli// ya wó di daane mo//**
     River fish   if increase, they fut eat each other emph
"When the fish population in a river explodes fish will prey on their kind"

A complex structure may contain a reporting clause with subject and the reporting verb *we* followed by what is reported. The subject, quite often, is an animal or bird but persons are not excluded as example Ex8 below illustrates.

Ex8: **Beilim we// siu ba gwoona//**
     Mosiman says   rest not to be rejected
"The Moshi say even a little rest is worthwhile"

This type of structure is common in Kasem proverb expressions.

There is also the type of complex proverb structure which exhibits two juxtaposed clauses mediated by the particle *se*. This type exemplifies a contrasting of comparable ideas, as in the example below:

Ex9: **Wirru we o kɔre gɛɛre mo// se o ba kɔre chwo-dɔrɔ//**
     Hyena says he fear failure emph se he not fear journey-long

"The hyena says he is worried by failure to find carrion and not by the distance he has to travel to get it"

Here *o kɔre gɛɛre mo* (he fears failure) is compared to *o kɔre chwo-dɔrɔ* (he feras long journey), two clauses that are otherwise structurally comparable.

Clauses may also be linked by means of other structural devices to form compound structures. In Ex 10 there is no overt linker while in Ex 11 *ye* is the element linking the two clauses.

Ex 10: **Kunkwola mo ke ka ba leu// ba ma de ŋwana da//**
Gourd   emph do   it neck leu   they then drop rope   there
"It is because gourd developed a long neck people are able to twist a rope around it"

Ex11: **Ba ba yage kukula yiga ne / ye / ba daa gwooni ka veiŋa//**
They not leave shortie   front   and they again complain his pace
"You don't elect a short man to lead the way and then complain about his pace"

The serial construction, an important feature of Kasem syntax, also occurs in proverb syntax as exemplified bellow:

Ex12: **Nabwonu/ mae/ o napere mo: o swo/ o kaane//**
pauper   use   his foot   emph   he marry his wife
"The pauper depends on his feet in his quest for a wife"

In this example the auxiliary verb *mae* (utilitative) and the verb *swo* "to marry a wife" are linked by the sharing of a common subject, *nabwonu* "poor man" in a serialisation not of verbs but of higher level structures that include a verbal item and other potential components. Not only are the verbs associated, they share the same aspect which is usually signalled by the shape of the secondary pronoun subjects which refer back to the initial subject. The secondary pronouns should in this case bear a low tone, as in the above utterance where the aspect is imperfective, or mid tone where the aspect is perfective. These are all standard features of serialisation in the Kasem language.

As stated above, the most popular sentence structure found with Kasena proverb expressions is the declarative, nevertheless we do come across non-declaratives although these are few and far between. In language, imperative structures usually function in the situational context as commands. The proverb utterance may have imperative structures such as in the proverb below where the sentential function is not really that of a command but a statement.

Ex13: **Te se n daare mo toom lira//**
Die and be survived is death's antidote
"The antidote to death is having living off-spring"

The hypothetical listener is not being condemned to death here although the expression is imperative, rather he is being told words of encouragement. This is a typical consolation proverb told to the bereaved when a parent or anybody dies leaving children.

Interrogative structures also exist in Kasena proverb idioms.

Ex14: Pɛ we n   sa   ye n we n tankona ba sea ?
Chief says you dance and you say your groin   not agree?
"If the chief commands you to dance you cannot say your groin aches"

The Grammatical Subject

The subject of proverb utterance derives from the cultural experiences of the people and their environment. Anything in their environment may be mentioned and discussed in the proverb. We do not however see examples deriving from the effects of social change. It is possible though, that some of the proverbs may have been borrowed from other Ghanaian cultures, modified and integrated within the genre. The similarities in proverbs that we notice between different ethnic cultures, in Ghana make it difficult to rule out borrowings from other cultures and by the same token diffusion of proverbs is difficult to authenticate. However even when proverbs are borrowed it is unlikely that they would be incorporated wholesale without adaptation, except where there is absolutely no need for this. Cultural and institutional similarities make it difficult to identify easily novel proverbs that have been introduced from other neighbouring societies, as may be the case between Kasena and Bulsa proverbs.

The Subject of the Entitlement

It is customary to entitle a proverb in Kasem. This is done by using an expression which invokes the ancestors of bygone days to whom the authorship of the proverb is attributed. This gives us the subject of Entitlement as in formulaic phrases like the following:

1. Faŋa tu mo   we... [It is the ancient sage who said...]
   Past owner emph say

2. Faŋa tu mo nɛ ye o we... [The ancient sage in his wisdom remarked that..]
   Past owner emph saw and he say

3. **Faŋa tu taane dem ba ji vwa,**   [The words of the ancient sage will
never err]
Past owner talk det not become lies

4. **Faŋa tu taane dem wó ji vwa?** [Will the words of the ancient sage
ever err]
Past owner talk det will become lies?

5. **Ko nwoŋi faŋa mo we...** [It issues from ancient times that ..]
It comes from past emph say..

6. **Ko tage ko nwoŋi faŋa mo we...** [It has been remarked since ancient
times that...]
It say it come from past time say..

In utterances 1-4, the subject is *Faŋa tu*, the ancient sage. In 5 and 6, it is
ko, the Kasem equivalent of the ambient 'it' in English that serves as
subject.

So important is the entitling phrase that when it does not occur at the
beginning of the proverb it comes at the end as a concluding comment. In
this position it is a defining clause such as, *Faŋa tu de o taane* (the
ancient sage and his talk).

The Ordinary Subject

There is more diversity as far as the subject of the core statement of the
proverb is concerned. The most common is however the third person
plural pronoun *ba*. This pronoun can be said to represents *nɔɔna*,
"people". We do not suppose it refers to the ancient sage since there is
difference in number.

Ex15: **Ba du mene de jwa keim ŋwaane mo**
They sow millet ......
"Millet is cultivated because of the expectation that it will some day yield
a crop".

This proverb when cited fully will read as follows:

Faŋa tu mo nɛ ye o ta o we ba du mene de jwa keim ŋwaane mo
(The ancient sage saw it and pronounced that ...)

Proverbs with *Ba* as subject are asserting or affirming a cultural norm, as it has understood from ancient times.

The second person singular *n* is another pronoun that functions as subject in the utterance.

Ex16: **N ná gwooni buga ka ja-m**
    You if underestimate river it catch you
"If you underestimate a pond it will drown you"

Proverbs like these are issuing a warning against inappropriate behaviours and they usually contain a condition and its fulfillment.

A bird or some animal may also serve as subject of the proverb utterance. A verb of saying such as **we** follows as in the example below.

Ex17: **Manlaa we n ná diini twio n ji ko vɔɔ**
    Chameleon says ....
"The chameleon says when on a tree assume the colour of its leaf"

Ex18: **Chworo ba ke kazɔgɔ lei**
    Hen   not do mortar thanks
"The fowl does not thank the mortar"

A pseudo-name may be the subject. For example, *A-nɛ-cham bu* (Mr I experienced hardships' son), as in the proverb **Anɛchambu sage de chwoŋa** (When the son of I-have-experienced-trouble takes his rest his weapons are on hand). *A-di-daane* (Mr I eat with others) as in **Adidaane de Adidaane mo di daane** (Mr I eat with others and Mr I eat with others eat together). "One good turn deserves another".

These pseudo names bear close resemblances to personal names and nicknames. For example, *Anɛcham* which is like the personal name *Aŋwedecham* (I live in pain) could pass for a real personal name except that in the context of the proverb it cannot be a name because personal names do not occur in proverbs. If personal names were to feature in the proverb its 'proverbiality' would be lost and the problem would become just a popular saying, wellerism or a *sinseira*. These names found in proverbs do not, like personal names, refer to individuals; rather they may describe hypothetical situations in which people can find themselves or maybe their personal characteristics. Situations and circumstances are thus personified by the coinage of names that refer to them.

This being as it may, the possibility nevertheless exists that the original composer of the proverb, in making the proverb had in mind the events that a neighbour experienced. That neighbour could not be named and instead a pseudonym constructed from a summary of the events and circumstances is thus used to provide the context for the proverb.

Other subjects include God, "who must kill before the Earth will consume", and other humans such as slaves, as in the case of the slave who must walk or go where his master wishes to go once the master's rope and its noose are around the slave's neck. Body parts are found as grammatical subjects for example, the hand which cannot deny the mouth except when it lacks the means to feed the mouth. We also notice kinship, friendship and other human relationships in subject position such as in the case of great friendships that are worth more than siblingship ties.

The Subject Matter of Kasena Proverbs

Kasena proverbs do not appear to deal with any particular favourite subject to the exclusion of others. As we have seen, proverbs deal with the broad domain of Kasena experience. There is no subject or issue that is too sacrosanct or too trivial to be commented upon in the proverb. Direct reference to the sexual act which in some cultures may be regarded as obscene is not avoided. Important life events like death and childbirth receive prolific commentary just like marriage and the status and condition of the unmarried adult.

Personal relations are naturally of great interest. Friendship, siblingship, filiation, kinship, or the lack of it, are discussed in the proverb just as conjugal relations and affinal relations are not excluded.

Kinship (*nubiu*) receives particular emphasis. We are told that human kinship ramifies widely: *Nabiinu naga dɔrma*. Patrilineal kinship which is the basis of the social structure is referred to in the context of *sɔŋɔ*, the compound house in which the family that grows around an agnatic lineage lives. The mud structure that serves as the physical shelter and dwelling place crumbles with time. It goes through what the Cambridge anthropologists have called a developmental cycle (see the Goody 1958 collection of essays on the subject). The *sɔŋɔ* may begin as a windscreen made from millet stalks where a couple set up home while they complete building their huts. It grows as this small unit, a conjugal family, grows and ramifies. Harmony and tolerance however, keep the members together, as proverbs tells us: *A ba lage konto tu ba jege sɔŋɔ.* (I don't want that man does not have a compound). When, after several generations, it has reached its optimum size, the land for compound farming becomes inadequate and competition and disharmony begin to rear their heads and witchcraft accusations become frequent, the membership of the compound begins to wilt and eventually it might be completely abandoned to become a *didwoŋo*, a farm and a burial ground for former occupants. The lineage, unlike the dwelling structure, should ideally grow and keep growing, hence the proverb remark that "To be survived by kin is the antidote to death". The *sayuu* (lit 'head house') is a major lineage whose members may not live in the same compound anymore. In fact they are likely to be dispersed throughout the clan-settlement or *nawuuri* or *kateiri* as these divisions of the chiefdom may be called.

From their proverbs we learn a lot about their conception of kinship and its place in the social structure. We are told that "One does not rob the domestic guinea fowl (i.e. lineage kin) of its eyes just to be able to salvage the vision of the wild guinea fowl (outsiders)". Kinship is like a scar that never disappears, *chero ye ŋɔn-dale mo*. Kin empathise with one another, "When your kin's head is going down your neck bends sidewards and it feels as though you were also losing the wrestling match", **ba ná jege n chero yuu ba vei tega, n ba ye gɛɛ mo**. However, it also pointed out that kinship should not be allowed to outweigh all other considerations. For example, "Siblings resemble physically but their stomachs (hearts) are not the same", **Nu puga bia nye daane mo se ba wo ba nye daane**. There are cases when "A dear friend may count more than a full sibling": **chilon-zɔŋɔ gare nu puga bu.**

In spite of the importance of patrilineal kinship, what Fortes (1969) refers to as complementary filiation receives reference. The mother's clan-settlement, we are told, should not be pointed at using the left hand. We are also told that the mother's clan-settlement is not really the place for the individual. The importance of the mother's clan settlement parallels her significance to the individual in this society where the father determines one's socio-political status. "If it were possible to roast the mother the desperate child would eat her but a mother could never do that to her child": **ba ná wɔge nu bu wó di se ba ná wɔge bu nu baa di.**

Chieftaincy is another subject we encounter many times in Kasena proverbs. This is interesting in view of the fact that Kasena have in the past lacked centralised statal structures comparable to those found among neighbouring peoples such as the Mamprusi and Moshi. The office of earthpriest, *tegatu*, is not mentioned in the proverbs, not even once to my knowledge. Perhaps this is not surprising since there are not many of such about in Kasena areas. The elder, *nakwe* often doubles up as *tegatu* in many Kasena clans.

The projection of the chief and the institution of chieftaincy is interesting in many respects. The chief is seen as a very powerful personality, so powerful that you cannot refuse to dance on the grounds that your limbs pain you, if the chief orders it; **pɛ we n sa ye n we n**

tankona wae? His child is better dressed than others and can afford to change his attire daily such that it becomes difficult to recognise him at all times. Kasena say, "When you are on bad terms with the chief, even the shepherds challenge you to a wrestling match" **Pɛ ná jege de nɔɔno nayera pwooli-m jaŋa mo.**

The chief's compound is also the centre of reference for the settlement. For example the slain leopard, an occurrence that is extraordinary enough to excite the curiosity of children, is carried to his compound. This reminds us of the customary entitlement of chiefs and kings in statal societies to certain big game killed within their territories. There does not seem to have been any legal requirement among the Kasena that big wild cats when killed should be sent to the chief. However trophies of animal parts such as the skin or a hind limb of the big game animals could be sent to the chief in token of his position in the chiefdom. This seems voluntary.

The chief is however reminded that power is not exercised in a vacuum. He must respect all his subjects even the poor nobodies (he may some day discover that the herbs he needs for his treatment are located in the farm of a nobody). Apparently, in spite of his power to compel a sick person to dance, as a proverb maintains, nevertheless, another proverb denies him the power and authority to dig up a poor subject's farm for the herbal components that are necessary to restore his health. He is reminded by the proverb that he is not indispensable; if he vacates his office there will not be shortage of replacements. He is told that he is not super- human; take away his privileges and he is just another man "who will eat even the seeds of the baobab".

As we have pointed out above, the proverb accords chieftaincy powers and privilege barely reflected in the everyday life of the people. However, it must also be pointed out that the portrayal of chiefship by the proverb is consistent with the way the folktale also represents the institution.

Authority is a matter of concern in the proverb. The elder should be respected even if he is puny. People ignore the puny elder at their cost. Seniority goes with age, and with it power in the ritual domain. The arm of the elder is difficult to twist, so says a proverb. The elder is however reminded that tolerance is the golden rule that an elder must observe if he wishes to be successful in the office of elder or head: "Mr I-don't-want-that does not have a house". Elders should know that wisdom has to be earned and must be demonstrated if it is to be appreciated by all; it cannot be claimed or derived from ascription. After all wisdom, the proverb says, is not like the *cheilima* fruit that it should grow in abundance within the stomach of the elder. Furthermore, elders must realise that the child who has travelled around, has seen and experienced the external world may have acquired greater wisdom than elders who have not had the benefit of going abroad.

The question of power abuse, or shall we say abuse of privilege, is also dealt with in proverbs. The elder is told that he must not take more than his due; one thigh from the sacrificed victim is in order but two thighs break the elder's bag. Authority is also a double-edged sword, it can sometimes place the elder in an awkward position or at a disadvantage: just as an elder takes the thigh of a big animal, the priced share, he must also accept the thigh of the puny bird, since tradition allocates that to him as his share.

We see economic activities that are important to the Kasena being discussed such as farming (including crop cultivation and animal husbandry) and hunting as well as marketing. However, fishing does not appear to have been a favourite subject for discussion, at least not in the corpus collected by us so far. Crop cultivation in particular receives greater mention and this is in accordance with the emphasis Kasena agriculture places on millet cultivation. We find references to the rationale for sowing the seed rather its consumption at a time when it is most needed as food. The proverb states that there is no greater pain than to have the elephant you long to see walk in your farm destroying in the process the tender millet as it germinates. The "dos" and "donts" of cultivation are discussed. The importance of endurance in farm work is stressed. The proverb maintains that "it is the farmer who has patience and endurance who is able to farm on till the mid-day" and in the same way, it is the husbandman who is patient who would some day get to eat the milk of a barren cow. Laziness is chastised.

Religion receives pride of place in these proverbs. God receives many references as Kasena philosophise about life and the destiny of man and woman. God is the ultimate arbiter in human affairs without whose acquiescence nothing happens in the world. In these statements, God is more than just an otiose God who is far removed from the world of man. The power of God is demonstrated through comparisons with the chief, the witches and the Earth which is so important to the existence of communities; even the dead are buried in it and the representations of the land of the ancestors suggests that it too lies deep down in the bowls of the earth. The earth, the proverb says, will not eat what has not been slaughtered by God. Implied here is a statement to the effect that though witches may be dreaded because they destroy life, nevertheless their power derives from God who acquiesces before the witch's craft will work. The powerful and wealthy chief's gift means nothing in comparison with divine gift. We are told that the person who has the blessings of God walks with a stride different from that of other humans.

Lesser gods and the ancestors are mentioned less often by comparison.

They are not to be trifled with, as the proverb says: "If you underestimate a river (which is the manifestation of a god) it will snatch you".

The technology, arts and entertainment of the Kasena also receive some mention. We hear reference to instruments of war and farming, the making of gourds from calabash and straw bangles and bracelets (*vale*) etc. Kasena music, drumming and dancing etiquette are mentioned. We are told that inability to appreciate a song induces anger and frustration in the hearer who is not sure that the song is not making insulting comments on him or her. The dancer is told she must not dance out of time when the drummer happens to lack mastery of his craft. We are reminded also that it is the rich who walk before the drummers and take the honour of being accompanied by them because they have the means to reward the praise singers.

The proverb expresses certain truths about life. Through the proverb we are told that truth itself is like a sore, the unpleasant truth hurts. The human lineage ramifies widely while kinship is like an unhealing or chronic sore. When a soothsayer prognosticates your future ask yourself if his predictions make sense against your situation and circumstances. Shame may not kill but it makes a person shy. Such a person avoids the company of others; it is as if he or she could or would grow an extra forehead to cover the face, in the attempt to avoid others. We could add that some people can be driven by a feeling of intense shame to commit suicide. A proverb remarks that the flesh does not say no to the desires of the heart: **boboŋa keim ba nyɔne year.**(i.e. the exertions induced by desire do not sour the body).

General human behaviour is discussed and the audience are reminded of what is proper behaviour and what is not and receive advice accordingly. A person does not mix stone pebbles in the grain of millet he or she wishes to eat or chew, just as a dog does not take a deep bite of its puppy for it would be inflicting pain on itself vicariously. Once in Rome a person should do as the Romans do; this we are told is the wisdom of the chameleon which says when you find yourself on a tree harmonize with your new environment. The person who wishes to share the meal of a child must learn to be persuasive. The female ant, which does not have much by way of a sexual organ does not assume that its husband knows this for a fact; it demonstrates its willing to engage in the act by offering itself to its spouse. Likewise, those who have a duty are obliged to contribute their widow's mite, even if circumstances make it impossible to discharge that duty fully.

What people see and observe in nature is also discussed in the proverb. We are told for example that when dogs are at play they take turns to fall for each other irrespective of the play partners' relative strength. The lizard that jumps from a height may receive no applause but it prides itself on its achievement as it lies where it dropped, nodding its head as if in self congratulation. The hedgehog is one piece of meat that walks majestically while the hawk watches but the sight of a tortoise on dry land amounts to its capture by observant humans. The bird that takes to flight in the night does so for a good reason. Animal behaviour regarding claims to territory is noted and commented upon as follows: while a donkey does not refuse to take a rest wherever it can find it, says a proverb, nevertheless, it does not bray in the territory belonging to another male donkey.

We can conclude that Kasena proverbs have as their subject matter those values that Kasena cherish so much, such as industry, love and concern for others, especially kin, respect for old age, patience, foresight etc as well as those that they abhor such as greed, abuse of power, laziness, disrespect etc.

The Personal Name as a Proverb

The personal name may be a nickname or a formal name. Name giving provides each Kasena person who is entitled to give a name to self or other with the opportunity to coin a proverb. Though there are stereotyped names like Adoa and Kadoa, (child born on rainy day), Abuga and Kabuga (child born on the way to river or at the river) Adda and Kada (child born after the death of a sibling in its infancy) etc which are not proverbial as they reflect the place of birth, the circumstance and even mode of birth, the majority of the names that Kasena individuals bear are proverbial in their own right. This does not mean that the names are necessarily coined from proverbs or are put to the same uses as proverbs. Rather, it is because they refer to reflections on personal circumstances and the name givers' attempts to philosophise and comment on life.

People use the opportunity of name giving quite often to comment on the state of their own relations with their neighbours, kin and the communities as well as their hopes and aspirations, their failures and frustrations etc. We have names like *Logojei* (the world has disappeared), *Fangajei* (the good old days are no more), *chirajei* (the ancestors edict no longer obtains), *Biateo* (Children's world) which like proverbs celebrate the past. Take the following *Keimtogedetu* (deeds follow their authors, i.e. what you sow is what you earn) and *Goronongdiga* (the murderer within i.e. those to fear most are the enemies within), which are just like proverbs in that they express the kinds of cherished wisdom based on observation of life which we find enshrined in proverbs.

Individuals have been observed to occasionally acknowledge the wisdom in a particular name by remarking on how "sweet" the name is. I have also come across people who have been reluctant to accept the privilege and the duty of choosing a name for a child on the grounds that they did not have it in them to propose names that would carry the expected philosophical load that others might praise.

Just as people appreciate the wisdom enshrined in personal names (and this includes the names of pets), there is also the awareness that name givers use names to do battle more like the way Anyi of eastern Cote d'Ivoire use the wax prints that bear proverbs for their names to comment on their relations with others in their society, Domowitz (1992). Names like *Kobereswoa* (it teaches a lesson) or to put it another way, "Now I know better" and *Yebere* (don't instruct) are names used by kin to attack kin and their meanings are often not lost on the target audience. These are names that we might consider less proverbial since they target specific individuals.

Despite the shared characteristics between names and proverbs, names are easily distinguished from proper proverbs. Among other things, names have a known author and cannot be used in isolation for illustrative purposes or to clinch an argument in the way that proverbs are used. However, there have been cases where names which were not initially intended to have wide currency eventually have caught on and begun to be quoted almost as though they were proverbs. One example of this is the name, *Liirinweeri* (take it out of the stream and make a fire to warm yourself). Most people in Paga and Navrongo chiefdoms know about this name and its meaning: it is a comment on ingratitude. Its full statement goes as follows: 'if you see a drowning person let him or her drown for your rescuing that person earns you nothing but future insults and ingratitude. It is better for you to have rescued a log awash in the flood, for it would serve your creature needs'. In this case, the name giver bore a private grudge which then became the basis for this name. Now others quote the name as a means of commenting on their own experiences vis a vis others as a way that conveys the message that they regretted the good they once did to somebody else. For those who put a personal name to this use, it has ceased temporarily to be a personal name and become a pseudo-proverb. Another of such names is *Nabwombajegechega* (the poor have no claim to the truth). The name means the poor and the meek in society are denied any claim to the truth or their entitlements; utterances and claims of the powerful on the other hand are taken seriously even when they have less merit. The proverb which says "The arrow of the powerful prevails against the wind" (*dedɛɛro chene wae vwio*) reflects this philosophy of might is right.

We may ask at this point whether, in view of the importance of proverbs, they are ever used as names. There is perhaps no reason for not using proverbs as names for individuals or pets however, this author knows of no such names. There are certainly names that hint at proverbs such as *Bokwasam* (Daughters compounds) which may allude to the proverb which remarks that "if a daughter does not ruin the lineage her child will do so", *bokɔ na wo de sɔŋɔ o bu jwa wó de sɔŋɔ*.

Kasena *Sinseiri*

In Kasem, the *sinseira*, (singular for *sinseiri*) is a separate oral literature genre. However, it comes close to wellerism, which Abrahams (1972:122) describes as a type of proverb, "dialog-proverb", or cliche imputed to a specific person. He goes on to remark that "This dialog-proverb form is really a joking device in English, but in many African and New World Negro groups wellerisms are used for less jocular purposes". The *Sinseira* is essentially a saying, a memorable utterance often attributable to an individual who may still be alive at the time of speaking. Such an utterance may have remained in the popular memory for a number of reasons, prominent among which is the fun it evokes. The *sinseira* may not have been intended by their originators as a joke or anything funny but people who have found them to be funny have turn them into jokes worth recalling in appropriate circumstances.

The etymology of the term *sinseira* supports the view that this is a category of sayings that are primarily jokes. Loud laughter depicting merry-making is qualified by the epithet, *-seira*, as in *mɔn-seira* derived from the verb *seeri*, the same verb that is the root from which *sinseira* is derived. Young girls have a way of laughing which depicts mirth or sometimes sarcasm which ends with *"heheya!"* This type of laughter is typically described as *mɔn-seira*, the laugh that has a dovetail to it. Why the adjective *seira* which derives from a verb which means to "wash" should be so used is not easily explained. However the mirth which characterises the *sinseira* cannot be denied.

The joke component of *sinseira* often centres on the initiator of the saying. Such a person's name may be appended to the saying. Often there is something about the originator or his character that others find awkward. Many a time the originators are people of low esteem: strangers, drunks, midgets etc., people whose appearance, demeanor or behaviour is idiosyncratic or evokes ridicule. We do not for example find *senseiri* attributed to chiefs or important people. This is not to suggest that powerful people do not make remarks that would be quoted in future. For example, Navropɛ Kwara, chief of Navrongo at the time the British arrived in the first decade of the 20th Century is said to have maintained that exogamy, as once strictly enforced, should be relaxed. In his words, "when fish in a pond increase considerably they prey on their kind". (*Buga ywona ná puli ya di daane mo*). This statement which has survived and is still quoted, is not regarded as a *sinseira* but as a statement of the character of a proverb that merits quotation in formal circumstances in the justification of a marriage between very distant kin, when such a union is questioned by the traditionalists.

The interest in a *sinseira* derives from the way in which it is uttered, the personality of the originator, the circumstances in which it was uttered and perhaps the fact that a certain person has coined a pet phrase which he or she uses frequently and in sundry situations. For example *Wε taa cho Gween* (may God check Gween) becomes a *sinseira* to be quoted by others because the author of the *sinseira*, a certain midget from the Paga chiefdom, was observed to use it frequently in his response to the teasing questions of the public. People would now use this saying in the sense of "God forbid", thus making it into a kind of idiomatic expression or cliche.

These sayings have been attributed not only to human beings but also to animals and birds. This springs from the observation of such animals, and the cries they make. Bird song and animal cries sometimes become lexicalised and serve as the basis for making statements that belong in the category of *sinseira* in Kasem. In this case the saying, although never attributed to a superior intelligence nevertheless has the quality of a proverb as it contains consolation features and advice for those who find themselves in peculiar circumstances.   A *sinseira* can also derive from popular music or slogans in a foreign language not understood by the Kasena. Since the introduction of cheap radios in the 1950s to date, Kasena have listened to broadcasts not only in English of which some can boast of some limited comprehension but also in southern Ghanaian languages which are incomprehensible to the majority of people. When a tune or phrase sounds interesting to the ears, attempts might be made to reproduce it by lexicalising it and attaching Kasem words to the tune. For example the drum signal tune for the official news on Ghana TV was lexicalised as *Pungu chwoŋa, ŋweena yerane, Pungu chwoŋa, ŋweena yerane* (Pungu road, only thieves, Pungu road only thieves). A talking drum signal which conveys a message in the Akan culture is thus given meaning which makes sense to the local community which may well have been worried by the anti-social activities that go on in the eastern corner of Navrongo town.

Though most *sinseira* have known authorship there are nevertheless a number of *senseiri* for which an author cannot be immediately assigned. Such sayings which may have began as true *senseiri* with known authors have been retained because of the moral truth that lies behind them. Thus to all intents and purposes these would be like proverbs and may even be treated as proverbs. A statement like *Wɔ mo go ye o wo pwoni*? (Who killed but did not skin the game for cooking) is one example. It has no known authorship but is not however strictly a proverb. Nevertheless, it can be cited in certain circumstance almost as if it were a proverb. *N ná jege wiiru bokɔ, n da-n ba kua kua*? (If you have hyena's daughter, you don't eat bone?) which has no known author seems to approximate to a proverb and may even be attributed to the collective wisdom of the ancestors.

Occasionally, a saying becomes memorable because of the peculiar circumstances under which the statement come to be made. In such as case it becomes memorable because people have found it interesting in some way, perhaps because it evoked mixed feelings of pity and disgust in people about the peculiar circumstances in which the author once found himself. The situation may be ridiculous, as in the case of the man foraging for shea nut fruits before daybreak but whose plight nevertheless strikes a note of pitiable because a scavenger also foraging for food attacked him in the process. A person by the fact that he or she is ethnically Moshie may command little sympathy with a people who still retain memories of the slave raids and atrocities committed by Moshie raiders, however, he is pitied and sympathized with for the loss of his purse in the market place. This the comment he utters on discovery that he had lost his purse becomes a memorable one although it was said in a different language.

Sayings can also become the means for ethnic stereotyping. There are only a few sayings that do this specifically. By attributing a saying that does not reflect positively on the utterer who though not named is identified as member of a neighbouring ethnic group or even somebody from a different Kasena chiefdom it becomes possible to make remarks that present others in an unfavourable light. Two such sayings come to mind, one concerning what a person from the Chiana chiefdom is reputed to have said and another identified as having been uttered by a Nankani-speaking person. These kinds of sayings are fictitious and the encounters that they relate probably never took place. There is no particular need here to discuss this type of sayings. The least said about them the better.

Senseiri, as popular catchy sayings, have a more local character and appeal than proverbs which are believed by the people to encapsulate universal truths applicable everywhere. Since sayings refer to individuals who are usually known to the group within which the saying circulates, sayings would vary from chiefdom to chiefdom and we can expect that *senseiri* that are popular on one side of the international border would not be popular or known on the other, precisely because there has been reduced interaction between the members of the Kasena ethnic communities found on either side of the international border since colonial times. It would also be expected that as time obliterates the identities of the persons to whom authorship is attributed many former sayings would fade away and fall into disuse or become proverbs.

On the language of Kasena sayings, it should be pointed out that although most of them are in the Kasem language those attributed to people identified as speaking neighbouring languages may be wholly or partially in that language. In the case of the saying attributed to a certain Nankani person, the language is Kasem rather than Nankani. Interestingly, the saying attributed to the person from Chiana, which is a Kasem-speaking chiefdom, the dialect is Chiana dialect, not Navrongo dialect. Part of the fun is to reproduce the utterance in a dialect which exhibits the peculiar features of the Chiana dialect.

Structurally, the sayings can take any form. However, we retain here their designation as statements. More often we are dealing with utterances that have become fixed sayings precisely because, regardless of their grammatical structure, they were originally exclamatory in function. That is to say, they were originally spontaneous and unpremeditated remarks let out on the spur of the moment by distraught individuals in their moment of trial.

A characteristic feature of sayings is the omission of a function word or verb in the construction of the sentence. Take for example the following: **Puŋu chwoŋa, ŋweena yerane**. (Thieves abound on the Pungu road).

This sentence can be expanded with the addition of the equative verbal *ye* to read *Puŋu chwoŋa ye ŋweena yerane*. (Alas, Pungu road abounds with thieves).

In the same way, *Lam wo gwoŋo ne, Asutaam* (Beauty is in the grave) is an ellipsis of two sentences or clauses thus: *Lam wo gwoŋo ne, Asutaam de o taane*. (Beauty is in the grave, Asutaane and his talk) or *Lam wo gwoŋo ne, Asutaam mo taga*. (Beauty is in the grave, Asutaane said this).

A *sinseira* may take the from of a question, albeit a rhetorical one, such as in the following:
A pa ko taa ye-m se-n vo Bolaa se-n ba?
(Would you wish you had to go to Bolga and return the same day?)

N ná jege wiiru bokɔ, n da-n ba kua kua?
(If you have hyena's daughter, you don't eat bone?)

Wɔ mo go ye o wo pwoni?
Who killed but did not skin the game?

A *sinseira* could also take the form of a declarative sentence as in the following:

Feila kam ta wo tage wolɔŋɔ
The Whiteman has not yet spoken evil

Kalwoa bam laam gwori da sia mo
The monkeys are now plucking each other's bambara beans

Imperative structures also occur in the structure of the *sinseira* as in the following:

Manlaa tan vei mɛmɛ se tega wo puri.
Chameleon, walk slowly so the earth does not open

Kasena *sinseiri* as would be expected, need not be single clause structures. More often a *sinseira* can be broken into several clauses with independent and dependent clauses combining or linked together. In *Peppeppeepe, a nakɔ wo pendaa ne*, we have a whistle sound followed by a simple sentence comprising subject, locative verb and place adverbial.

Peppepeepe, //a nakɔ /wo /pendaa ne///

ᴏ‌∝-   S   P A
(Peppepeepe, my siter lives in Pindaa)

The structural complexity of some sayings is exhibited by the combination of several clauses as in the following utterance:

Didwonkwogo yage ne, a yage a nɔne dem; nam done se-a si, a done nanjoa kam?
Let me go, Spider! How can I let go of my meat. Then get on with it, eat me! How can I eat a fly

We can have in a saying a set of imperative structures combining with declaratives that functionally are rhetorical questions, such as is illustrated by the following:

IMPERATIVES

1. Didwonkwogo // yage / ne //   **2. nam / done //se-a / si//**

   ∝-   P   C   A   P   //   S P

  (Spider,   let go me)   (Then chew so I rest)

DECLARATIVES

3. **a / yage / a nɔne dem//**   **4. a / done / nanjoa kam//**

    S   P   C   S   P   C

   (I   leave   my meat det ?)   (I chew   fly det ?)

We come across potentially autonomous sentences which may not at first appear to be related logically and yet combining to constitute a saying, as in the example below:

Boŋo ba di sabare, Wagadogo chɔge logo

A goat does not eat thorns, Ouagadougou has spoilt the world

Where the sentence, **Boŋo / ba di / sabare //** (A goat does not eat thorns) combines with the following:

Wagadogo / chɔge / logo // (Ouagadougou has spoilt the world)

    S   P   C

The two sentences seem not to bear any logical relationship until they are situated in the context of the trips of poor needy local girls going to Ouagadougou in recent times to earn a living by prostitution and eventually being returned as a funeral bundle.

Another kind of sentence complexity is suggested by serialisation as in the following *sinseira*:

Ka kare ka di// ka kare ka di //zem da-n di (It roves about searching for food, it roves about searching for food, serves you right, let's see you eat today). Here we have three independent sentences or clauses juxtaposed the first two of which are reduplications and exhibit serialisation of verbal elements sharing subject markers and common aspect, thus:

Ka kare :: ka di //   **(ɴ) zem da:: -n di //**

 S   P   S P   S   A   P   S P

 (it rove::   it eat)   You today again you eat

The pronoun **ka** here is an impersonal pronoun, and its repetition in the second clauselet serves the purpose of a structural device necessary in Kasem to anchor the second verbal in the serial chain..

Note also that it is possible to analyse the entire sentence more simply into an embedded or rankshifted serial clause functioning as a minor sentence in a vocative mood followed by an imperative structure thus:

[Ka kare :: ka di// ka kare :: ka di] // zem da-n di ///

∝_   ∝!

An analysis like the latter would mean that somebody called Kakarekadi is being mentioned by mentioned by name and mockingly told off.

Side by side with complex structures like the above can be found sayings that contain only minor clauses that do not exhibit verbs. The following are examples:

Pedea// Angola /// (Courage, Angola)

∝_   ∝_

The saying *Boboŋa biseim* (Greeting made in the imagination) has a similar structure but the following exhibit more complexity although no verbal is in evidence.

Feila chulu // gwaleyara jeŋa swɛ // (The Whiteman's taboo, the Slave

∝_   ∝_   raiding's bracelet)

Similar to the *sinseira* are the nicknames that circulate among members of a peer group. A group of friends might hear somebody use an unusual expression which they repeat among themselves to poke fun at the originator. With time this frequently used phrase might become the nickname that this group would use to address each other. Among Kasena women this is common. This author recalls that his mother and her friends used to call themselves by a nickname which was a phrase attributed to a certain mad woman in Navrongo market. The mad woman had coined a tune to the words, *Amo ne mae tento*, (really, look how big I am). This type of popular use of language is to be found in all Ghanaian societies, including the schools. For example a teacher earns a nickname because he or she frequently uses a certain expression. With time this same expression becomes the jocular name for the peer group of classmates. This author can recall countless examples of these nicknames some of which continue to be used later on in life.

CHAPTER THREE

Interpretation of Proverb Texts

Introduction:

In this chapter we will now attempt to introduce some Kasena proverbs and comment on their literal meanings and their applications in situations. It will be seen that some of these require more explanation than others.

My approach to the interpretation of Kasena proverbs recognises that a proverb has several components which are similar to the three components discussed by Siran (1993). They include the 'signification' of the proverb, or that aspect it that can be translated into another language i.e the literal text of the proverb. Then there is what Siran calls the 'value' of the proverb, that aspect of the proverb that is not translatable but is nevertheless understood by the users and their participant audiences, interlocutor or those at whom the proverb is directed. It is here assumed that a proverb would not normally be quoted at audiences that could not understand the proverb. Siran (1993:225) regards the 'value' component of the proverb as " a sentence left unspoken that listeners must substitute for the text of the proverb if they are to understand what is meant here and now". I would substitute for sentence, the sets of concepts and ideas that constitute the background against which the proverb can be understood. That is, when the proverb statement is taken at its literal value, it subsumes various ideas, beliefs and norms some of which may be culture specific. Thus the Kasena word *nabɔ* may, for lack of a better term, be translated by the English kinship term 'brother', but the *nabɔ* is not simply a 'brother' [male sibling], he is a male sibling where a female is the point of reference.

Finally, there is the meaning of the proverb which Siran defines as what "..enables listeners to make the substitution and which provisionally can be characterised as what, in the text, translation lets slip". Meaning, here is the symbolic meaning of the proverb seen from the totality of its references and uses or its potential meaning. In the context in which Siran invokes it the concept would seem to exhibit similarities to the "odd job word", or Needham's (1975) polythetic class. In Siran's view the proverb's meaning is an open-ended space which cannot be exhausted but within which any particular or actual usage can be situated. We might also conceive of the meaning of the proverb in this case in terms of its connotative meaning, having dealt with its denotative meanings.

Below, I attempt to capture the signification of the proverb by translating it into English. This is not always as easy as Siran's definition would suggest for it is not every utterance that is amenable to straight forward translation. There are certain aspects of Kasena material and normative culture that defy translation into an Indo-European language like English since proximate equivalences are lacking. However, what is lacking in the translation is compensated for by the elaborate explanations that follow. Those aspects of Kasena social structure that might shed light on the issues that the proverb statement refers to covertly, if not overtly, are thereby elucidated. Some proverbs, it will be found, require more explanation than others in this respect.

In attempting to analyze the 'value' of the proverb its literal interpretation will be taken into account, first and foremost. Its literal meaning is discussed to show how that statement stands in the context of the social and cultural experience of the Kasena people and how understanding the culture and society of the Kasena suggests the motivation of the statement in the first place. It is assumed that each proverb makes sense even in its literal form, even where the proverb statement is evidently hyperbolical in character. It is only when that sense is appreciated that the value of the proverb emerges and its symbolism can be appreciated.

From the interpretation of the literal meaning of the proverb, the general applicability of the proverb is discussed and where possible summarized pointing out the moral and ethical meaning of the proverb. Not all proverbs lend themselves to such treatment. Where summarizing the proverb is not easily accomplished concrete examples of its application are suggested.

Unlike Siran, I take the view that Kasena proverbs are mostly symbols rather than being partly symbol and partly sign. It can be argued that an understanding of the 'signification' and 'value' of the Kasena proverb usually is adequate for the understanding of the proverb and it equips the user to employ the proverb in appropriate situations in future. This is not to deny that some people have a better appreciation of proverbs than others. However, this is a function of cultural competence reflected in the extent to which a person is immersed in the traditional culture. There must be very few Kasena proverbs which are arbitrary in their applications such that the appreciation of the symbol alone is not enough to appreciate the situations in which it might or might not be used. This feature of arbitrariness has been assigned to the proverbs of the Vute of Cameroon by Siran (op cit 236). While, the Kasena riddle has this characteristic of arbitrariness, since the correct responses of the riddle have to be learnt rather than deduced from its metaphorical statement alone, Kasena proverbs strike me as different.

1. **Wiiru we o kore gɛɛre mo se o ba kore chwo-dɔrɔ**
   The hyena says he is worried by failure to find carrion and not by the
   distance he has to travel to get it

Commentary: *Wiiru*, hyena, is a favourite character in Kasena folktales
notorious for his inordinate greed and voracious appetite. He is stupid
because he allows his stomach to rule over his common sense and
morality counts for naught with this character. For example in one folktale
he sells his mother on the advice of his clever and cunning "friend", Nase,
the rabbit who never wishes Wiiru well.

This character is modelled on the African hyena, an animal Kasena
regard as despicable. In their search for food and carrion, hyenas are
known to visit human settlements at night to prey on whatever they can
get. This could mean travelling for a long distance from their wild habitat
and risking danger to get to the human settlements, hence the statement
that hyena is worried by failure to find food for his belly more than by the
long distance it may take to find its prey. Most other predators, in
contrast were not known to frequent human settlements except for the
occasional incursion.

The proverb admires the dedication of the hyena in its quest for food.
In the context of seasonal food scarcity, people like the Kasena and their
neighbours know only too well the dangers and indignities that famine can
impose on a person. The difference is that there is no seasonality to
hyena's quest for food which makes hyena's behaviour in this regard
atypical of human conduct.

The message of the proverb is that certain ends justify the means
necessary to achieve them just as an exceptional appetite compels the
adoption of exceptional food search strategies. This proverb could also
have passed for a *sinseira* (a popular saying). In a sense, this statement
seems to fall into the class of utterance that typifies more the self-centred
inclinations of ordinary individuals than the community-spirited ancestors.

2. **Namɔra ba mɔne na-tuntwogo**
   The calf does not poke fun at the horn-less cow (on account of its
   handicap).

Commentary: Horns are good for a cow since they are its means of self
assertion against other bovine creatures. The calf has no horns and these
should develop with time; however until horns have appeared a calf
remains a hornless beast. In this respect, the calf should not task the
hornless cow over its inability to have horns. The proverb insists that it
would be foolhardy to laugh at the hornless cow since a calf cannot be
sure that it will ever grow horns in future. After all, when the hornless
cow was a calf it probably never imagined that some day it would not be

able to grow horns like other members of its kind.

In the stock of idiomatic expressions available to Kasena, to say that a person, particularly a child or subordinate, 'has now developed horns' (o nwoŋi nyea) is to imply that that person has become assertive to the point of being unruly.

The proverb seems to be making the point that no condition is permanent. The future is not entirely predictable. It warns the lucky ones who for a moment forget that their accomplishments could be due to good fortune. They should therefore have sympathy for the unlucky ones who through no fault of their own find themselves in a predicament. Worse still, it is foolhardy to preempt one's future, for no one can tell what tomorrow might bring.

The proverb appears to be directed especially firstly at the arrogant youth who do not respect unsuccessful others because they do not know any better; and secondly, at those who have the tendency to poke fun at the handicapped. More generally, it is a rebuke aimed at the well-off and the fortunate in society who happen not to sympathise with those who fall short of society' expectations. In a more or less egalitarian society, it is unwise to boast. Folktales and stories are told of how people who were once proud of their looks and had laughed at or showed disrespect and to others not so fortunate, e.g. the sick, the poor and the physically deformed or handicapped. Eventually, they paid the price for their folly when they too developed similar disfigurement. In many African societies people do not ridicule the sick or the handicapped. It is almost taboo to do so, nevertheless people make insulting references to the physical handicap and disabilities of those they quarrel or fight with.

The interested reader may refer to saying # 32 below which points to the folly of self-assurance in the belief that adversity was too distant to ever strike and the associated tendency for those who feel this way to ridicule their unfortunate neighbours, as was the case of the mother of sons who used to taunt her co-wife for her inability to have sons.

3. **Kua cheiŋi kabeila**
    A bone has occupied the space in the soup bowl
    Bone prevents the diner from getting at the soup in the bowl
Commentary: *Kabeila* is a clay utensil usually shaped like a semi-sphere, except that it narrows at the mouth. It has a flat bottom which enables it to stand. The soup or sauce is put in the *kabeila* while the thick stiff porridge that goes with it is served in a separate bowl made from calabash. Enamel ware has since replaced the latter in most Kasena homes. The sauce may be boiled leafy vegetable mixed with ingredients and condiments like salt, pepper, locust bean cheese and bits of dry meat

or fish. When fresh meat is available it might be cooked with the vegetable sauce and served in the same utensil. Bone is not usually extracted from the meat before cooking it.

The main Kasena meal is eaten by cutting a morsel of porridge and dipping it in the soup in such a way that it is covered with enough soup before it is eaten. When a sizable bone sticks in the soup bowl it creates difficulties for the eater who cannot easily dip a morsel of thick stiff porridge in and fetch a reasonable portion of sauce. Customarily, meat is eaten at the end of the meal.

The question that the proverb seems to be asking is whether it is worth the trouble to allow the bone to remain in the stew or soup bowl, seeing that it is only a bone that is taking up so much space and making it hard to eat one's meal. If a bone is soft enough it may be eaten or else whatever juice or marrow remains in it is sucked out and the dry bone dropped for the dogs. We have here a problem which is not unsurmountable and the proverbs would seem to suggest the solution of removal.

This proverb resembles a cliche. It may be used to describe the situation where a powerful person is an impediment to the realization of another's desires. We are reminded of a similar proverb which runs as follows: *kapaa ná cheiŋi buga ŋyeŋo ye dwei* (when the cobra claims the pool the crocodile does not contest).

4. **Ko ná ni vora ba wó jwoŋi veene**
    When necessity compels, soothsayers will accept hibiscus sabdariffa seeds for fees

Commentary: The *voro* is a soothsayer who assists those in need of his services to communicate with the ancestors and divinities. For his service the *voro* takes a fee. This may be a hen, money or grain but rarely *veene*, hibiscus seeds, which are not staples. The seeds of the hibiscus plant are hard and take long to boil and become tender. Even then they are not served except when mixed with other grains like millet and beans. Kasena take the position that the fees that the soothsayer would take or demand would be for the divinity that guides his performance. It is said that a soothsayer lacks the option to refuse the fees provided by the clients. However clients would be expected to settle their fees in the customarily recognised medium, if they are not to offend the divinity being consulted and jeopardize the seance.

The proverbs informs that necessity can compel a soothsayer to take his fee in any form or medium. For example, in the past when food shortages prevailed in a bad year hibiscus grain served the same purpose that millet would normally serve.

The proverb advises on the need to adapt to changing situations since even gods whom Kasena regard as inhuman and inflexible do recognise and accept that circumstances can compel adaptations.

The proverb can be quoted at those who seem to be uncompromising in their attitudes and behaviours and it serves as warning to those who stick by the rule in all circumstance and refuse to accept the need for accommodation.

5.   **Anɛcham bu sage de chwoŋa**
     The son of I-have-experienced-trouble takes his rest with his weapons on hand.
Commentary: Kasena names reflect the experiences of the name giver and his or her background and lineage history as well as the circumstances surrounding the birth of the individual. There are nicknames as well as formal names allocated to the individual at birth or sometime thereafter. In the case of the nickname it is the experience and attributes of the person who bears the name that are reflected in the name utterance. A name such as *Anɛcham* reflects on past unpleasant experiences. In this example the name *Anɛcham* is not a formal name since it is a generic which does not refer to a known individual, although we should not be surprised to come across individuals bearing it as a formal name allocated at birth. *Chwoŋa* are the arms (quiver with bow and arrows) that are used for defence and offence as well as for hunting.

The point of the proverb is that a person learns from his or her own bitter experiences as well as those of his or her parents and kin. Where a person has come to grief in tragic circumstances the memory remains with the offspring. The memory may be kept alive through ritual observances and taboo or totem practices and prohibitions. The lost of a parent is not a thing that an average Kasena person would forget since a person benefits so much from the protection of the parent, particularly the father, in this patriarchal kind of society. The deceased parent is expected to watch over the living offspring and to intervene for better or for worse in the affairs of the living.

To appreciate the proverb, it has to be recalled that in former times physical harm could befall a person at a moment's notice, even in the relative security of the home, and it was necessary to be prepared for self defence. In the past it was not unheard of for big game to visit the settlement or enemies, especially slave raiders, to mount unexpected attacks. The diaries kept by the White Fathers in the first decade of the twentieth century testify to the frequency with which big game animals such as leopards, buffalo, elephant etc made incursions. It seemed to have continued up to the mid 1950s. Big game animals were however only one kind of danger in the past. Slave raiders were common and group or private vendettas existed too. There is the story of the man who was surprised by his enemy as he made sacrificial offerings on a shrine in the outer courtyard. Having noticed his armed enemy waiting in hiding for him to finish his ritual for the attack to commence, he had the presence of mind to pretend not to have observed him. Feigning to be exasperated with the peculiar demands of his fetish he complained loudly, enough for the enemy to overhear, "What a demanding fetish; it requires you to dance in and out of the house before you complete your sacrificial offering". He was allowed to dance in only to emerge with his bow to defend himself.

The proverbs is saying that if *Anecham* suffered because he was careless his son will not repeat that mistake; he will have his weapons by his side even when he sleeps.

The proverb is not only describing human tendencies but also warning that once bitten the victim should be twice shy. As another proverb reiterates, when a buffalo has killed your father the sight of its excrement alone is enough for you to take flight.

6. **Kanyambwoga nam mo ka kweeim**
   Spotting a tortoise amounts to its capture
Commentary: The proverb refers to the sighting of the tortoise on dry land and not necessarily in the water, since the tortoise is an amphibian. On land the animal is a sluggish and tends to recoils into his shell when there is danger. Though this is adequate protection against some predators it is hopeless against human predators. Thus a person who sights a tortoise on dry land is assured of cheap meat.

This proverb is used to suggest that a situation is one of hopelessness. People preempt the future by having savings to tide them over at a moment of need. Savings and the buffer stock may however get depleted. A person might thus finds himself or herself at wits end, with no endogenous support. A woman responds to another's request for material help such as money or food by saying, "I have nothing left for myself; i.e, what you see is what you get" and drives home the point by quoting this proverb.

7. **Bumburi toom nwoŋi de ni**
   The death of the *bumburi* frog issues from its own mouth
   It is the *bumburi* frog that proclaims its own death
Commentary: *Bumburi* is a species of large frog that Kasena consider good to eat. It makes so much noise thereby unwittingly advertising its whereabouts. Its capture and death are thus blamed on its own doing. The proverb is remarking that if the poor creature did not as a habit make so much noise it might possibly escape the notice of its predators, especially

children.

The proverb is used to refer to cases where the victim is to blame for his or her fate and misfortune.

8. **Beregɛo koro mo tigi tento puu: konkwonpwoŋo de ko keira**
   It is foolhardiness that accounts for the pile of plucked feathers
   Unwillingness to heed advice accounts for the pile of plucked feathers

Commentary: This proverb which could also pass for a *sinseira;* it has the quality of seriousness that proverbs have yet can hardly be the kind of statement that can be attributed directly to the ancestors. It imitates the song of mother dove. The dove seems to blame its young one for not heeding her advice thus facilitating its capture by boys hunting birds. It seems to say "Ignoring my warnings repeatedly has brought about your capture and this pool of feathers plucked from your body by your enemies".

The proverb implies that parental duty or indeed that of those with authority over others, is to advise and warn since people are ultimately responsible for their fate. However, if the child or minor should refuse such advice because it claims to know better and as a result should get into trouble the parent or person in authority should not be blamed for neglecting his duty and responsibility. and responsibility. The one in whom jural responsibility vests in this case may be liable for damage suffered by others as a result of the failure of the ward to heed advice but this is where liability stops. Another proverb may say that when children or jural minors chew raw fig fruits it is the stomachs of the elders that suffer the pain but it in no way absolves the recalcitrant from the injurious consequences of his or her behaviour. In any case his culpability is limited to only the jural damage.

9. **Bu yei durim mo se o yeiri vwɛɛm**
   A child knows how to run but not how to take cover

Commentary: It takes time to equip a person fully to cope with life and its exigencies. The proverb illustrates this with a scenario taken from predatory behaviour. Escaping from the pursuit of an enemy requires quick motion but if the enemy is faster then other strategies are called for if the quarry is to outwit the predator, such as an ability to take cover, use deception and other subtle strategies of defence. Children, because they are younger, may be physically capable and should be responsible for adopting those physical behaviours that would get them out of harm's way. However, they lack knowledge and stratagem which spring from experience which in turn is perceived as a function of age. As minors are thus handicapped it becomes the duty of parents and mature adults to supplement their efforts and to equip them adequately with the means of survival. To escape from harm's way requires the capability to get away from the danger and where this is not enough to apply the mental faculties. Children cannot therefore be blamed if their lack of experience and training makes them falter and fall prey.

The point of the proverb is that adults should share the blame when their wards through inexperience get into certain kinds of trouble.

10. **Wɛ mo de baleiga yia**
    It is God who treats the eyes of the lizard
    When the lizard has conjunctivitis it is God who doctors it

10b. **Wɛ mo su baleiga yia**
    It is God who provides the lizard with water to wash its teary eyes

10c. **Wɛ ba yage de bu-kayaa kafae**
    God does not abandon his useless child
Commentary: The lizard is house bound. It lives in the compound and is always to be found on the walls. However, it is not a domestic animal. It is not regarded as food, although children may hunt it and even roast it for meat. To most people, it is harmless, unlike the mouse. People do not therefore care for it as they perceive no benefit from it, unlike the domestic fowls and the livestock for which treatment is sought when they are perceived to be ailing.

Domestic livestock and poultry are in some ways like children. When a child has conjunctivitis, or any ailment for that matter, parents and kin assume the duty of providing treatment. This is not necessarily or purely altruistic. The child whose biological parents are alive and around is very fortunate. Some people are unfortunate enough not to have immediate kin or protectors. The *bu-kayaa* (the useless child) and perhaps the orphan, one who has lost both parents in childhood, or the *chuchuru*, a person classified as a reincarnation of an evil bush spirit, seem to fall in this category. This class of person is not perceived to be of any use now or in the future to anyone and therefore no resources would be expended on it. However, these are wards of providence on which they might depend, even if they cannot be sure of the support of their kin.

The proverb is saying that God who made them kinless takes care of His own. God helps the needy whatever their condition when society fails them. Like the wild lizard they may have neither mother nor father nor kin who are responsible for its well-being yet surprisingly they suffer no want. The lizard does not have to worry about who would wash its face in the mornings or who would treat it when it suffers from conjunctivitis. In times of personal crisis those who have kin and friends can expect that their well-wishers would console them by providing water, as is customary, to wash away the tears but the lizard or the destitute does not enjoy that privilege; in their case heaven comes to their aid.

This is certainly one of the numerous proverbs that project Kasena attitudes to God and their religious beliefs.

11. Tete zuŋa ba zaŋe kafae
The night bird does not fly without good cause
A bird does not take to flight in the night without cause
Commentary: The same proverb may be presented as *Tete zuŋa ba jaane kafae*. Kasena have observed that birds too rest or go to roost at night. To see a bird take to flight at night therefore implies that it is being disturbed and a predator may be after its life.

The point of the proverb is that when the unexpected happens there is usually a cause for it, even if that cause is not immediate. There is no smoke without fire, as Ghanaians say. A similar proverb says, the noise that emanates from the hole does not remain there forever *"kore kore ba maŋe bɔɔne ne"* or the creature that bestirs itself in the hole will soon emerge.

12. Manlaa we n ná diini twio n ji ko vɔɔ
The chameleon says when on a tree assume the colour of its leaf
Commentary: The chameleon, a common reptile in the wet season, is an enigma in Kasena experience. It is not regarded a capable of causing physical harm to man and it is not to be killed by humans. Its lean and emaciated look and its unsteady movement seems to suggest to the Kasena the old and the ancestral. Some clans have it as their totem. Encountering the chameleon on the path has specific foreboding for Kasena. Usually it prognosticates death but in some cases it foretells the advent of good fortune. Magic derived from the cult of the chameleon is used by some families to protect their crops from thieves. However, there are many who find it revolting to behold and some people are scared to death by it. People in the latter category may harm it on impulse, and children kill it for the fun of it, although this is forbidden.

The ability of the chameleon to change its skin colour and pigment to reflect its surroundings is the basis of this proverb. This is the Kasena equivalent of the saying "When in Rome do as the Romans do". The chameleon camouflages its presence by assuming the colour of its environment thereby escaping from its enemies. It needs to do so in the savanna environment of Kasenaland where its enemies are many and the sparse vegetation would otherwise have made it easy to spot. The proverb urges adaptation to prevailing circumstances and situations as a survival strategy.

13. **N ná ba jege bu se ba jwa bwoŋi n yere ko buga**
If you do not have a child to ensure that your name will be remembered then dig a well
Commentary: Childlessness among Kasena is a great misfortune. There are several arguments for the importance attached to children: in one respect children are seen as an investment against the future. They will maintain the aged parent but people do not wait to age before they depend on their children. There was in traditional times a division of labour by sex and age. Thus children were seen as producers even from tender ages when they helped parents to drive away poultry or birds pests from the crops and they tended the livestock in the cropping season. It was and still is prestigious to have children. The common argument advanced by Kasena for having children is that they perpetuate the family name. In this respect children are the way to immortality. As another Kasena proverb affirms, the antidote to death is to have children who survive the deceased. The proverb however offers consolation to the childless. Good deeds to society ensure that society treasures its benefactor's memory. A well is a considerable endowment in this savanna ecology where water is often hard to come by, especially in the dry seasons. Water becomes tantamount to life, a fact confirmed by the traditional history of the people which shows how a clan has kept in memory the salvation of their ancestor due to the timely emergence of a reptile like the crocodile which led the hapless ancestor to a water source, as Paga legends illustrate. Refer also to Malam al-Hasan Mole's (a Dagomba cleric) view of a priority of fruitful expenditure of resources in an interview with Ferguson (1972:347) where making a well comes second only to building a mosque. In al-Hasan Mole's view, the well will retain the memory of the builder until it is closed by God. This may be the Islamic view of charitable deeds but its similarity to local perceptions is obvious.
The point of the proverb then is that good deeds are also an important social investment almost comparable to having children.

14. **Ko pɔe tega ne mo se ko ba pɔe wɛ ne**
It is what is beneath the ground the rots, not what is above ground
Commentary: Death results ineluctably in decay. Interment speeds up this process. For Kasena death is not the end of life but a mode of transition from one plane of existence, the mundane, to a higher plane. Yet at the moment of death and bereavement the surviving kin are distraught with

grief to the extent that they deny themselves food and other necessities of life. In some cases it begins to be feared that the bereaved might take their grief to the point of suicide.

This is a proverb that is used in the context of bereavement. Its message is that the dead may rot but the living can be consoled that the dead derive satisfaction from the fact that through their living kin they continue to exist. Living kin must not therefore grieve excessively for the dead. Kin are valued for their own sake and for the duties and obligations that kinship statuses impose on them. The bereaved are sometimes heard to voice their loss in lamentations which describe the deceased's roles in life vis a vis the bereaved. Thus from another perspective, the proverb is saying that the bereaved should derive consolation from the realisation that though a relation may be dead others have remained alive to fill the social vacancy created. Those who grieve so much for deceased relations are thus reminded that excessive grief is not good, especially if it leads self pity and to self destructive acts. The living kin remain the consolation of the dead and they do the dead a favour by living and not by dying, as is often threatened.

15. **Kunkwola mo ke ka ba leu ba ma de ŋwana da**
    It is the gourd that stretched out its neck and a rope has been tied around it

Commentary: The gourd is for storage and carriage of fluids like millet beer and milk. It is shaped like an hourglass and is usually hollowed out from a calabash. Between the two bulges is a long thin neck. The bigger end is where the fluid is kept. For ease of carrying it a rope is wound round the thin neck.

In cultures like that of the Kasena-Nankana, it is not unusual for the victim of misfortune or handicap to seek an explanation for the misfortune by asking the popular question, why me. If the gourd were a person or animate it might complain of the liberty loss which is symbolised by a rope tied round the neck since other vessels do not usually have ropes tied round their necks. The anticipated reply in this case would be that no one is to blame for the turn of events. Its appearance, shape and structure suggest what could be done to enhance its utility in the absence of handles. Thus in some way the gourd can be said to bear the blame for abuse and degradation humans subject it to.

The point of the proverb is that man should examine his or her own culpability before seeking an external scape goat to bear the responsibility for some of his or her misfortunes. The Kasena ideology on witchcraft in fact blames the victim, his or her kin and affines in the first place and only secondarily the external witch. For example the victim is believed to open himself to the predations of witches by his own behaviours and weaknesses.

16. **Ba ba yage kukula yiga ne ye ba daa gwooni ka veiŋa**
     You don't elect a short man to lead the way and then complain about his pace
Commentary: The path was in traditional times narrow making it necessary for people to walk in a file. There was no system of path maintenance as obtained among some other African peoples with centralised authority structures living in forested country such as the Ashanti.

   The walking arrangement may under certain circumstances favour women and children walking in front while the menfolk brought the rear. This was often for the security of the women and children themselves. However, the important person for the occasion, the leader of the party or the person familiar with the course of the journey was expected to walk in front. These practices find expression in the language of the Kasena. An important personality like the Pɛ, chief had **kɔga tɔgena** (back followers) elders.

   All things being equal, a person who is short in stature is not usually preferred for the front position and there is a Kasena proverb which states that when a short person takes the lead it is either in a journey to his affines compound or to his mother's brothers' village. Thus it becomes necessary sometimes for short people to lead. The disadvantage is that they have shorter paces and therefore slow down the progress of the group.

   The point of the proverb is "You can't eat your cake and still have it". Once it has been found necessary to accept a situation that is less than ideal then one must also be resigned to the attendant disadvantages. It serves no purpose to complain about the associated problems.

17. **Manjɔro-gɔgɔ vei de ko kaane mo**
     The sex maniac's wife accompanies him on his travels
Commentary: A sex maniac, it is conceded here, cannot control his urge. He is at liberty to indulge himself; however he must not infringe the sexual rights of others. Other people have rights to their wives and their daughters and these cannot be usurped by another. A person had access to women for sex only through marriage and although men sometimes befriended widows whom they visited at night the widows' affines did not often approve of this, even if they did not or could not do anything about it. It was a serious ritual offence for the widows to engage in sex before the celebration of the deceased husband's final funeral rites. Worse still

sex in the open was considered as a taboo. The options open to the unmarried sex maniac were few indeed given these strictures. The precaution that the sex maniac takes is to ensure that he is married legally and to as many wives as his means and his charms allowed. Since sexual activity was forbidden to a woman who had not weaned her baby a husband who felt he could not contain his urge had to have more than one wife to ensure that at least a wife was available to him at all times. Polygyny, the taking of more than one wife was thus an ideal culturally for this and other reasons, even if not many people succeeded in being married for long to several wives concurrently.   The point of the proverb then is that those who have special needs have a duty to make provision for themselves; it is unacceptable to expect that society should be inconvenienced on their behalf.

18. **Buga ywona ná puli ya di daana mo**
    When the fish population in a river explodes fish will prey on their kind

Commentary: When fish multiply in the river the tendency is for the fish to prey on their own kind. The cannibalistic tendencies of fish have been the basis for this proverb. Fish seem to be somewhat usual in this respect as many of the mammals Kasena are familiar with rarely exhibit such tendencies. Kasena seem to put this to the fact that fish spawn their young at a more rapid rate. It is here assumed that since a pond that does not increase in size substantially, food must run out before long leaving the fish with no other choice but to prey on their kin. We can detect in this type of proverb a concern for uncontrolled population growth and the need to cull natural resources to restore balance.

Scarcity undermines kinship norms and sentiments, compelling a return to lawlessness exemplified by the rule of might as bigger fish are compelled to eat smaller fish in order to survive.

This is a proverb which is associated Pε Kwara, chief of Navrongo at the coming of the British in 1905, who was said to have invoked it when he advised that the rules of exogamy needed to be relaxed somewhat to permit intermarriages within the chiefdom. Kasena chiefs have always played the role of arbitrators in marriage disputes.

The context of the proverb is set by the wide ranging rules of exogamy which Kasena try to abide by. For them, it is forbidden to kin of opposite sex to intermarry or contract relationships that are sexual and non-platonic. The histories of the various clans and lineages however, reveal inter-lineage or inter-clan relationships, real or putative, that bind them. It is not uncommon to find groups of clans tracing descent ties cognatically or lineally to common apical ancestors. Arguably, a strict adherence to the established norms of exogamy could preclude marriage within the chiefdoms thus compelling suitors to seek spouses from outside the chiefdoms and the ethnic group and thus placing extra hardships on wife-seekers. If we accept kinship as a solidarity mechanism, exogamy arguably could be seen as providing additional and complementary solidarity between groups within the society that lack kinship bondage. Given therefore a concept of community that in traditional times did not extend far beyond the chiefdom and rarely beyond the ethnic group, exogamy would have less of a perceived benefit where inter-ethnic relations were concerned. This seems to be the basis for the injunction that exogamy be made less restrictive, as the above proverb maintains. However, as the spans of kin groups themselves widen and they expand numerically, the quality of intra-kin group relations declines, thus necessitating the deployment of mechanisms such as affinal relations to effect greater solidarity.

The stress on the prevailing expansive exogamic rule is manifested by the increase in number of unions that violate the rule. There have been cases of kin intermarrying and where attempts to break these unions have failed rituals have had to be performed to nullify the existing kinship tie by breaking symbolically the calabash to allow affinal relations to be established. This is however possible only where the kinship tie is a very distant one. Some couples have been compelled to live in concubinage as a consequence.

The proverb in question tends to be quoted to justify marriages in which the couple are distantly related. The point is that such marriages may not be ideal but they should nevertheless be endorsed. The proverb is a reflection on life's experiences. Its message is that conditions may induce unethical behaviour and depending on the circumstances, this might be sympathised with rather than condemned. There is sympathy for marriage between certain distant kin as exemplified by the proverb which maintains that "you marry kin with the assurance that she would provide you with enough sauce for your meal". That is to say a wife who is a distant kin might be motivated by kinship considerations rather than solely conjugal feelings to take better care of her husband.

19. **Am' ba lage konto tu ba jege sɔŋɔ**
   The person who cannot tolerate others cannot live in a compound house
   He who complains persistently has not compound house
   Commentary: The Kasena compound house, *sɔŋɔ*, is also a term which stands for the lineage that dwells in this structure. As a kin-group *sɔŋɔ* may comprise people whose parents once lived in the same compound

house but who may have since dispersed and now live in different houses or compounds in the clan-settlement. The typical compound house is inhabited by many agnates and their wives and wives relations (the maids). Large compounds are considered desirable and are often the source of envy for others who find themselves living in smaller compound houses. Nevertheless, living in such a large compound house has its problems; it requires tolerance. If the household head is difficult and lacks diplomacy in his dealings with subordinates he may well find that his kin have left to found their own compounds within the clan-settlement. Although the exodus does not negate the lineage head's authority over these offshoots, it restricts the effectiveness of that authority. It is less effective over agnates who now live in their own compounds within the clan-settlement.

The proverb calls for tolerance and neighbourliness, essential ingredients to communal living.

20. **Kukuri-tekka ba ka tu wua kwori ni**
The dog that is destined to die does not respondent to its owner's whistle
The dog that is destined to die is not saved by its owner's whistle
Commentary: On the chase the hunting dog should obey its master's instructions. These are given by means of a whistle which the dog is trained to recognise. The instructions are necessary as they can safeguard the lives of master and dog. A dog that is destined to die may not respond to its master's voice and will get into danger. For example, some dogs may challenge ferocious beasts like lions unless restrained. In some respects the proverb is a warning to underlings who claim to know better than their seniors. Well-meaning advice is ignored leading to tragedy.

The message of the proverb is that our destinies are not subject to our actions or omissions. However, we are not always responsible for not having done the right thing that would have ensured our well-being. What has been ordained is beyond our power and will happen since even basic precautions will not be taken. What will be will be. Similar to this proverb is the Kasena saying that "If you are destined to fall off your donkey, you do not see it ears".

Kasena in fact believe in "*a jaane a nwoɲi a Wɛ sɔŋɔ*" (What I have brought from my God's house) or "*a tage a Wɛ sɔŋɔ*"(told so in my God's compound). Personal destiny is a life trend charted in advance by each one, before birth and confirmed in statements made before God. An otiose God endorses these pronouncements. Refer to Fortes (1987b) for a similar perspective on destiny held by the Tallensi.

21. **Lulwei ba jege dam de o vaŋeno**
The blind is in the power of his leader
Commentary: Blindness has until recently been common in the rural parts of Kasena where onchocerciasis has been endemic for those communities close to the river tributaries.

A blind person is led. He or she holds on to one end of the cane or stick and the person who leads holds the other. The latter is usually a boy of ten to fifteen years who may not always be experienced. Onchocercal blindness affects the aged more often as the cumulative damage caused by the killing of microfilarial worms in the affected person takes time before ocular vision is impaired to the point of blindness. Since the blind person does not see to know where he or she is being led he is totally dependent on the boy leading the way. Choices about where to go or where not to go no longer reside with the blind person and this is the measure of handicap and lack of empowerment. The paradox here is that rather than the aged leading the young as custom and tradition expect, here, it is the tender young who lead the old.

The proverb has not only literal relevance, it applies in many other dependency situations where the dependent lacks the means of self assertion. The proverb reflects on this lack of empowerment in people's lives and the sense of helplessness.

22. **Chaveera ba goe se ya gwoori tiri.**
Shame does not kill but it causes the forehead to bend
Shame may not kill but it leads to the hiding of the face
Commentary: Shame is bad; perhaps not as bad as death since it does not kill. However it leads to lost of face. It makes the one shamed to feel shy, consequently, he or she would try to avoid the company of others in the attempt to hide away. It is almost as though the forehead of the person in shame has overgrown and covered not only his or her view of the world but also prevents others from seeing the one shamed. The logic here seems to be that sight provokes popular recollection of the shame that is attached to a person.

23. **Bɔɔla ba pe natwonnu**
Lovers do not shut the windows
Commentary: The *natwoŋo* is a small opening, like a chimney in the hut and through it air, light and sunshine may enter the traditional Kasena mud thatched hut which usually has no conventional window on the side wall. However, being an opening located on the floor of the mud thatch roof (*nayuu*), it must be closed in the evening when it is likely to be cold and especially before rain or the storm breaks. This is necessary if rain

water is not to pass down into the hut. A broken clay vessel may be used to cover the *natwoŋo*.

The word *bɔɔla* in this proverb refers to a lover or a friend of the opposite sex. Both men and women are allowed to have platonic relations with the opposite sex but these, though referred to as *bɔɔlo*, do not provoke jealousy. A wife however would be jealous if she got to know that her husband had taken another woman for a love relationship. Husband may tolerate a platonic relationship between the wife and another man in the same village. The couple would be guilty of an adulterous relationship if their relationship involved a sexual encounter.

The proverb is based on an observation of the hostile relations that seem to exist between two individuals vying for the affections of a common love. The competition may degenerate into hostility and those involved might become vindictive. Between such a pair even basic favours like closing each other's chimneys to forestall the destruction to property by rain water might be neglected.

The proverb talks of those who share a common love but it would seem that it is women who are married to the same husband, co-wives, who are being discussed. The proverb seems to assume that the competing lovers live close enough to each other to be in a position to help each other out by seeing to it that the chimney of the absent competitor is closed when it is necessary. These are favours that can be expected of those who live in the same compound. Really, it is co-wives who are most likely to find themselves having to do each other these kinds of favours. Men are unlikely to have opposite sex friends living in the same compound since the compound has an agnatic core. The men are agnates and the women are either wives or kin-women. Kin are forbidden to share the sexual favours of the same woman. It would seem therefore that the proverb is hinting at the negative personal relations that can exist between co-wives. Ideally, such women are expected to live together and to cooperate. Wives have sometimes brought over kin into their conjugal relations to serve as co-wives. This is in preemption of their husband some day taking an unrelated woman as second wife and thereby introducing conflict into their marital relationship. It is understandable that the proverb should stop short of using the example of negative co-wife attitudes in the construction of this proverb. No matter how bitter the relationship co-wives are expected to help each other out in times of crisis and it would be unforgivable for a woman to fail to secure the absentee co-wife's property on account of petty jealousy.

In another respect, the proverb is critical of the idea of a man having amorous relations with other women. It is not uncommon for some men to seek the sexual companionship of widows within the clan-settlement and to concentrate so much effort on these relations to the neglect of their wives and children. Wives have sometimes left their husbands in disgust for their inability to shake off such relationships. The point of the proverb is that because a girlfriend lives in her own compound she is of no use to her paramour in times of critical need. She would not for example be around to close the *natwoŋo* when the rain is about the fall and thus prevent avoidable destruction to property.

24. **Wolo na lage kukuri-kokɔra nɔna to mo twi mim o ke ka kuri ne**
    He who relishes the meat of mangy dog is he who must be prepared to feed the fire that will cook it.
Commentary: Dog meat is eaten by many Kasena who enjoy it as a delicacy. When the dog is fat and good looking Kasena relish its flesh. Traditionally the womenfolk did not eat dog meat and could not therefore be expected to prepare the meat or cook it. Therefore men must do the cooking, in spite of the fact that the division of labour assigns culinary chores to women. In this case the meat must be cooked outside the compound, usually in the outer yard by a group of men and boys.

Mangy dog, usually a dog which due to its old age and poor feeding has meagre and tougher flesh, takes longer to cook. It is thus unappealing even to the male eaters and few would take much interest in cooking its meat. Therefore, just as women cannot be expected to cook dog meat, those who consider mangy dog unfit for consumption cannot be expected to bother with the chore of cooking it. There would be shortage of people willing to involve themselves in cooking it. This implies that the few interested eaters must perform the menial tasks when it comes to it. These include not only fetching firewood and fuel stuff, a task that men usually regard as beneath their dignity, since women would not permit the use of their wood for this purpose, but also having to sit by and attend the fire till the meat is ready.

The point of the proverb is that those who hope to benefit from any chore must themselves get involved in its execution. One cannot expect to reap the reward of the labour expended by others. Self interest cannot be discounted in any province of life.

25. **Ba du mene de jwa keim ŋwaane mo**
    Millet is cultivated because of the expectation that it will yield.
Commentary: The millet is a very important staple for the Kasena who are cultivators. Kasena grow several varieties of millet: two varieties of finger millet, an early maturing variety (pennisetum sp) and the late millet variety (pennisetum typhoideum) as well as the varieties of guinea corn (sorghum vogelianum) . Important as it is, millet has peculiar demands.

The supply of moisture has to be right before millet will do well and this requirement is rarely met. When there is drought for several weeks the crop wilts and dries up. When it rains frequently in the growing season the weeds grow faster than farmers can hoe them out. The crop moreover does not do well with excessive rainfall. Strong gusts of wind can and do ruin the crop just as much the various pests common in the wet season undermine yields. All this raises the question why Kasena bother to cultivate this crop in spite of the numerous uncertainties. The answer to this question lies in the faith of the people in their ancestors and gods and their hope that poor yields are not necessarily a perennial problem. Their faith in the future, in spite of the uncertainties, is explained by their faith backed by their experience which shows that present difficulties are not a permanent fixture. An agricultural year that begins badly may yet end well just as a good year may be ruined by a succession of bad weather conditions. That hope and faith explain the willingness of Kasena to commit seed that has been treasured throughout year to the ground rather than consume it.

The message of this proverb is that it is expectations of gain that explain why there is investment.

26. Te se n daare mo toom lira

The antidote to death is off-spring

Commentary: Death means for the Kasena a physical removal from the world of the living. Socially, the dead retain some role in the world of the living which they may play out vicariously through their living descendants. A dead husband for example retains his rights to the widows until the performance of the final funeral rites, after which the widows can elect to remarry or stay single or, as Kasena say, "to sit by their deceased husband's grave". Moreover, the deceased elder continues to be regarded as the head of family, if he died in that office, just as his property continues to be vested in him until the final funeral rites. Consequently, prior to the celebration of the final funeral rites his youngest son acts for him in all matters formal. This boy or junior son will on formal occasions be addressed as though he were the deceased. All these practices illustrate the belief that to be survived by living off-spring implies a continued role in the world of the living. More importantly, the living off-spring are the means for future re-births into the lineage of long deceased kin or their 'reincarnations', so to speak. Names like *Kwotua* (father has returned) illustrate these beliefs.

Death does not therefore triumph completely over the kin-group so long as its members remain alive to keep the lineage in existence. The living kin will safeguard the interests of the dead and provide them with their material and spiritual needs, though they be dead. The message of the proverb then is that though death is inevitable human beings in their wisdom mitigate the results by ensuring that they have kin, particularly close family members. Thus while the proverb which says that decay occurs underground and not above it attempts to console the living, this other proverb consoles the bereaved indirectly by reminding them of their duty to the deceased which they should discharge by living rather than through suicide, the perceived ultimate mode of expressing anguish and sorrow.

27. Napere pɔe gare nakuri pɔe
The dusty foot is better than the buttock that shows evidence of continued use

Commentary: *Napere pɔe* refers to a foot that has grown pale as a result of walking in the dusty harmattan weather. The item *pɔe* is an ideophone in the Kasem language which describes a whitish or pale colour or appearance. Until recently many people walked barefooted. By the same token the buttocks that have remained seated for all day show this by their pale appearance. Traditionally people dressed scantily at home as they reserved their best clothing for use when they went visiting. Here, pale feet symbolise travel while pale buttocks symbolise sedentary idleness. Far from a rolling stone not being able to gather moss, Kasena take the view that a responsible person is one who exerts himself or herself. In the case of a man he should be mobile and willing to journey abroad, and to undertake risky ventures.

The point of the proverb is that it is better to be mobile than static. Personal needs for example can best be met when a person bestirs himself. The one who visits homes gets invited to meals, especially when these have been prepared for work parties. The mobile person is also abreast with news and events and is well prepared to take advantage of new situations. In sum,. the advice offered by this proverb is that it is better to be up and doing than to remain immobile. It is better to suffer inconvenience than to shun danger by not taking risks.

28. Nabwonu mae o napere mo o swo o kaane
The pauper relies on his foot to find a wife

Commentary: Among the Kasena it took several visits to the fiancee's family before a person was even acknowledged as a suitor. Thereafter the suitor and his family and friends visited the home and kin of the wife-to-be as often as possible armed with the customary courtship presents for the parents and kin of the girl, the wife-givers. Usually there would be many other eligible persons vying for the hand of the maid. Eventually one of these would win out though not without a hectic competition. The bridewealth legally required is settled after the consummation of the marriage. Even then, it can be settled in installments spread over time.

It would seem from the above descriptions that the wealthy would be more favoured to win as they have the means to give more generously. Nevertheless, poor people sometimes prevail either because they are loved by the girl or her parents consider a particular suitor more satisfactory, regardless of his means. The poor man who does not have the wealth to deploy in the search for a wife can nevertheless do well if he is seen to be a more caring person able to show concern for people around him. A good reputation counts. By his visits and his serviceability, particularly to his in-laws a poor man too earns the respect and sympathy of wife-givers. Not only are wife-givers likely to persuade their daughter to marry such a person, they might not insist on his settling fully bridewealth claims. Kasena culture permits wife-givers to give waivers or to accept tokens in place of the complete sets of bridewealth goods. It is acceptable for an impecunious son-in-law to present hoe blades in place of sheep as mourning presents when an in-law's final funeral rites are being held.

The message of the proverb then is that material wealth does not prevail in all circumstances and that concern for people also counts in the courting of personal favours. There is a Kasena saying that supports this: *tan jege nɔɔna se-n yeim wonnu* (If you have the sympathy of people this counts more than material wealth). The above proverb can be said to illustrate further the previous proverb (see # 27) which advises on the need for a person to exert himself if he is to succeed in life.

29. **Duum doa mo jaane nabwonu kaane ka jwoori sɔŋɔ**
    It is the early rains that begin the sowing season which return the estranged wife

Commentary: The early rains can begin at about March, the height of *wulim wɛ*, the heat season. Some people might sow their low lying fields in the bushlands at this time, if these early rains are judged to be heavy enough; however, it is not until late May that most farmers would begin to sow their millet crop, the main staple. Kasena in Navrongo maintain that in the good old days, the advent of Easter was the time to sow their crops. It is said that the heavy rain that would begin the season would fall on the eve of Easter Sunday. The following day local non-Christians would commence sowing while their Christian brethren went to church service. It is said that the ritually powerful Gundoona, earthpriest of the Yogbaanea clan-settlement who lived at about the time the British first came to Navrongo, circa 1906, could sow his millet in the dry earth long before it was time to sow crops and yet obtain a good yield. In recent times, nobody is rash enough to start sowing millet until late May or June, no matter how early the rains began.

The first heavy rains that begin the sowing season are important for the Kasena for whom it was necessary that sowing be synchronised. Often a key person in the clan-settlement or the neighbourhood began the process and others followed suit. Acting in unison was necessary if a common policy on livestock management was to be achieved. Usually two to three weeks after the commencement of sowing it would be announced that owners of livestock should see to it that their animals did not roam about freely and cause damage to crops. After the majority of farmers have harvested their crops the livestock would be let loose with the result that those whose crops did not mature early could suffer losses.

For a community which depended on subsistence agriculture the first rains that initiate the sowing season were good grounds for the estranged wife who had absconded to her natal family and did not feel like rejoining her husband to now return to carry out her duties. It was a satisfactory face saver and parents would take advantage of this to persuade their daughter to go back to the conjugal home as her failure to return could harm their own interests. Failure to rejoin the husband at this time can only imply a determination to seek separation or remarriage. An adult woman of marriage age did not have much of a place in her natal clan-settlement. In traditional times she could not farm independently of her agnates and while she would be expected to help out on the farm she would be provided for through her mother. Often her position would be a precarious one as her brothers' wives would take precedence over her in the distribution of farm produce.

This saying which is more of a maxim than a proverb is commonly cited against estranged wives who spend too long a time with their agnates (patrilineal kin) and fail to return to their husbands. The point of the proverb is that conjugal life made collaboration possible as a division of labour along sexual lines was the norm. The failure of one spouse to discharge his or her duties amounted to irresponsibility and it placed in jeopardy the domestic economy of the couple. In strictly subsistence cultures like that of the Kasena-Nankana a breakdown in conjugal collaboration posed serious dangers for livelihoods. Thus by a wayward wife's refusal to return on time she furnished her husband with the pretext to seek a second wife.

30. **Kabaa ná boŋe ka kwo sɔŋɔ veiŋa ka leini ka logo lei mo**
    When a slave contemplates flight he sings songs native to his

hometown

Commentary: Slaves were not common among the Kasena but chiefs did possess a few slaves in the past. Occasionally, vagrants were captured and attached to households. The predatory activities of more powerful, more centrally organised neighbouring kingdoms like the Mossi of Burkina Faso can be cited here. Their armies carried out campaigns in the zone occupied by acephalous peoples like the Kasena resulting in the capture and enslavement of the less well organised peoples. Thus the concept of slavery was well understood among the Kasena, even if they did not themselves keep slaves on a regular basis.

As a captive, it is natural for a slave to look for the opportunity to escape. The proverb observes that the mere thought of escape evokes in the slave thoughts and longing for home and the ways of the native land. The point articulated in this proverb is that the feeling of nostalgia and the longing for home is expressed in non-material forma and symbols such as the recollection of native folk songs and music.

31a. Kenkaa jɔgɔ ba twogi zore

The cockroach's pants do not solve the problem of the naked pauper

Commentary: The jɔgɔ, a kind of pants worn traditionally by the Kasena male was a triangular piece of non-European cloth that was wrapped around the waist in such a way that the private parts were no longer exposed. It is still the garment that a man's loins should be girt in as his corpse is laid to rest in the grave. Kasena did not make their own cloth and they had to obtain it from the Moshie or others at a high price. It meant that in the pre-colonial past, for some Kasena it was an expensive item to have. Thus a small piece of cloth for use as a loin cloth was beyond the reach of the poor.

The cockroach seems to have a thick covering of wing which resembles a pair of pants. The problem with it is that it does not appear to be adequate as it leaves much of what we may call the roach's waist exposed. The proverb laments that such a jɔgɔ does not serve its true purpose and the cockroach remains the poorer for it; its needs remain unrequited and it cannot do anything about that.

Another interpretation would be that the pants that have been eaten by the cockroach and are left in tatters can no longer cover the waist fully and it would be a pity if the owner has to wear them. Cockroaches are known to eat clothing when these have not been stored properly or placed out of their reach. The poor man who is unfortunate to have his pants chewed up is thus in an unenviable spot. His choice is between going naked, a shameful thing to do, or wearing a pair of pants which do not quite serve their purpose and moreover advertise his condition.

This proverb serves to express the helpless condition in which a person finds himself when he seems not to have any other recourse or way out. It is a lament on poverty. Poverty makes it difficult to meet essential human needs, not even those that others might take for granted.

31b. Kenkaa jɔgɔ ba yi teiŋa
The roach's pants do not cover the waist

Commentary: This is in essence the same proverb as the previous version i.e. # 31a above. Here we are told that the cockroach's pants do not cover its waist or those pants already chewed up by the cockroach do not serve their purpose. The owner is thus left helpless and in shame whatever he does.

32. Gɛɛre mo tei kenkaa jɔgɔ
Necessity compels the wearing of the roach's pants

Commentary: This proverb, like the two previous ones discussed above: # 31a and # 31b can have two possible explanations. One explanation is that necessity compels a person to dress up in a pair of pants that has been eaten by cockroaches and an alternative explanation is that the cockroach wears its rather short pants because it has no choices.

The pauper, like the cockroach, can afford only one loin cloth and if that one should happen to get torn or worn out then he is really unfortunate. The cockroach likewise can only make do with what nature has provided it.

The message of the proverb then is that poor people have limited options; necessity therefore compels them to adopt measures and strategies that others would frown upon or consider inadequate to solve their problem.

33a Lelaala peina ba zoora
The penis being inserted hurriedly does not achieve penetration
33b. Lelaala bu ba lora
The baby being delivered hurriedly does not get born

Commentary: Proverb #33a and #33b and related. They have a common subject and message although they use different metaphors. In fact, they are one and the same. In the first version it is sexual behaviour which serves as our metaphor. That proverb seems to refer to illicit sex where the partners are in a hurry to get it done with. The message is that the satisfaction hoped for might elude lovers when they do not exercise patience in the act. Penetration may be difficult without enough preparation and ejaculation may occur externally. In the same way childbirth occurs in its own time. The desire to have a child born quickly, perhaps because of the pains and pangs the mother experiences, may lead to disastrous results if care is not taken. Kasena, in this writer's experience, did not have specialist birth attendants as such and any old lady might try her hands at delivering the baby, when necessary. There were thus occasions when the child did not appear soon thus causing the mother much labour. The placenta or the after birth might not drop or some other anomaly might occur to complicate the process of parturition. Traditionally when the waiting got too long the woman might be requested to confess her sins, especially, adulterous relations that she might have been involved in. This probably still happens, although on a lesser scale as most complications would be taken to the hospitals and clinics.

The message of the proverb is that when things are done in too much of a hurry the results are poor. Patience is necessary to get a good job done.

34. Ba ba bwei tampuuri ye ba lwoi weeru

One does not ask the midden's permission before tipping rubbish
Commentary: The *tampuuri* or kitchen midden is located just beyond the outer yard of the compound and next to the principal compound farm. Waste products from the homestead and domestic refuse are disposed of here. Nobody requires permission to tip rubbish in the midden. It is the place for refuse and since the refuse eventually decomposes and serves as useful fertiliser there cannot be any reasonable objection to dumping ordinary refuse there. It is the source of manure for the farms and for that reason sometimes an unreasonable head of compound might demand that lineage members seek permission before they scoop up the decomposed refuse for their farms. The *tampuuri* has not only economic importance but also social, symbolic and ritual significance. It is the place where certain children believed to be 'returnees' from the other world (perceived to go through a cycle of repeated deaths and rebirths) and engaged in playing a mischievous prank on parents are symbolically dragged about to communicate society's desire to disgrace and abase them in the hope that by shaming them they might desist from their pranks. Some of such children are eventually christened *Tampuuri*.

The message of this proverb is simply that the needy do not insist that their permission be sought before benefactors can offer to assist them. As another Kasena proverb would have it, those who are in need and those who are eager to exhibit generosity have common cause: "Mr Needy and Mr Generosity are one and the same". (*A-jei-a-laga de Ban-jwoŋi ye bedwe mo*).

35. Naao ba ke bwolo lei

The cow does not thank the valley

Commentary: The cow feeds in the *bwolo* which is low land that is not put under cultivation every year. The *bwolo* may be near the compound or located some distance away from the settlement but it is never too close to the compound, unlike the *kaduga* which surrounds the compound.

The proverb's point is that if it were possible for a cow to express gratitude it would not thank the *bwolo* and this is not out of ingratitude. The cow depends on the grass in the *bwolo* and goes there all the time. Thanking the *bwolo* each time it visits the *bwolo* would be too monotonous and would seem superfluous.

This proverb is often used to express gratitude. It is an intimation that because it sounds monotonous to be saying thank you all the time a person may occasionally omit to say thank. This apparent omission should not be interpreted as a sign of ingratitude or lack of appreciation for benefits derived from those upon whom one is dependent. Verbal expression is just one mode of showing gratitude. Alternative ways of achieving that objective exist. The monotony of verbal expression soon becomes meaningless.

36. Chworo ba ke kazɔgɔ lei

The chicken does not thank the mortar

Commentary: Hens and domestic fowls are attracted to the mortar because after pounding the grain it is winnowed and grain will fall to the ground for the picking. For the same reasons that the cow does not thank the valley, so does the hen not thank the mortar since its visits to the area where the mortar is located are frequent.

Gratitude does not have to be expressed verbally on each occasion but can remain unexpressed or demonstrated in some other way. Customarily, verbal gratitude is expressed after the benefit has been conferred and used. No where is this true than in the case of food or beverage gifts. It is only after a meal has been eaten is it proper for the beneficiary to say his or her thanks. When a person does another the honour of buying him or her a drink of millet beer, it is customary for the receiving party to say something like, "we shall eat before we perform thanks". As the mortar continues to provide for the fowl's needs, it makes not so much sense to say thank you. Among kin, verbal expression of appreciation is expected only where the gift is one that is special in some way. Between strangers on the other hand every act of kindness should draw profuse expression of thanks. Proverbs # 35 and # 36 may be regarded as version of the same proverb. They are themselves quoted in expressions of gratitude and appreciation. They are aimed at conveying to the benefactor, the beneficiary's feeling of indebtedness for the present gesture as well as acknowledging previous benefits. In the strict Maussian sense, gift-giving implies a triple obligation: to give, to receive and to make a return or counter gift. Statements like the above acknowledge that the flow of reciprocities is uneven and tipped in favour of the person to whom these proverbs, as remarks, are addressed. They are thus an acknowledgement of a state of indebtedness and are themselves part of the counter flow of prestations.

37. Ba ba bere kwogo churu chwoŋa
One does not point out the way to the land of the dead to the zombie. Commentary: The *kwogo* is a kind of zombie, the spiritual remnants of a person that survives death temporarily. Kasena believe that only witches may become *kwogo* after their death and for this reason the corpses of notorious witches are prepared in such a way as to make it difficult for them to become zombies and continue harming the living. The *kwogo*, it is believed, can live for some time before it is destroyed. It is said to be protected by its living kin and sometimes used by them to harm others, to protect their property or to steal the property of others.

Churu is the abode of the dead. Views seem to differ however about the location of *churu*. There are accounts which suggest that some people by accident have stumbled upon the sites where their deceased kin go after death to continue life. These sites are said to be located in a remote area either within the Kasena-Nankana area or in another land. Each clan is said to have its own abode for the ancestors. A vague location near Salaga in the East Gonja District of Ghana has been cited as the place where some of the deceased members of some clans go. It should be noted that these beliefs are not generally held and it would appear that for the majority of Kasena no living person could ever have been to *churu*.

As the *kwogo* has tasted death it should therefore require no education on life after death. Certainly not from the living!. Death is a *deja vu* for a *kwogo*. The point of the proverb is that you don't carry coals to Newcastle. A person who has experienced certain hardships needs no education on those experiences. This proverb is used as a rebuke aimed at those who ought to know better but do not appear to have learned their lesson.

38. Ba gane bu mo ba tore jeŋa o tampɔgɔ ne
It is by persuasion that one gains access to the child's bag
Commentary: A child, especially a boy is provided a bag in which to carry food. A shepherd boy carries bits of food in such a bag when out with the livestock. Long before a child has reached the age of working as a

shepherd parents would have started preparing it for this role by providing it with a small bag capable of holding groundnuts or grain meant for the child. Parents are expected to be partial to the youngest children. When food is short it is given to the younger siblings. Senior siblings are not however, forbidden to share with the child but they must seek the consent of the child. Experience shows that it is not easy to gain access to the contents of the child's bag. The child might protest with cries if senior siblings attempted to share its food. Crying is effective as it draws attention to the unjust behaviour of the those trying to confiscate the child's ration and this is sufficient deterrence. However, by persuasion and sweet talk it is possible gain access to the contents of the bag.

The proverb's message is that gentle persuasion can go a long way. It is better than the exercise of brute force.

39. Kaleiŋa ba ka nu swolim yaga
The kaleinga fish does not fail to inherit its mother's slippery skin
Commentary: The *kaleinga* fish is, like all fish, slippery and this property it has inherited from its mother. It is a quality that does not come as a result of choice.

The point of the proverb is that there are traits that may not be passed on by heredity necessarily but are learnt or acquired from parents perhaps through the subtle processes of enculturation. The proverb applies particularly to negative behaviour traits such as theft. Kasena state that such a propensity is in the blood of the lineage or family.

40. N ná gwooni buga ka ja-m
If you underestimate a pond it will drown you
Commentary: Kasena say water has no ladder (*na ba jege nateini*) to be used by a drowning parson to save his life. They also remark often that it is impossible to know by sight how deep a pool of water is likely to be. It is therefore unwise, the proverb advises, to conclude from the surface size of a pool or stream that it must be fordable. To make such an assumption is foolhardy.

On another note we note the literal belief that a pool or stream is the dwelling place of a god. The size of the water body, the abode of the god, is irrelevant to the accurate assessment of the god's potential and power. It is considered dangerous to contest the power of the river god or any other god for that matter. Kasena have stories of how river gods have trapped and killed people from water kept in special pots (*chuchoori*) hen.

The point of the proverb is that appearances can be deceptive. It can be dangerous to underestimate an opponent on superficial evidence without objective grounds for doing this.

41. **N ná yeiri leiŋa ka pa-m chuchwooru**
   If you do not know a song it makes you mad

Commentary: To know a song is to be able to understand its message and to sing it for one's entertainment. Kasena say it is not everybody who 'hears' songs. By this they mean that a person can listen to a song and not understand it. Kasem is a tone language and tone and vowel quality are phonemic or significant and can be the basis for a distinction between minimal pairs or sets of words. However a composer is at liberty to vary vowel length and change the tonal patterns of words in song in order to achieve the necessary effect in rhythm and artistry. These artistic devices make it all the more difficult for some listeners to follow the message of the song. For example *yínákúkúú* (tear drop) becomes in one song *yìnàkùkúú* while *nàwùùrï* (division) becomes *nàwúrí* (a place in Burkina Faso).

The argument of the proverb is that for those who are able to appreciate a song it becomes a work of art but those who do not have a sense of appreciation of music a song can be exasperating and a source of offence. The worst part of it is that Kasena songsters are known not only for their adulation of their subject but also for the insults and negative comments on their neighbours and acquaintances.

The argument of this proverb then is that the unfamiliar can evoke in some people anger and hostility. It is common knowledge that in some cultures foreigners and things foreign are called names and stereotyped negatively. Although the fear of the unfamiliar may not be universal nevertheless it is a widespread tendency.

42. **Gwoli delo na mage ka-kwea to, mo de de jwa wó mage ka-bia**
   The club that beats the senior wife will some day beat the favourite wife.

Commentary: The *gwoli*, a club with a round head is a typical Kasena weapon often carried men and boys for self defence. It is used in fights when the aim is to injure but not to kill the adversary. Shepherd boys occasionally mount clubbing contests and some clans are believed to have had magic against the effect of clubbing. Husbands may occasionally beat their wives with their clubs when provoked. This is not approved behaviour and it can result in a wife seeking justifiable separation from her husband for the cruelty involved as well as for the symbolism of the act.

The proverb remarks correctly that husbands are more likely to treat the unloved wife in this fashion and this is likely to be the older wife for whom a husband may care less. A senior wife with whom a man has had issues is also less likely to seek divorce or separation in her mature years. By contrast husbands feel less secure where their young wives or the newly wedded wife is concerned. The latter feel less committed to a husband, especially if they have not borne his children and could leave if they are not happy with the marriage. Love wanes with time and the longer a woman has remained married the more difficult it becomes for her to leave an unsatisfactory union. The point being made in this proverb is that given time the rough treatment visited on the senior wife will some day be experienced by the darling wife. The proverb warns the junior wife that the rough treatment that a old wife receives at the husband's hands is an index to future maltreatment. It is only too easy for an inexperienced newly wed to misinterpret the brutal behaviour of a polygynous husband where co-wives are concerned.

The same proverb is presented as *Kafena kalo na mage ka-kwea to, mo ka ka jwa wó mage ka-bia* (The whip that canes the senior wife will some day whip the favourite wife). The point is that the differential treatment meted out to new comers or those whose favours are courted needs to be measured against behaviours and attitudes that apply to others in the environment. Bad behaviour has to be generalised rather than particularised or interpreted as episodic.

43 **Chilachiu we puga ná sua vɔna wuuri mo**
The chilachiu bird says when the stomach is full the wings flap noisily
Commentary: The bird *chilachia* is notorious to Kasena for its propensity to doze or look sleepy. The proverb maintains that when this lazy bird has had its fill of food it suddenly comes back to life and wings flutters noisily.

The point of the proverb is that there is nothing like a full belly; it does wonders to a person's spirit. Behaviour undergoes a transformation in times of plenty. People engage in festivities and celebrations and merrymaking. Kasena marriages for example are contracted more often in the season of plenty that in the time of food shortages.

The general point is that contentment induces responses that are out of the ordinary.

44. **Badeinu ba jege badein-yoro**
A bachelor is not finicky
There are no proud bachelors
The *badeinu* (bachelor) is a man who has no wife and the archetypal

bachelor is one who had remained unmarried up to and beyond his mature years. Such a person may also be referred to as *badein-dwoɲo* (lit. Old bachelor).The term *badeinu* has no opposite although a morphologically symmetrical term would be *kadeinu*, a widow. Just as Kasem has no lexemic term for spinster it also lacks a lexeme for widower.

A bachelor does not enjoy great respect among the Kasena people for a number of reasons. For them, a respectable person should have at least one wife, if not several. In a culture where celibacy was never practised sexual desire was expected to be requited within marriage. An unmarried man was regarded either as too poor to find the means for marriage or else he was one who did not have kin to support him in the quest for a wife. It could also be that he was not truly a man. Where an individual lacked the resources to be used to woo and take a wife traditionally and to some extent today, the onus fell on his kin to find him a wife. More importantly, a person lacking the resources could nevertheless earn a wife by his good deeds and behaviour as we are informed in the proverb: *Nabwonu mae a napere mo o swo o kaane* (A pauper can depend on his feet to find a wife), see # 28 above. A disreputable person on the other hand, it was expected, would not find it easy getting a wife as wife-givers would discourage their female wards from entering a marriage relationship with such a person.

In the view of traditional society, to be a bachelor meant not to have a wife to cater for your immediate needs such as cooking your meals, fetching water for you and performing other sex related chores that it was culturally unbecoming for a man to be seen to perform. It was never considered a respectable thing for a man to depend on other people's wives for his domestic needs, be they kin or non-kin. More importantly, the bachelor did not have a woman to bear his children. A man was not entitled to claim paternity over any of his biological children born out of wedlock. So, if in spite of the various opportunities at a man's disposal he still could not find a spouse society regarded him as worthless. Such a person on his death could be subjected to degrading rituals that stigmatised the deceased one for his failure to live up to an important societal expectation viz. To wed and become a parent.

45. Zun-bwɛo ba jege pwogo
A male bird has no nest
A male bird does not nest

Commentary: The male bird does not have a nest since it does not lay eggs or nurture the young, in Kasena view. Ornithologists now accept that among some species of bird both male and female collaborate in nurturing the young birds.

The point of the proverb is that a man is not a home maker, from the Kasena cultural perspective. The place of the Kasena man is the *bichwoŋo*, the open space in front of the compound. There men spend their time when they are not on the farms. They receive guests here and important business should be discussed here as the ancestors themselves thus become witnesses. The place of women by contrast is the *diga*, the room or the space where cooking is done. Children are born there and until the boys are old enough to join the men they remain with their mothers in the *diga*. Men are expected to enter the *diga* at bedtimes. On funeral occasions it is customary for men to sleep outside in the outer yard or *bichwoŋo*.

In this proverb a room or the interior of the compound is compared to the bird's nest. This proverb goes to support the point made by the earlier proverb, # 43 i.e that a man needs woman in his life. The division of labour along gender lines enshrined in traditional notions and practice made it necessary for the two sexes to unite in marriage.

It is customary that a guest be not allowed to leave the compound without entertainment of some sort. A special meal would most likely be prepared for a respected guest, especially one who has come a long way. This proverb is quoted at the visitor to a Kasena compound as he bids farewell. The menfolk would remind such a guest that menfolk of the compound with whom he may have been talking cannot grant his request to take leave until he has sought and obtained permission from the womenfolk. As another Kasena proverb maintains, a visitor may enter a Kasena compound forcibly and uninvited but he or she cannot leave without permission to do so. (*Veiru zoore de dam mo se o ba nwoŋi de dam*). The menfolk of the compound imply by this proverb that the job of giving hospitality to guests is entrusted to the womenfolk and the men cannot be certain if the women have plans for the guest. Custom forbids that a guest be asked if he would stay long enough for a meal. Since it would be disappointing for an honoured guest to leave without taking the meal that is being prepared for him or her, it becomes necessary that he or she should be granted permission by the women to leave. Before a guest, the menfolk pretend that they are not aware of what their wives are up to. The proverb in a sense summarises these ideas.

46. Ba kwei kukura ka bɔle ne mo

A dog is acquired while it is in its infancy

Commentary: A family needing a dog looks for a puppy to adopt and this is because a dog is best trained while it is yet a puppy. Training an old dog is not likely to meet with the same degree of success as when a puppy is trained and this is because old habits are difficult to change. The same for humankind too. Teaching and learning should be carried out as soon as it is opportune to do so.

The message of the proverb is that children are better trained and socialised while they are young and more receptive. Catch them while young, the proverb seems to be saying.

47. N kara ná saare gare n ni ná saare

It is better for the harvest to fail than for the mouth to cease to function

Commentary: The *kara* is a supplementary farm where some of the food crops are cultivated. Unlike the *kaduga,* the compound farm, this is located some distance from the compound and therefore, unlike the *kaduga,* the compound farm, does not benefit from the manure derived from the kraal and household refuse. The *kara* is less valuable than the *kaduga.* The former is cultivated occasionally while the *kaduga,* on the other hand, is under cultivation every year. Occasionally, the crops on the farms fail thus bringing untold hardships. However, these difficulties, the proverb maintains, cannot be compared to the calamity of not having a mouth at all. The implied argument of the proverb seems to run thus: Without a mouth you could not then be able to feed and starvation would be inevitable. Traditional Kasena could not have been familiar with intravenous feeding or any other non-oral form of food intake. They knew that the quantity of food consumed affected health and for this reason the sick were encouraged to eat even when they did not feel like doing so. When a person has no appetite for food it is said that 'the mouth has spoilt'.

More importantly, a person whose mouth had 'withered away' like a drought stricken farm could not be expected to socialise effectively since the mouth is the organ that enhances verbal communication, an essential ingredient for socialisation and survival. For the beggar, the ability to speak enables him to ask for alms. The importance of the mouth and verbal communication in self-defence and survival is conveyed in the saying, 'you save yourself by means of your mouth', (*n ma-n n ni n jwoɲi ntete*).

The proverb seems to draw attention to the importance of language skills and the need to be civil to others.

48. Yuu ba koe ba

The head is not older than the neck

Commentary: Seniority in age establishes precedence in Kasena society. In sequential order first usually takes precedence over what follows. The only case of apparent reversal is furnished by the seniority accorded the last born of twins in which case the first to emerge is said to have been sent by the last to be born. The latter being senior and therefore in a position of authority has sent the junior into the world to investigate and determine whether it is a fit place for both to be born into. In their scheme of dual symbolic opposition, Kasena view what is up or above as taking precedence over what is down and below, just as the sky and God of the above (*Baŋa Wɛ*) take precedence over the Earth, which is said to be wife to the sky God.

As the head rests on the neck and is therefore above it there is the possibility that the head would be perceived as taking precedence over the neck. The proverb expresses the view that both parts of the body are of equal importance and each needs the other to function properly. The point of the proverb is that precedence and even seniority are not incompatible with complementarity. It may be tempting to see the members of the body as different and unequal in some respects, but they are equally important as they compliment functionally.

The message is about team work and the importance of collaboration as against the danger of invidious comparison and the laying of stress on the relative worth of individuals at the expense of the team. Kasena have a conundrum in the form of a folktale to illustrate this. *Kanichɔɔ* (I have telescopic sight) saw the python which had swallowed the maid enter a deep river and *Kanyɔnakawe* (I drain rivers) drank up the water in the river to enable *Kazambworikale* (I retrieve from the mud) to retrieve the maid from the thick mud on the river bed. *Kabitwa* (I revive the dead) brought the dead maid back to life. At the end of the folktale the audience are asked which of the actors should be entitled to marry the maid. Kasena insist that all actors played a crucial role in the recovery of the girl since without one the others might not have been able to recover the girl. Their collaboration rather than their individual merits was more important in the maid's rescue.

49. Momwɛ ná gaale ni ko daa dae lam
When the nose is longer than the mouth this ceases to be a sign of beauty

Commentary: Some Kasena think that a long nose is a measure of good looks. This comes out abundantly in their folktales. The proverb makes the point that when the nose happens to be too long, then this is not beauty anymore. In other words too much of everything good ceases to be good.

Moderation is the golden rule in human affairs. In their folktales, Kasena show how beauty without blemish eventually serves as a camouflage for monstrosity while beastly appearance becomes a masquerade for beauty.

50. Baleiga ná dale de twio ba wó ke ba daane mo
When a lizard hides behind a tree both become targets
Commentary: Kasena boys learning to use the catapult start by hunting lizards which, in the past, they might roast and eat. The lizard is thus the target of the young hunter but children cannot be bothered if the tree is hit instead of the lizard or if both get the stone in the process.
The point here is that an accomplice or an associate or his interests for that matter cannot always be isolated from those of their friends or kin when the latter are marked for punitive action by their enemies. The proverb seems to be saying that my enemy's friend is my enemy vicariously. Another Kasena proverb which shows how things that are associated come in for similar treatment is the following, "it is because of its association with the bean that the stone pebble tastes butter". In other words nobody would waste butter on stones but when the stones happen to be found in beans, a meal that it is customary to eat with butter seasoning then by dint of the association the little stone pebbles which the cook failed to notice and remove get to 'taste' the butter meant for the beans.
A proverb like the above teaches that discrimination between individuals who are associated is not always politic, especially when circumstances do not favour that discrimination.

51. Wɛ ná wo go tega baa di
If God does not slaughter (man) the Earth would not consumed
The earth will receive only what God has killed
Commentary: The Sky God is husband to the Earth, as we have seen, and the two in Kasena thought constitute a dyad. Same sex twins are named *Atega* and *Awe* or *Katega* and *Kawe* with the one named after the sky being senior in that he or she came out of the womb last. The Sky God as husband should provide for the Earth in the way that a good husband provides for his wife. A good and faithful wife is expected to depend on her husband rather than on other men for her maintenance and other needs. Thus the Earth eats only what God provides her.
The point of the proverb is that God sanctions events. Without His permission nothing evil can befall a person. He prevails over the other gods, who are seen as his agents. Powerful as the Earth is it submits to the will of God. The proverb thus affirms the omnipotence of God. It is cited to show that powerful as the witches and the lesser gods and evil forces might be, nevertheless God is Almighty. Without His consent no agency is capable of harming man.

52. Ja wɛ n ba se n yeim lam

If you have the blessings of the Almighty looks are unimportant

Commentary: It is better to court the favours of God than to be endowed with good looks. Kasena concept of good looks is abundantly reflected in the folktales where a person who is endowed with good looks is usually sought after and in the case of a girl, can afford to spurn her suitors. It comprises among other things a person who is in perfect health and is tall, has a smooth skin, few scars or other blemish on the body, and the facial features are proportionate. The nose in particular is strait. Of the beautifully crafted person they say, *n sane je n dwei*: ".. you would feel like washing your hands to touch.." That is to say the hands are ordinarily dirty and should be washed first.

Good looks per se, the proverb warms, are nothing in comparison with good luck and fortune. Kasena remark of a maid who is sought after by men as one "whose head has suitors" (*O yuu jege nonɔna*) which implies that it is a question of luck more than physical beauty per se which accounts for the attentions paid to a maid by her numerous suitors. The requirement of exogamous norms that kin should not intermarry often means that in the past, a man looking for a wife must woo a girl he did not know previously and will not get to know well until he married her.

The point of the proverb is that God's blessings are the ultimate and count more than human accomplishments or natural endowments.

53. Bu ye wɛ mo

A child is God's responsibility

Commentary: A child is a helpless human being; it depends on God. It is God who makes childbirth possible and also protects the tender infant. There is also the view that each individual comes to earth from God's house and that when children die prematurely they have merely returned to that abode, unlike older persons who go to the land of the ancestors after they have lived for some time on earth before dying.

The proverb reflects on the high infant mortality rate among Kasena in former times and the wonder that some of them survive at all.

54. Bein-lɛɛro mo zaŋe bein-dwonnu lwom

It is fresh faeces that provoke the odour of old excrement

Commentary: dried up faeces do not produce smells that are necessarily unbearable; in any case, the scent from old faeces cannot be as bad as that of fresh faeces. However, the scent that fresh stool emits reminds people about the odour of old faeces. On the other hand not all fresh excrement may be very odious, yet even the mere sight of fresh faeces that might not be revolting nevertheless induces revulsion in people because they recall the odour of past faeces.

The proverb is making the point that new events though they might not be very unpleasant in themselves can nevertheless evoke unpleasant memories of the past. This is illustrated by Kasena mourning behaviours. It is customary that when a person dies all kin, friends and even affines, some of whom might never have known the deceased personally come over to mourn. On these occasions the mourning is loud and copious tears are shed even by people who barely knew the deceased. The tears, in the latter case, are due not so much to sympathy felt for the deceased as it is a recollection and exhibition of grief over the loss of a dear one in the past.

55. Ba ba du mene dedwoŋi baŋa ne
One does not sow millet on millet

Commentary: Kasena are experienced cultivators of grain crops. Traditionally they cultivated several varieties of millet the main types being early yielding ones (including *chaara*) and late ones (*men-pwoona*) as well as guinea corn or sorghum. The typical Kasena farm is one that is likely to have several types of crops growing together. Their agricultural practice insists that millet crops be reasonably spaced. Therefore when tender millet appears to bunch together the crop is thinned. Without spacing millet, the crop will not thrive to the extent expected due to competition for nutrients and sunshine. Some crops like beans and creeping plants which may not compete for sunshine with crops like millet may be inter-cropped with millet. This is considered good practice since these different crop items mature at different times and rates while their moisture requirements and demands on soil nutrients also may differ.

This proverb is drawing attention to bad farming practices and warning that when the same type of seedlings sown too close to each other there is the danger that the crop would fail. The proverb not only makes practical sense, it also has wider applications and can be extended to any domain imaginable.

The proverb is not counseling against choice or discrimination, if this were so then it would be contradicting other proverbs such as the one which urges that if it comes to a choice between the domestic guinea fowl and its wild cousin the former takes priority and one would not therefore rob the eye of the domestic fowl to provide the wild one with an eye, see # 107 below. This proverb implies that it might be justified to remove the eye of the wild guinea fowl so that the domesticated one can have sight since the domesticated fowl is poultry.

A Kasena proverb maintains that 'one does not bypass one needy mouth to give water to another'. In this proverb, as in the proverb about millet seedlings being planted on top of each other, it is unwarranted discriminatory that is under criticism. The advise seems to be that in matters where things are substitutable, favouritism is unnecessary, but where choice between alternatives is nevertheless compulsory, perhaps because there are limitation on available slots, random sampling might be a away out. It is better that those items that belong in the same class are provided with equal opportunity for inclusion.

In some respects, the above proverb reminds us of Proverb # 49 above which cautions against discrimination. Kasena have another saying which sheds light on this proverb: *Ba ba mage bu ba woli odwoŋ* (one does not beat one child in support of another). The English proverb that says the goose should be sauced like the gander is a good paraphrase of this proverb.

56. **Bena-bwɛɔ ba keeri kodwoŋi teo ne**
   A male donkey does not bray in another male donkey's territory.
Commentary: One male donkey does not bray in the territory of another with impunity. A foreigner cannot take undue liberties in a foreign country. To do so would amount to an abuse of hospitality which can precipitate sanctions.

The point of the proverb is that animals recognise property or territorial rights so humans should not fail to recognise the rights of others and act accordingly. The rightful owner who is backed by a legal right will fight to protect that right and would enjoy public backing and moral support for his actions.

57. **N ná kwɛɛre de n bɔɔlo bu o ja n peini o maa wu wua**
   If you play with your girl friend's child he will play a whistle tune on your penis
Commentary: The proverb is motivated in part by the resemblance in shape between a traditional Kasena whistle, *wua* and the phallus. Kasem word *bɔɔlɔ* refers to either a love affair or a platonic friendship relationship between man and woman. A divorced or widowed woman might have an open and regular love affair with a man. It is not however unusual for a man to have a platonic relationship with a married woman. He may for his part help her on her farms and occasionally make her gifts of foodstuff and guinea fowls. She might occasionally cook for him and his friends nice meals when they visit. More importantly, these reciprocities associated with a relationship which resembles the "*pok nong*" of the Bulsa discussed at some length by Kröger (1980) might culminate in the provision of a wife for the boyfriend, if he needed a wife. Women who have claims on the hand of their brothers' daughters may

exploit that leverage to find a wife for their male friend.

Kasena men also engage in love affairs with widows whose husbands' final funeral rites have been observed but who thereafter have elected to stay out of a conjugal relationship with the deceased husband's relatives. Such widows, if they happened to have children with the deceased, might continue to live with the deceased husband's lineage. It is a widow's option to elect one of the junior agnates of the deceased husband as a consort or to remain unattached in the lineage for the sake of her children

These opposite sex relationships usually involve visits and socialisation. And where the man's visits are regular, he may well try to fraternalise with his girlfriend's children as a means of easing restraint and suspicions. The danger, according to the proverb, comes when the boyfriend becomes too free with his hostess's child. This can result in the latter taking liberties with the former as familiarity breeds contempt.

In Kasena society, children are socialised to behave with profound respect for their seniors, particularly those in the parental generation. To say of a child that he or she "does not fear a person": *O ba kɔre nɔɔno*, is to intimate that the child has not been given good home education. Such a child can also be described as 'spoilt'. Children are never expected to be very free with adults; they should not, for example mention people of the senior generation by their full names. They might use their reduced names, which are a lisped version of the full name usually coined by toddlers as they first lisped their parents' names. Refer to Awedoba (1996) for a description of Kasena names and genders.

The proverb warns that although seniors may sometimes try to condescend to patronise their juniors and inferiors they should keep their status differentials in perspective or else they risk a perversion of their good intentions to their ultimate embarrassment It is alright to reduce restraint in the relationships involving inequality of status but this should not be done overly as it can give a subordinate ideas or the opportunity to take the superior for granted as too much familiarity breeds contempt.

58. Sabia lage ya tiina yiga mo

Money loves to be found where the wealthy are

Commentary: Those who are rich have no difficult adding to their wealth since money seems to attract money. Wealth is generated by investing wealth and those who lack it therefore have nothing to invest and cannot therefore grow wealthy. Wealth and poverty are here perceived obliquely as cyclic processes. The point of this proverb is not too different from the Biblical saying that to those who have more would be added. The proverb is an observation that fortune favours the fortunate ones. It is an irony that those who are better endowed and whose basic needs are taken care of should be on the receiving end while those who are most in need continue to want for even their basic needs. As another Kasena proverb maintains, curdled milk like to be admired by its owners who do not want it to eat.

59. Ŋwea ye ba zeili ba jaane mo
Life cannot be caught without a hot chase
Commentary: Life is so precious that it cannot be given away without a fight. The instinct of self preservation is present in living creatures which will fight to protect their lives. This looks like a proverb based on hunting practices. A traditional hunter cannot expect his game to stand still and be shot at. The hunter must therefore pursue his quarry by adopting cunning ways of ambushing the game. Even when shot he must be prepared to chase the wounded game until it drops out of exhaustion or through the effect of the poison in the arrow. This is confirmed by another proverb which quotes the duiker as saying that "it is better to be on your feet till sunset than to boil till dusk". The point of the proverb is that survival is an important consideration for all living things especially humans. They will fight to survive in life or in what they do.

60. Yi mo yeiri na se zwɛ yei na
It is the eye which does not know the ancestor but the ear knows
Commentary: The *na* is a person of the great great grant parental generation or someone who is older still. In a society where life expectancy was not much, certainly not more than 60 years for the average person, most people could not have been born during the life time of their great grandparents, not to mention their *na* who is several generations antecedent. However, many Kasena would have heard about their *na*, the great great grand father or his antecedent, from their parents and grand parents. The *na*, it is customary, receives mention in sacrificial rites and on other important ritual occasions. Appeals would be made to those in the category of *na* in times of crisis and need. There are many occasions then when the living remember the *na*. A traditional Kasena child who hangs around his parents and grandparents would not fail to hear about the *na*.
     The point of the proverb is that cognition can be by word of mouth or by sight. What a person may not have witnessed visually he might nevertheless have heard about. It is not only seeing that is believing but also hearing.

61. Ba ba mae yi ba laŋe (lɔre) yɛ dwoa
The salt content in soup cannot be determined by the eye
Commentary: The eye cannot help us to know how much salt there is in

food since the salt content of food does not change its appearance. In the case of *sean* or *chasega*, the local salts made from distilling the mild potash from the ashes of millet stalks, the colour of the broth may change with the addition of this potash salt. Taste is the means for assessing the salt content of a dish among the Kasena. Sight is a form of experiencing, albeit the external while taste is a form of experiencing that is internal or introspection. The latter has an in-depth quality and therefore embodies insight and greater appreciation. The proof of the pudding therefore is in the eating, as the English would put it. Each organ has its specialised function in experiencing life. Good judgement should be based on an insightful knowledge of what is being judged or assessed rather on external assessment which lacks insight.

62. Diira dedɛ ba chɔge dwoa
Lots of condiments do not necessarily spoil the broth

Commentary: The Kasena spice their broth with various condiments including salts which were scarce in former times. Though salt is the most important ingredient such that broth without salt would be considered as tasteless and insipid, this item was in former times a luxury which only the wealthy could afford, as the missionary, Gagnon (1956) remarked. Perhaps this explains its role in pre-marriage prestations. It used to come into Kasenaland through transactions with caravans which may have obtained the commodity from the Sahara region. Although there were local salts made from burning millet stalks these did not have the taste of cooking salt and were a poor substitute for conventional salt. In addition to salt, cheese made from locust bean, fish, pepper, guinea fowl meat are used as condiments in the preparation of sauce. Groundnut powder was usually mixed with the other ingredients to make the broth palatable.

The proverb seems to be saying that one cannot have too much of a good thing that happens to be scarce in the environment. In some respects it appears to contradict other Kasena proverbs such as the one that stipulates that too much of everything is bad.

63. Kazɔgɔ yera kwɛ de swanno mo
The mortar is coated with chaff

Commentary: The proverb maintains that it is only natural that a mortar should be coated with the dust of millet husk and chaff. This is where the millet is pounded and later winnowed to remove the chaff. The mortar in which millet is pound is rarely cleaned and usually is located some distance from the homestead. Any woman who might wish to use it can do so. It becomes in a sense collective property as women within the clan-settlement cannot be denied access. It is constantly under use, for which reason it is not felt that it should be cleaned after use. This contrasts with the maintenance of the smaller mortars that individual women own and keep within the compound for pounding the ingredients that go into the preparation of food. The latter which is never used to pound millet with husk, is carefully cleaned and maintained.

Actions have their logical consequences just as things have their characteristics. The proverb's message is that one cannot eat his or her cake and still expect to have it.

64. **Bone yeini de kaane daane mo ye de tu kwogo**
    Goats warn each other before they get down to the salt lick
    Commentary: Goats always warn each other before they get to the salt lick. Domestic animals frequent salt licks in the vicinity and when they go there they do so collectively. Kasena do not allow domestic livestock to roam free in the wet season when they pose danger to crops on the farms. However, in the dry season when the crops have been harvested the animals may roam about freely and it is perhaps at this time that goats frequent the lick. The lick may be located some distance from the clan-settlement, perhaps in the bushlands. While there the animals may be in danger as wild predators could be about.

The comment of the proverb, which is certainly based on the behaviour of a herd is that despite the anxiety on the part of each animal to lick the salt, nevertheless, there seems to be an understanding that precautions are called for if the herd is not to be surprised as each and every animal concentrates on the salt.

The proverb warns that success and self preservation often depend on a joint action and group understanding. Between companions and associates there should be an unexpressed understanding that though the occasional disagreement and infighting are unavoidable they must not be allowed to degenerate into enmity or feud or to undermine the viability of the collective enterprise or collective safety. Even in those traditional societies like the Tallensi and Nuer where feuding was enshrined in the social structure as described by Fortes and Evans-Pritchard there were still situations when people were expected to put aside their differences and to collaborate for the good of the collectivity. Though Kasena kinship does not work in quite the same way that Fortes' various accounts of Tallensi social structure describe, Kasena people did and do recognise the need not to allow differences within the lineage, kin-group or any other social grouping to get out of hand.

65. **Vala gurim mo ka boboom**
    The beginning of the straw bangle is its ending

Commentary: The straw bangle known as *vala* in Kasem may be warn on the wrist or waist for adornment. It is also used in shepherd boys' games where it is rolled on the ground. Though the weaver of the *vala* uses sticks of grass he or she in the end produces a circular artifact by joining the beginning and the end. This is done in such a way that it is not easily noticed where the end or the beginning of the bangle is.

The proverb implies that so long as there is a beginning there must also be an end and vice versa. We cannot understand the end without knowledge of the beginning. This proverb remind us of the Akan symbolism of the *sankofa* motif or icon which suggests that life is cyclic and much history can be learnt from the present just as knowledge of the past sheds considerable light on the present and the future.

66. Dɔɔm yeiri a nu tega
   Sleep is oblivious of mother's death
Commentary: The occasion of a mother's death is a crucial moment in a person's life. Kasena believe the burden, ritual and non-ritual, that a person has to bear on the death of a parent is greater in the case of a mother. It is the bereaved child's duty to bury the deceased mother. Despite the grief, the child must bestir himself or herself as there are rituals to be carried out as well as sundry other chores. Until burial, it is hard to find time for sleep. The hardship is worsened by that fact that the corpse might remain unburied for several days, as is the norm when old people die. This is hard time for a person, with all the public attention that is focussed on the bereaved child. At such a moment the bereaved child's reputation is up for reassessment. Observers wish to see how a person comports and acquits himself at such a moment.

The proverb makes the point that despite the activity imposed on the bereaved child by the mother's death sleep is inevitable. It overtakes the bereaved child against his wishes and to his embarrassment. The spirit, it might be said, could be willing but the body is weak. What is more when he succumbs to slumber, the child is likely for a moment to forget his grief and the momentous event of a mother's death. Kasena have a statement to the effect that sleep is the younger sibling of death. In other words, sleep resembles death in that the sleeper is rendered unconscious of events in the immediate surroundings. Sleep dissolves, albeit temporarily, the worries and cares of this world.

67. Beeru woporo wo sɔŋɔ chwoŋa ne
   The person who habitually returns home late learns his lesson on the home bound journey
Commentary: The person who loves to stay out of home till late in the

night may not heed warnings so long as he remains in the comfort and security of another's house. It is only as he returns to his own home alone in the still night after all the convivialities that he learns the wisdom in the advise against staying out late.

Kasena believe that many dangers lurk in the night. They favour the dispersed patterns of settlement in view of the need to have farm space surrounding the compound. Compounds are often sited some distance away from each other. At the height of the wet season thick vegetation covers even the paths which adds to the dangers the solitary person walking home in the darkness is exposed to. Fear is heightened by the beliefs and supported by reports of ghosts and spirits moving about at this time of day as well as reports of wild creatures and were-cats prowling about.

The point of the proverb is that if a person will not listen to advice the best thing to do is to stop bothering the person with unwanted advice. The best advice will surely be the lesson learnt the hard way. Verbal warnings do not have the same effect as close encounters with the unpleasant, i.e. with fear and danger.

68. N ná yeiri boŋo n mɔne ko tɔnɔ

If you did not know the live goat you would laugh at its dried up skin Commentary: It is customary to skin a slaughtered goat. The skin was valued not for its meat value but for its leather. In the past, a goat's skin was worked into a garment which was worn around the shoulders. The skin had to dry in the sun for a while before it was cured and then made into a garment or put to some other use. The skin of a beautiful goat retains it beauty while the goat lives. When it is killed, skinned and that beautiful skin dried changes occur; it shrivels and loses its former smooth feel, appearance and elasticity. It becomes unrecognisable even to those who once admired it. The person who has never known the live goat may thus be forgiven for ridiculing the dead goat if all he or she has to go on were the evidence of the dried up skin. Compare this proverb to its antithesis in Buli where we are told that "If you did not know the goat (when it was alive) you had better inspect its skin", Agalic (1983:33). What the Bulsa proverb is saying is equally true, especially in these days of commercialisation and its associated problems. For example, if livestock suddenly goes missing, the likely explanation is that some thief might have stolen it and sold it off to the butchers in town. The owner would therefore be advised to visit the butcher's shop and inspect the skins of slaughtered animals left outside to dry.

The argument of the Kasena proverb in question is that it is unfair to pronounce judgment without taking into consideration the background history of the people who receive negative assessment based on tenuous evidence. Critical assessment, from the point of view of this proverb, should be diachronic and take into account the past and not be based simply on synchronic evidence.

69. **Ba ba lwoi sɔɔro ba dare bu**

One does not prepare the *sɔɔro* in anticipation of the birth of the child

Commentary: The *sɔɔro* in Kasena culture comprises leaves and roots boiled so that the resultant infusion can be used in the ritual of bathing the neonate. The proverb says that it is waste of time and energy to fetch the leaves and the necessary herbs in advance in expectation of the child's birth. This can be explained at one level by the impossibility of predicting exactly when the child will be born, or indeed if it will be born at all. The leaves and the other materials necessary for the rite can always be found in the bush when needed but if stored away for more than a day they might dry up and become useless medicinally. At another level, an event as important and critical as childbirth has to be handled with circumspection. There are forces, it is often believed which are not on man's side and it would be foolish to tempt these forces or fate itself by pre-mature jubilation. Kasena practice insists that the neonate has to be shielded from ritual danger by keeping it confined for a period to allow the lineage head to negotiate, as it were, for the safety of the new comer.

The proverb is a warning against those who tempt providence by their lack of patience. There is time for everything, the proverb seems to be saying.

70. **Ba ba sɔ tampɔgɔ ba tiŋi bu**

One does not weave a boy's bag for the unborn child

Commentary: This proverb echoes partially the above proverb, # 69, where it is advised that the collection of leaves to use in preparation of a neonate's bath should wait till after the child's birth. The bag in question is meant for a son who will grow to become a shepherd boy and will need it to keep food in while out herding the sheep or cattle. In the short run, the proverb is warning that though a parent might prefer a son, in this patrilineal society, he should not act as though he were sure that the issue could not be female, if a child will be born at all, given the possibility of still births and taking into consideration the many pregnancies that do not end in childbirth. Furthermore a male child may be born deformed or might even be perceived or diagnosed to be a *chuchuru* child, one of these children who in the past were regarded as incarnations of evil bush spirits that will not only be of no benefit to parents but could eventually harm the kin group. Such children in the past were disposed off. A parent in any case has several years between a child's birth and the age at which he will begin to herd sheep and this should be time long enough for the weaving of the shepherd boy's bag. Traditionally, a child begins to herd sheep at the age of ten.

71. Ba ba teiŋa tontoŋeno keila

One does not press the cheeks of the worker

Commentary: It is contrary to custom to refuse to feed the person who has volunteered his labour. Where the work involves harvesting or processing foodstuff, the owner cannot be too critical of his helpers if they happen to eat the crop in its raw state as the work progresses. It is considered ungrateful for a person to be so hard hearted as to refuse food to his workers since it is food that sustains the worker, in Kasena view. Kasena sometimes say, *a toŋa a kana ŋwaane mo* (I work for my stomach).

Kasena expect that when others come over to assist the farm owner to harvest groundnuts the volunteers should be given some of the produce when they leave at the end of the day. The quantity that the volunteer will take home depends on the generosity of the farm owner. For other types of farm work which do not entail harvesting the farm owner should reward the helpers with a meal and millet beer.

The proverb makes the point that every kind of work entitles the worker to some reward, even if it is not monetary, and it would be unfair to the worker to expect that he or she should harbour no expectations for compensation at all.

72. Yi kɔre didwoŋi

One eye fears another

Commentary: Another version of the same proverb says that one elder's eye fears another elder's eye. (*Nakwe yi kɔre didwoŋi*).

It is generally perceived as disrespectful for one to look at another strait in the eye or to stare. One way of showing annoyance is to look at another from the corner of the eye. Kasena describe this as *n tiŋi yi tega n ni* (literally, to put eye on the ground and look) or 'to look with the red eye' (*ni de yi-seŋo*). The way a person looks at another also can suggest the intention to frighten. Finally, when a child stares at a person eating food, this is considered as bad breeding. This proverb thus expresses a truth that holds in both the literal and metaphorical sense. Every person is expected to show respect to other persons and although children may be forgiven for not exhibiting respect to other children and sometimes to adults, adults should show by word and deed that they respect other adults. This is not to say that people do not make eye contact in their dealings with each other. This should however be distinguished from rude staring. To say that a person did something *yifula yifula* is to imply that he or she did something unpleasant to another full view without bothering to disguise his or her act. Thus one desists from saying unpleasant things about others in their presence except where there is an open quarrel or fight. Courtesy demands that unpleasantness be disguised and not disclosed openly.

The proverb is referring to the need for indirection and the application of face saving devices among cultured individuals.

73. Am' yei ma mo se a yeiri jagala
I accept what is within measure but not excesses
I know enough but not excess

Commentary: The word *ma* is an ideophone describing the brink, the point where the uttermost limit has been reached. The proverb says enough is enough and that it is unacceptable to exceed this. To do so is to cause overfloat which leads to waste.

This proverb is used to signal that patience has its limit and that it can run out. Parents sometimes quoted the proverb at their children when they have to put naughty children in their places.

74. Bia done kapera ba wɔe nakwa wo
When children eat raw fig fruits it is their elders who suffer stomach ache

Commentary: The fruit of the fig tree when ripe is soft and sweet and is not deemed to cause ill-health when eaten. It is not however a favourite fruit among Kasena. The unripened fruit of the fig tree which is not sweet may be eaten raw or used in the preparation of broth. Mothers believe that taking broth made from figs can improve the rate of lactation in a woman who is breast-feeding. The raw unripened fruit, if not processed, is considered not so safe to eat, especially if taken in large quantities. It does not digest well in the stomach and can thus cause stomach upsets. Adults are expected to know this but children can be expected to be less careful and might when hungry eat more of the fruit than would be safe. Both children and adults eat the fruit nonetheless, and hungry children may over indulge themselves to their detriment.

The point is that when children get the subsequent tummy problems from eating too much of the raw figs it becomes the duty of the adults or their seniors to worry about how to cure the stomach ache. The individual suffers the consequences of his actions due to a lack of caution and failure to heed the advice of his seniors or those who know better but parents and those who have jural authority are not exempted. The latter suffer even more since they not only feel for the suffering child or dependent they must also exert themselves in the search for treatment and whatever expenses are entailed in fees due to the healer or prescribed as part of the healing process will have to be settled by the parent or elder concerned . The moral behind the proverb is that youth are impetuous and do not always heed advice. They do what the elders and their seniors advise against. Nevertheless when things go badly wrong as a result it is to the elders and those in authority that the inexperienced sufferer must turn to for help. The elders have to suffer the consequences of the youth's irresponsible behaviour. Elders as elders are jurally responsible for their juniors in Kasena law. A man is responsible for the misdemeanors of his wives and children and other dependents and he must answer for it. By the same token, complaints will be directed to the lineage elder or parents when a dependent wrongs a member of another lineage. The chief, in dealing with cases brought to his notice, does not deal directly with individuals about whom complaints have been levelled. Rather the chief summons the appropriate clan head or lineage head whose duty it is to produce the culprit. Whatever fines have been imposed by the chief are not necessarily settled by the culprit but by his or her seniors.

75. **Napwoŋo ko chwoŋa naseŋo ko chwoŋa**
   Red takes its course and white takes its course
Commentary: The three primary colours in Kasena perception are black, white and red. Similes are used to describe more accurate colour shades. The three colours do not necessarily constitute a triad; rather, it would appear that black articulates with red to form one set of dyadic colour terms and with white to form another dyadic set. Each of the three colours covers a range of colour hues. White describes light colours and pigment shades and red (*naseŋo*) might cover brown, red, orange, yellow etc. As far as their associations and connotations go these cannot necessarily be classified in terms of positive and negative regardless of the situation and context. Red is certainly desirable when we talk of fruits since ripened fruit is described as 'red'. White connotes positive attributes when applied to the emotions, in contradistinction with black. A young tender maid enjoying the freshness of youth is described as *busankan-pwola* (fresh white girl), happiness is fresh white stomach (*wo-pwolo*), frank person is white person (*nɔn-pwoŋo*).
   The message of the proverb is that things that are different do not mix and should not be mixed together, if confusion is to be avoided. The factors and conditions that engender them are different, after all.

76. **Zurigaluu mo tei dam**
   Strength resides in numbers

Commentary: The word *zurigaluu* is an ideophone which describes the bunching together of things, particularly living things. The metaphor is based on ant behaviours. Food that is much too heavy for one individual ant is nevertheless carried away by the collective effort of the ant colony.

The point of the proverb is that strength lies in unity and collaboration.

77. Naao wó gaao ne ye ko yuu wó kura ne mo

A cow may spend its time in the bush but its head is in the hearth
Commentary: Cattle ranching is not customary among Kasena now or in the past. Their husbandry practice involves leaving cattle in the charge of youth who herd livestock in the wet season. The primary reason for herding the livestock seems to be the danger that unattended livestock pose to the crops.

In the wet season the animals are sent where there is good pasture. Settlements have open spaces reserved for the pasturing of livestock. These, however, are often not adequate due to the pressure on land. Kasena practice compound farming which means that 80% of farm land is in the immediate perimeter of the compound homestead. As settlement pastures are exhausted the animals are moved to fresher fields. From time to time the boys take the cattle to the bushlands outside the settlements. In the dry season however, after the harvest, cattle and other livestock are left to roam about in search of food. In the night unattended cattle come home to the cattle yard which is an enclosure within the compound. It only become necessary to search for the herds that fail to come home.

The point of the proverb is that although the cow is found often times in the uncultivated bush this does not make it a wild game animal. The property rights of its owners are upheld. Its head which is symbolic of the whole animal belongs to its owner and will be cooked by its owner whenever it is slaughtered, regardless of how the meat of the animal is shared. In the metaphorical sense too the cow's head belong's in the hearth of its owner who decides on how to dispose of his cow.

This proverb is often used to emphasise that each individual occupies a status in the community and has rights to others just as others have jural rights to each individual. A person, thus perceived as property, is owned by the lineage. A person may rove about and go to places of his choice nevertheless mobility does not make a person kinless; each person has a home and kin somewhere who will acknowledge his or her kinship claims and provide the opportunities for the exercise of that person's civic rights and obligations when necessary.

78. N ná lage doa ka ne n nawara ne

If you long for rain it will fall on your parapet wall
Commentary: The *nawara* (parapet wall), in this proverb represents the set of rooms that a woman calls her own. She sees to the plastering of the walls of these rooms which she regards as her responsibility to keep in good repair. Her reputation as a housewife in the clan-settlement may be measured by the care she takes of her rooms. Women are known to decorate the walls of their huts with black and white stripes in their effort to make their huts attractive to the visitor. Put differently, the proverb is warning the person who has a longing for the rain that he or she could experience such a down pour that just that individual's hut is inundated. The pattern of rainfall in certain times of the year is such that it might rain in a section of the clan-settlement but not in other sections or in the adjacent settlements.

Rain is considered a great blessing yet it can cause problems for people, especially if it falls out of season. It can ruin social and economic activities. Too much of it destroys crops and dwelling places. Although Kasena claim to have masters of the rain who are capable of inducing it or withholding it yet experience shows that it rains when rain is not wanted just as communities needing rain might pray for it in vain.

The parapet wall that encircles the mud platform which is such an essential component of Kasena-Nankana building architecture is the most exposed part of the dwelling hut and therefore most vulnerable to the deleterious effect of rainfall. It is coated with plaster from time to time in the wet season to protect it from the rains. While the plaster coating is still fresh and wet the wall is most vulnerable to torrential down pours. Rains moreover can come at short notice in a culture where there was no foolproof process of predicting rain. A woman who has misread the signs and has prepared her parapet wall may find she has laboured in vain as rain washes away her efforts at a moment's notice. The proverb captures the precariousness of the condition in which Kasena living in a savannah ecology with very seasonal and erratic rainfall find themselves.

The point of the proverb centres on the paradox that good things can have their undesirable features. When there is an abundance of the good things that are desired their negative effects become obvious. People will pray for events like rain which unfortunately are beyond their control. They will habour feelings of regret when undesirable effects begin to manifest themselves.

79. **N ná lage tuu ko nɔm n men-chena ne**
    If you long to see the elephant it will walk in your crop of tender millet
Commentary: The tender millet that is growing on the farm symbolises the

farmer's hopes. Should this crop suffer the farmer's expectations for the year are dashed. Kasena did not have substantial surpluses. Food reserves were and are still lowest in the sowing season which begins in May or thereabouts, as by then farmers would have used up any surplus food from the previous season in ancestral rites such as the *faao* harvest ritual or in funeral celebrations which have customarily embodied an element of conspicuous consumption. For most traditional Kasena, the peak of the famine season tallies with the period of the first rains when sowing is going on in earnest.

An elephant is a thing that people rarely saw even in the past. Today the only place to see a live elephant is in the zoo in Accra, the Ghanaian capital. Thus many perceptions of this animal depended on secondhand accounts about the animal's size and what it looks like[9]. Against this background it is conceivable that some people should crave for the sight of a live elephant. However, those who are familiar with the elephant's habits will also remark on the destruction it is capable of causing, particularly to crops and farms, not to mention the danger that a wild elephant on the rampage would pose to humans. The presence of an elephant near the settlement was not therefore quite the good news that it might be expected to be. In the past elephants were wont to visit settlements.

The point of the proverb is that one should not knowingly court danger, especially when one does not have the means to handle that danger. It is better that certain curiosities remain curiosities, unexplored.

80. Na ba jege nateini
Water has no ladder

Commentary: A ladder enables people to climb out of a pit or up a height. The *nateini* among Kasena is usually a wooden ladder made from a notched beam. This enables people to climb up to the *nayuu* or raised platform which is the mud thatch for the dwelling hut. A river, pool, lake or some other body of water may pose a danger to those who fall into it, if they cannot swim. Cases of drowning occur in the wet season when torrential rains flood river banks and wash people away as they attempt to cross swollen rivers and streams. Nevertheless, drowning is also one form of death that may be attributed to vengeful or retaliatory actions taken by river deities against men who have contracted with them but have failed to carry out their end of the contract.

This proverb is a warning to children who love to play in streams, rivers or pools to be careful of the danger. It could be but is rarely generalised as a warning to people to beware the unknown.

81. **Ba ba mage ba ni mo se ba ke ba nia**
One does not experiment by beating people but other modes of experimentation may be acceptable
Commentary: Beating is painful and provocative, it is therefore unwise to test people's pulse or their temperament by beating them. Although this is one thing that should not be tried out the idea of experimentation in itself is a good one.

Human beings are not Guinea pigs to be treated as objects of experimentation, so says this proverb. The proverb advises on the need to carry out experiments if discoveries beneficial to man are to be made. It could be concluded from proverbs like this one that the notion that traditional societies are conservative to the core may not be applicable in all cases.

82. **Magem ná mage konto sarem (sareno) ye sa konto**
Though the beat may be wrong the dancer does not dance badly
Commentary: A good dancer is expected to dance to the tune of the drum beat. The drum beat assists the dancer in his or her performance. However, where the beat is wrong or out of tune the dancer does not for that reason have the excuse to perform badly. There is mutual support relationship between drummer and dancer to the extent that when the music is ill-suited the dancer's performance can be affected. Similarly, poor dancers have been known to discourage drummers to the point where the session is called off. To say of a person that *o sage o gwɛɛne jɔŋɔ* (he or she terminated the *jɔŋɔ* dance by his dance) is to imply this. In Kasena dances it is usually the dancers who are rewarded with a tip in appreciation of their skill and not necessarily the musicians. However, the tip usually belongs to the drummer and not the dancer. Nevertheless drummer and dancer can display their skills and expertise independently and would be so assessed.

The message of this proverb is that even in collaborative events there is still always room for individual accountability. Merit due to an individual, or individual responsibility for that matter, is not negated or nullified by the collective character of an event. The proverb also implies that two wrongs do not make a right.

83. **Ba lwoni dwoŋi sɛo mo se ba ba lwoni dwoŋi kio**
We copy dances but we do not copy the actions of others
Commentary: Kasena learn to dance well by imitation of their favourite dancers. This behaviour is to them commendable as individuals thus aspire to the high standards set by others in the community. In this context *sɛo* refers to an approved or admired performance or specific standard of

excellence. The word *kio* is derived from the noun *kikio*, actions, behaviour or doings. It is of a higher degree of abstraction. While a style of dancing is comparatively transparent and limited in its range of potential consequences, behaviour is opaque and cannot be understood out of context. Behaviour which is appropriate to one person or set of circumstances may not be so for another person is similar or different circumstance. Thus, it is not in every domain that a person should ape the behaviours of others.

The proverb is urging that copy cats should not imitate others blindly. This is a proverb which usually ends the folktale in which a character such as Ayiying, the prince, was claimed forcibly by the half-bodied spirit agent for a husband[10]. It pursued the hero everywhere he took refuge allowing him no sleep till the chief, his father, finally decided that the spirit must be burnt alive to get rid of it. The spirit's response was to change into a beauty and to confer wealth on her husband. At the end the chief decided that his son should rather be burnt. This was carried out but the spirit revived the hero at which point the chief's favourite wife decided if her daughter-in-law could pull off the stunt so could she. Thus she had her husband thrown into the fire but she lacked the magic to bring him back to life, thereby illustrating the adage.

84. Ko di ko muri mo se ko ba tɛ ko mura
Rumour is not like food that some should fail to receive their share.

Unlike food, quantity is not a factor in the circulation of rumour
Commentary: Food is sometimes scarce and not everybody gets to share it. The food supply is subject to seasonal fluctuation. When it is short those who have it tend to hide it away in order to keep it to themselves, contrary to the ideal norm which favours the sharing of food between kin. Differences in people's circumstances imply also inequalities so that while some individuals and families may have sufficient food others might not have enough to eat. Food is thus unlike rumour in that as rumour circulates it grows rather than diminishes. Given time all and sundry eventually get to hear a rumour that is current in the community since those who peddle it lose nothing by spreading it. There is however a proviso: rumour mongers try to ensure that the individuals the rumour concerns do not get to know that they are its disseminators. Thus rumours are whispered in private, just like scarce food that is concealed and eaten in private.

This proverb is cited to show that anything done in secret may yet out. Certain types of information are not privatised since those who have it lose nothing by sharing with those who have not, provided they wish to listen. Even the walls have ears.

85. **Wɛ ná le-m n ze swoi se n zeŋe nuga de chana de, ka ta wó nyeene mo**
If you are cursed by God even the soft rays of the moon will be enough to melt the butter that you carry
Commentary: The proverb seems straight forward enough. Kasena butter is made from shea nut and is usually thick when it has cooled and congealed. The sun's rays in this ecology can however melt it if it is exposed long enough. Freshly made butter is usually left to thicken over night and this means leaving it either inside the hut or outside in the inner living yard. Nights can be warm but usually as it approaches dawn temperatures drop somewhat and it begins to feel cold. In the early part of the dry season, November to February, the mornings can be chilly. It is not expected that butter that has ready congealed would melt in the night unless heated over fire.

The point of the proverb is that God is All powerful such that He can melt butter at a time when butter ought rather to be congealing. Not only is it within the power of God to work miracles, the wrath of God is dreadful. If a person is cursed by God nothing can safe that person. Kasena believe that good luck like bad luck comes ultimately from God. The lesser gods might assist or punish and undermine man but it is God Almighty who sanctions events. As another proverb viz # 51 says, "If God has not killed the Earth will not consume".

86. **Chilwon-zɔŋɔ gare nupugabu**
A dear friend is better than a full sibling
Commentary: *Nupuga bu* is the mother's child or sibling. In Kasena culture, those who share a mother in common also share their mother's witchcraft propensity since witchcraft is believed by them to be transmitted matrilineally, i.e., through women rather than men. It is expected that those who are of the *Nupuga bu* category will stick by each other and defend one another against any accusation of witchery, if this becomes necessary, since when one is accused the other maternal siblings and cousins stand equally accused too by implication.

The proverb makes the point that in spite of the close kinship between siblings nevertheless, an intimate friend is better than a sibling. The reference here is no doubt to the intensity of friendship which, though of the short run, as Bloch (1973) would have it, is based on merit as opposed to kinship which is a relationship of the long run. The latter is ascribed at birth. As the saying goes, we achieve our friends but our kin are imposed upon us. Kinship can withstand stress which means that kin sometimes take the relationship for granted in a way that friendship could not be taken because of its fragility. Thus, what people do to maintain friendly ties, kin do not or may not necessarily do.

87. Fee fee mo ti bonaga yu-kwolo
By eating small bits of the donkey's head it will be consumed eventually
Little drops make an ocean
Rome was not built in a day

Commentary: Meat is not an every day food item for Kasena. Though they rear poultry, and keep livestock, in the past no Kasena would slaughter even a fowl for domestic consumption. There is therefore a strong craving for meat. However, not every animal is good to eat. Their totemic beliefs determine what meat to eat or not to eat. Donkey meat, for some unknown reason, has never been a favourite of Kasena; however Kasena do not have taboos against its consumption. This writer's impression is that Kasena will eat donkey meat reluctantly. Since their norms forbid the throwing away of food it holds that donkey meat will always be eaten rather than thrown away. When in the Kasem language anything is described as *bonaga nɔna* (donkey meat), it implies that the item in question is in abundance and nobody is keen on having it. It is therefore with difficulty that the head of a donkey, which is certainly not the best part of any animal's carcass, is consumed. It takes time to accomplish this, given the ambivalence that people feel about eating this type of meat.

From this proverb can be derived the observation that with time and some patience, even unpleasant tasks can be completed.

88. Nabwonu diini o bonaga ye ka tigi tega ne mo
The handicapped man mounts his donkey while it is lying down

Commentary: The term *nabwonu* can mean a pauper, a handicapped person, a weakling or an aged person who has become senile. The horse has always been associated with chiefs and princes. There is however no equestrian culture among these people similar to what has been reported of Dagomba, Staniland (1978). For Kasena, it was the donkey that served the needs of the average person and even this was not exactly a poor man's beast. However, donkeys did not cost much when purchased from the Moshie. The donkey's main use was as a means of locomotion but it walked rather trotted. Thus, the donkey appealed more to the handicapped and those who could not walk much. Although a handicapped person might have difficulties mounting his donkey he could solve the problem by making the donkey lie down. This is easier said than done, given the remarkable stubbornness of the donkey. The handicapped would do well to mount his donkey while it remains on the ground, the proverb points out.

The message of the proverb is that a person should know himself or herself well and then should preempt those personal limitations in his or her approach to difficult situations.

89a.   Siseiŋa na vei mε to bonaga de wó yi da
Where the horse is going the donkey too will get there eventually
Commentary: The donkey, as we have seen in Proverb # 88, is the average person's "horse". It is not much valued as a means of locomotion since it walks and does not trot, unlike the horse. What is more, it is stubborn and can on occasion refuse to respond to its master's bidding to move. However, with patience the donkey too will eventually arrive at its destination.

The message of this proverb is, patience and perseverance can overcome obstacles. Substance, artistry and style are here compared. It is to say that artistry and style may be aesthetically appealing but it is substance that matters ultimately. It is not so much manner as the result that matters in the long run. This is a proverb that may be cited to confirm a situation where a person acknowledges his comparative disadvantage but remains satisfied that the disadvantages notwithstanding the objectives can be achieved.

89b Bonaga tu na vei mε to naga tu de wó yi da
Wherever the donkey rider will go the walker will also get there eventually
Commentary: This proverb is in essence just another version of # 88a. The person on donkey back is now compared to the person on foot. The advantage of the person on donkey back is perhaps that his journey is less tiring in the first place, which means his chances of earlier arrival are greater since he may not have to stop so often to rest. The person on foot does not have these options. When he is tired he must stop to take a rest. Therefore, in the short run, the person on donkey back covers longer distances within the same time span than the person on foot, however through endurance and patience the man on foot will eventually make it too. This proverb, regardless of its origin has a historical reflection that goes back to the early decades of the twentieth century when the pax Britannica allowed Kasena to walk the distance between home and Kumasi, the Ashanti capital, to trade cattle. In the same convoy might be Moshie traders taking their goods on donkey to the same markets in the then Gold Coast.

The proverb commends endurance and patience. Never despair, the proverb seems to say.

90. Bam-peno tu mo di na-kadogo yela

It is the patient man who eats the milk of the barren cow

The message of this proverb is again the same as that for proverbs # 88, # 89a and #89b, although the metaphor is different. Milk is a special diet item for Kasena who do not keep many herds of cattle and, for that matter, it is worth waiting for it. It seems contradictory to expect a barren cow that cannot bear young to lactate. However, some cows, just like human beings, reproduce late. This makes it really difficult to be sure that a person or a cow is really barren, it is time that will tell. It is thus a wise precaution to be patient and wait rather than to get rid of the seemingly barren cow too soon. In the case of human reproduction, the same injunction seems to hold to a limited extent. Kasena say that when the "blood of the couple does not harmonise" (*ba jana wo maŋe daane*), the woman does not become pregnant. The truth of this is illustrated for them by the knowledge that some couples who have failed to have children nevertheless each succeeded in getting children of their own after they had separated and remarried someone else.

The message of the proverb is that patience moves mountains and that obstacles are surmountable. Miracles are possible given time and patience.

91. Sabu yeiri choro

Money knows no kin

Commentary: Modern money, *feila sabu*, literally, "European money" the universal medium of exchange, is valued by all and sundry. This interest in money goes back to traditional times as the notion of money is by no means recent; there seems to be ample evidence that there was money in one form or another. Cowries, cyprea moneta, was introduced fairly recently but prior to colonisation, as evidenced by its name, *subu-pwoŋo* or white money. This assertion can be justified. Borrowed ideas and artifacts usually come in with either the term by which they are known in the lending culture (as in the case of the English word "bucket" which in Kasem is *bɔkte*) or the borrowing culture supplies a descriptive phrase to stand for it (*luuzuŋa* <metal bird> for aeroplane which may also be pronounced as [alopile]) or a term for an item that is analogous to the borrowed item may be used to refer to it. In the case of money none of these processes appear to account adequately for the term *sabu*. That being so, one is tempted to suggest that there could have once been a form of indigenous money, known as *sabu*: perhaps a special form of limited purpose money that the Kasena once used. It is not possible now to identify the particular object that might have served this purpose although one is tempted by the phonological similarity between *sabu* [seɔ bu] "shea nut" and *sabu*, money. There is however a slight difference in pronunciation effected by subtle tonal changes. For example, the term for money is pronounced with a sequence of low and rising tones while that for shea nut is mid tone followed by rising tone.

The proverb is used in a rather circumscribed context to point to the dangers that an overly concern for money can result for kin. The point here is that commercial relations and kinship relations are not of the same kind and should not be confused. When the kinship sphere is not clearly differentiated from the commercial it can lead to the undermining of personal kinship relations.

92. Chwoŋa ba jege ni
The journey has no mouth

Commentary: Kasena talk about *chwoŋa ni* or the edge of the path or road which is literally, the mouth of the path. However, *chwoŋa*, as journey, they maintain has no mouth. Thus the path does not communicate with the traveller.

The message of the proverb is that when one is on a journey one loses touch with the place of departure and the destination. The traveller is thus, so to speak, between and betwixt, as Turner (1969) would have put it; he or she is temporarily ignorant of home events and in a state of apprehension and uncertainty especially about what the place of destination holds for the traveller. Telephone and telegraphic facilities were introduced not too long ago, perhaps in the 1930s or 1940s and they have been unavailable to the average person. Even today, only the privileged few have access to the telephone or any other means of telecommunication[11] Prophets of course have always claimed to be capable of telling the immediate future and were consulted for this purpose now, just as in the past. In one respect the path did have a mouth and did communicate with the wayfarer. This took the form of prognostic signs, such as hitting the auspicious or inauspicious foot as a person walks to his destination. For a person whose succeeding sibling is male the left foot means good luck and the right stands for ill-luck and vice versa.

93. Dayoo we o wo wonnu mo ye o wonnu se o keila wonnu dae o wonnu
The rat says he can only call what is in his belly his property but not what is still in the mouth.

Commentary: The proverb reflects the distinction in meaning and significance between what is in the mouth or what is being prepared for consumption and what has already been introduced into the digestive system of the human body to be absorbed and to enhance survival of the living person. The word *di* in Kasem covers all this and its derivative *wudiiu* (literally, things eaten), means food or the nourishment that is destined for consumption or is safe to introduce into the system and will if eaten become part of the system. When Kasena wish to signal that things, including persons, are not safe or are bad they might resort to the metaphor of food by describing the person or thing in question as "not food" (*dae wudiiu*). This suggests that their concept of *wudiiu* takes account of its generic safety and beneficial character.

The notion of *wonnu*, "things" refers to food in this proverb. Food in the mouth which is yet to be introduced into the system is *ni wonnu* or "mouth things" while the food that has now reached its destination is *wo wonnu*, "things of the stomach"[12]. Verbs like *done* "chew" and *mu* "to suck" show the preparations that take place within the mouth where teeth, tongue and mouth fluids are at play while *li*, "to swallow" describes the internalisation process. What is yet in the mouth is easily expelled either voluntarily, or under duress and coercion. Thus the rat says he could not be sure that the food in the mouth really was his to boast about until it has entered the stomach.

The gist of the proverb is that it is futile to boast prematurely about ownership when claims have not been consolidated. Anything can always happen in the interim to dispossess a person. Hopes and expectations are not the same as a fait accompli.

94. Bɔna we o yaa maɲe o lage o tembaaro sɔŋɔ veiŋa mo vwio maa ke o nazaŋa

The mosquito says he was contemplating a visit to his in-laws and fortunately the wind blew him there

Commentary: The *tembaaro* or wife's father or wife-giver is like kin in many ways yet in many others he is not kin since relationship to affines is conditioned by the exigencies of the marriage.

A person is considered a good son-in-law if he visits the wife's parents often to be of assistance to them in whatever way possible. We find the same expectation among the Taita of Tanzania, (see Harris 1962). Nevertheless, such visits can be costly to the visitor given the expectation of gifts from the son-in-law on each visit. True, as the relationship develops with time a man begins to feel more relaxed in the presence of his wife's parents and the expectation of gifts from him on each visiting occasion diminishes. Sons-in-law visit when necessary.

The mosquito is a great nuisance among Kasena people who traditionally have dreaded it more for its painful bite rather than its disease vector potential. The insect abounds in at the height of the rainy season (August-September) and bites become unbearable especially on a still night with little breeze. The view that the mosquito has no power to resist the wind and is compelled to follow wind direction derives from experience and observation. The mosquito, feared as it is, has no power over the wind and in this respect is like the son-in-law who must respect and revere the Wife Giver who has power to dispossess the husband of his wife. This is not to imply that husbands' marital rights count for nothing. Though a wife-giver retains much influence over the married daughter and could recall her, wives themselves have been known to defy their parents where they have felt their own interests to be on the line. The occasion when a disgruntled wife-giver or parent can punish the wife-taker or husband is after a marital row precipitating the return of the daughter.

The proverb is about opportunism, a human characteristic. It teaches that a smart person, like the mosquito which does not resist the wind, yields to the pressure of powerful forces graciously. Rather than resist, where it is fruitless to do so, advantage might be taken of any beneficial turn out of events, even if they were not originally part of one's scheme.

The proverb seems to suggest that there could be silver linings in the dark clouds; these must not be left to go begging. It refers to opportunistic behaviour that does not have to be negative.

95. Pɛ we n sa ye n we n tankona ba sea ?

If the chief commands you to dance you cannot say you waist ache
Commentary: The Kasena *pɛ* or chief enjoys much respect among his people although he was not a ruler who wielded physical sanctions that could be deployed to coerce those who did not obey him. His authority flowed from religious sanctions as he was and still is perceived as a religious functionary and custodian of the *kwara* shrine. In the colonial era he enjoyed more authority backed by the colonial regime which required local agents capable of playing a role in its concept of indirect rule. The colonial regime empowered some chiefs like the Navro Pio to hold court, hear complaints and pronounce judgement on customary issues. There was in colonial times a special police force set up by the British to help the chief to enforce law and order. It came to be referred to jocularly by Kasena as "the chief's maidservants". The chief became more feared by his people as he wielded these new powers. As Kasena still say "you never know if tomorrow your case could go before the chief for adjudication". Signified in this statement is a fear of the chief based on his judicial role and the suspicion that he might be inclined to take reprisals against those who happened not to be in his good books when cases in which such people have an interest come to his attention.

The point of this proverb is that those in authority compel compliance and it is unwise to resist or rebel against that authority since it is backed up by punitive sanctions.

96. Nɔɔno ba zwɛ kasolo o de o men-dona ne
One does not drop sand in the grains of millet that one intends to eat in the raw state

Commentary: millet is an important staple crop among Kasena whose diet centers on millet and sorghum. It is used to make the thick stiff porridge called *gole* or TZ (acronym for the Hausa "tonzaafi" or 'hot *to*' in Hausa) by the educated. Millet also may be roasted while still fresh and eaten in that state or allowed to dry and then ground into flour to be mixed with pepper and butter and with water added to make a snack that will be eaten as an afternoon meal. Millet seeds were sometimes eaten in raw, while fresh and juicy or in the dry condition. When consumed in these states there is always the danger that small stones found in the grain could become a nuisance when chewed. Millet heads are dried on the gravel surfaced floor (*konkɔlɔ*) before being stored away. When grain is required for consumption, the heads of millet are pounded and winnowed and although this clears much of the husks and chaff it is inevitable that impurities including pebbles should remain.

   The proverb remarks that no sensible person would deliberately put stones or sand in millet grain, least of all in grain that is intended to be eaten in the unprocessed form by oneself. To do this would amount to self inflicted punishment or flagellation given the pain that a person feels when the teeth chew stone pebbles.

   The point is that everybody looks out for his or her self-interest and this is to be expected. Self interest is of course relative to others. It might include in the first degree one's immediate family, in the second degree parents and siblings and so on along lines of kinship segmentation.

   The proverb is cited in self defence by those against whom accusations have been leveled for wilful negligence of duty. In playing this proverb, a person seems to be arguing that his actions were for the best, since his or her interests were not different and it would therefore be preposterous for him to have acted against self interest.

97. Ba ba dɔne pɛɛre vɔrɔ
One does not sound a gift hoe to know its metal

Commentary: One does not look a gift horse in the mouth, the proverb seems to be saying. The *vɔrɔ* is the native hoe manufactured by Kasena blacksmiths. It was a very important tool in former times as agriculture depended on it. The blacksmith toot a fee or gifts from those who requested for a hoe to be made. So important an item is it, it continues to feature in many Kasena prestatory rites including marriage and affinal prestations and funerals. It may well have been a form of currency in the past.

These days it is possible to take the hoe for granted as cheap scraps of metal is smelted and used to make this farm implement. Hoes sold in the market place differ in quality and the buyer has to make sure that he does not buy inferior hoes which might not last as long as expected. Buyers check the quality of the metal used by sounding the hoe and they do so by tapping blade with a knuckle to see how the hoe blade sounds. The quality of the sound that emanates as the metal is sounded suggests to the expert ear the quality of the metal used in the manufacture and its durability. Some would lift the hoe blade to ascertain its weight The heavier it is the better the quality.

The proverb expresses the view that a gift item is not a commodity and there has to be a distinction between gift and commodity in the attitudes and behaviours exhibited in relation to them. If a gift hoe were sounded to establish its quality it would seem as though the recipient distrusted the giver or was at liberty to reject the gift if its quality did not measure up to expectation. A recipient does not have these rights. Gifts are symbols. A gift hoe blade regardless of its quality, would serve just as well, as a token of friendship and concern for the prosperity of the recipient. It is the sentiment that is important in the gesture and not necessarily its utility or quality. It is for these reasons that the proverb has literal application as well.

The proverb also appears to reflect on the ambivalence of feeling when a useless object is proffered as a gift. Even in that case it would be bad form not to show enough appreciation of the present or respect for the giver.

98. Chene na dɛ mɛ de zo to de ta wó da daane mo de nwoŋi

The way out for the nail (arrow) is the way in

Commentary: The proverb takes us back to the days when children played with bows and arrows and individuals and communities used them in hostile skirmishes. The arrow is often barbed to make its extraction difficult when it is lodged in its target. Yet unless it is extracted quickly its poisons enter the victim blood stream and eventually lead to death.

The proverb observes that the way to take out the arrow is through the hole that it has punctured in the body. The operation involves cutting the area where the arrow is lodged to enable the arrow to be extracted.

The point of the proverb is that the solution to a problem or difficulty lies in the problem itself. Until a problem has been studied squarely, solutions might be hard to come by.

99. Wɛ ba di jena mo se de ŋwe jena

God settles debts although He is not a debtor

Commentary: This is another of those statements of Kasena religious philosophy. God Almighty is a gracious and fair judge who does not fail to give man his deserts. He does not owe man since man himself is on this earth by the sanction of God who is the ultimate owner of the universe and all in it.

The point of this proverb is that those who wrong their neighbours in the knowledge that the aggrieved lacked redress err since God the final arbiter will some day settle scores.

100.   Tu-pwola ba lwoori nunugiri, ka lwoori ŋwea mo

The baby elephant does not pray for obesity it prays for life

Commentary: Obesity was something that traditional Kasena seemed to appreciate in a person as they saw it as a sign of well-being and prosperity. Even today, observers are worried when a person seems to lose weight. They suspect that he or she has fallen on hard times; that is to say food may nct have been available, he or she might have been worried or troubled or else the person has been ill or in poor health. Given the life style of the average Kasena person, obesity was uncommon, nevertheless some cases of obesity existed and it was believed some chiefs cultivated obesity as a status symbol, while for others it might be due to a hereditary trait. The elephant which is noted for its huge size is in a special position. Its young should not worry that it does not have the gigantic and portly appearance of its parents since this will happen as a matter of course.

The proverb's advice to the baby elephant and to mankind is that what a person is ordained by nature and heredity to be, will soon come to pass given time. Long life, *ŋwea* or *momɔ-dedɔrɔ* (a long nose) however is important and this is what people should pray for since not all people attain long life. All in its good time, and so long as there is life there is hope. The case of the meek baby elephant that cannot imagine that some day it too would develop like its adult parents is bears comparison with the calf that, in its arrogance, is scornful of the cow that has not been fortunate to develop horns.

101. Voro ná voge-m n vo n wone

The soothsayer may diagnose your problem but you must interpret his prognostication

Commentary: the Kasena soothsayer rarely tells his client the meaning of the augury. The soothsayer is an agent of his patron deity and his job is to conduct or facilitate a seance. As answer to a Kasena riddle would have it, the soothsayer divines and although he is supposed to help others find solutions to misfortune nevertheless he is incapable of preventing the death of his own son. A soothsayer may himself be unaware of the meaning of the prognostication. Thus, a consultation at the soothsayer's shrine is done by those who are adept at it. The seance involves the operation of symbols some of which have prescribed meanings. There are however other symbols ascribed individual or idiosyncratic meanings by the client himself who does not necessarily have to let the soothsayer in on the meanings ascribed to the symbols. Keeping the soothsayer ignorant of what special significations the client has attacked to the objects used as signs or symbols is considered necessary to ensure that the consultation is not biased. The procedure of soothsaying Kasena style involves posing a set of queries to the deity of the shrine. The questions must be those that have relevance to the peculiar circumstances of the client. The articulation and combination of chosen signs and symbols is the basis for interpretations of events and messages from the ancestral world.

The proverb advises that a client must relate the findings at the augury to his own circumstances. The general advisement here is that people must not take or follow the advice offered by others blindly. The recipient of advice must pause to ask himself or herself whether the advice offered makes sense in the light of personal and individual circumstances and experiences. This is further confirmed by the proverb that states that "It is the hunchback who knows best how to turn himself or herself" (*Choatu mo yei ka pipirim*). That is to say, it is the hunchback who knows how best to cope with and manage his or her handicap.

102. Ka duri ka to wɛ gare ka chore ka to wɛ
It is better to run till sun down than to boil till sunset
Commentary: The duiker is said to demonstrate by its behaviour that it is better to experience exhaustion as one runs till nightfall than to end up as game in the hunter's pot because one was too tired or too lazy to get away. This proverb again celebrates industry and a willingness to fight for life and its benefits all of which is better than to surrender to death or to an unpleasant fate without a fight.

103. Sɔŋɔ tu we o baa da bebala yenyɔna ŋwaane se o jwoni maŋe da
The head of compound says he cannot neglect his ritual duty to the ancestors on account of the sad countenance exhibited by the billy goat
Commentary: The head of compound is responsible for a minor or major lineage whose well-being depends on the rituals that he should perform to appease the divinities and the ancestors. These entail the sacrifice of a

fowl or goat from time to time, as required by the deities and the ancestors, and very occasionally a cow. Pain flour water may be used in some instances as libation to the ancestors, who also require a 'drink' from time to time like their living descendants.

The ancestral shrines, out of sympathy for the living, seem to prefer the use of the expendable billy goat to a she goat for sacrifices and other rituals. These rituals are considered very important as the prosperity of the individual and his family depended on maintaining harmonious relations with the ancestors and clan deities through prescribed sacrificial rites. Traditionally, and even today, it is unusual for a person to kill livestock for food, although important visitors are generously received and a fowl, or in some exceptional cases, a goat or sheep might be killed to prepare a fine meal for the visitors. Goats may be sold when there is need for cash in the family.

The destruction of an animal's life is unpleasant but necessary, this proverb says. People love to see their livestock increase and it is not without a sense of misgiving that they part with livestock. Livestock constituted in former times, a Kasena person's material wealth. However, goats, especially billy goats, must be disposed of when it becomes necessary. Concern for ritual and other benefits far outweigh the sympathy that the herdsman has for his stock.

The message of the proverb then is that in life prioritisation is a necessity. Some values take precedence over certain others.

104. Chega jei ye ŋɔne mo
Where truth is located is a sore spot
The truth is painful

Commentary: The Kasem word *chega* means truth or right. Its opposite is *vwa* or lies. A sore is painful and truth is like that; it can be painful to those it goes against and even those who have a duty to say the truth do not always find it an easy thing to do. This is because people are often unwilling to accept the painful truth. Thus those who are not influential may be denied a claim to right and truth. Some personal names such as the following draw attention to this: *Nabwombajegechega* (The poor have no claim to truth or right) and *Nabiinabachegatea* (People do not tell the truth).

The proverb tends to be quoted at those who react adversely when told the unpleasant true. Such attitudes, the proverb implies, do not show that people cannot perceive the truth, rather they are unable to bear the pain that stems from the unpleasant truth.

105. Dam ba di gaao

Power does not eat grass

Commentary: The concept of *gaao* is polysemous among Kasena. It can mean the grass we find in the unsettled areas and hence the bushlands or wilderness where people do not live. *Gaao* also refers to anywhere else other than hometown. Thus Kasena in diaspora or those living outside the Upper East Region have usually been described as living in *gaao*.

The literal meaning of the message of this proverb is thus ambivalent. It can mean that power cannot be exercised over foreigners or that it cannot be wielded in a vacuum or void where people are not found. Whichever interpretation is adopted the underlying meaning of the proverb remains the same: power is exercised over people.

It is people who make the exercise of power meaningful to power holders like chiefs. The proverb is therefore a warning to the powerful when they appear to exhibit traits of arrogance and dictatorship.

106. Sabu ná gɛa mini mo wó di
Where money has failed only fire will succeed

What money has failed to do only fire will prevail

Commentary: Money, as universal medium of exchange, has come to dissolve whatever spheres of exchange may have once existed in the indigenous economy; see Bohannan (1955) for a discussion of spheres of exchange. Kasena pretend to be surprised that the culture of money should pervade all spheres including even the domain of kinship.

In some sense, the proverb does not lend itself to an easy interpretation. It can be said to signify that where money does not prevail only fire will make inroads. Fire is here perceived as the all conquering element next to which is money which can destroy as well as make.

107. Ba ba le sɔŋɔ sugu yi ba ke ga-sugu yi ne
One does not rob the domestic guinea fowl of its eye to save the sight of the wild guinea fowl

Commentary: The domesticated guinea fowl is of the same species as the wild guinea fowl in the bushlands. Both are sources of meat for Kasena but they are not at par. The latter is nobody's property.

Sight is very important to Kasena who are used to noticing parents and kin lose their sight prematurely and become dependent on others. They say eyes cannot be purchased in the market. If it boiled down to a question of sight restoration for one at the other's expense it would make no sense to rub the domesticated fowl in order to benefit the wild fowl for which one does not have exclusive rights. Self interest compels that the domesticated guinea fowl be given preference above its wild cousin.

This proverb is used to emphasise kinship sentiment and the priority that should be accorded it in dealings with the world. Kin come first. Kasena live in societies where lineages play an important role; the local community is essentially lineage based. The concept of *sɔŋɔ* (compound homestead) symbolises the lineage, the residential group which comprises agnatic kin and their wives. From this is derived the *sa-yuu* (head house) which is the major lineage. Kin belonging in the same clan-settlement are *sam tiina* (lit. people of the houses).

The message of the proverb then is that the lineage and kin compel loyalty at the expense of everything else. All things been held equal, the kin have prior claims on loyalty.

108. N nu ná wó lua sɔŋɔ ne n ba-n ga kenkɛ n laŋe

If your mother happens to be at the funeral house you will surely taste bean cakes.

Commentary: As part of the final funeral rites it is customary for women from the clan-settlement as well as kin and affines to converge at the funeral house to help prepare various delicacies necessary for the deceased "to send" to the land of the ancestors. One of such delicacies are the bean cakes "kenka" fried in butter for the purpose. These are not ordinarily prepared for consumption in homes nor are they available in the market place, unlike "kwosa", the Hausa variety which is easily found in the market places today. The traditional variety is not salted, rather potash is added to it and it tastes different.

Women who assist in the preparation of the funeral meals are allowed to take some of the items cooked home to their families. Otherwise, the bulk of the food is shared out among the funeral functionaries and kin-groups involved in the celebrations after the deceased has 'received' his or her share. A child is thus certain that its mother will bring home funeral food and looks forward to the mother's return, especially at the time of food scarcity.

The message of this proverb then is that those in privileged positions do not fail to fend for their kith and kin. Thus nepotism is a natural expectation in people.

109. N nubu ná wó kekanɔ yuu ne n ba-n ga kekan-sene se-n laŋe

If your relative has climbed the diospiros mespilifornis tree for its fruits you will surely get ripe fruit to eat.

Commentary: The diospiros mespilifornis tree does not, like the shea tree, butyrospermum parkii, lose its fruits as they ripen, rather in the former case the fruits remain on the tree till they dry and then they may be dispersed by the birds and wind. Thus access to ripened fruits necessitates climbing the tree to retrieve them. Although many Kasena children learn to climb trees as a matter of course yet it is not all who can do so or are bold enough to climb on to the slim boughs that bear the ripened fruit.

The message of this proverb is thus the same as that for #107 i.e kinship implies reciprocity and a philosophy of being one's brother's keeper. In short, kin can depend on each other for support.

110. Choro ye ŋɔn-dale mo, de ba saara
Kinship is like the chronic sore its scar never disappears

Commentary: What Kasena regard as *ŋɔn-dale* is a chronic sore i.e. a sore that is very visible on the body and does not heal. Even when it appears to have healed it leaves behind a scar which some day will become sore again. Kinship is like that. It is, as Bloch(1973) would have it, a relationship of the long term. It can suffer temporary set backs but it does not disappear forever as it can withstand strains in the relationship.

111. Chero ba jege cher-balaŋa
Chero ba jege cher-bu
A witch is a witch irrespective of size

Commentary: Kasena dread witches for the harm that they are believed to cause to their own kin. The witch is perceived as the enemy within. Witches are believed by Kasena to have spiritual powers above the ordinary which accounts for their ability to cause psychic harm to those who do not have witchcraft powers; they are said to fly, to see things that remain invisible to others and feast on people's souls. It is believed that the older a witch is the more powerful he or she is likely to be. However, even the weakest of witches is believed to be capable of harming people. Thus one should not underestimate the potential of any witch to cause harm, certainly not on grounds of age, size or physical appearance.

The message of the proverb is that the harm that the wicked are capable of is not to be measured by their visible outward appearance.

112. Nabiinu naga dɔrema
Human kinship ties are widely ramificating

Commentary: Kasena social structure is premised on patriliny but they trace kinship ties bi-laterally as well and they may trace them back many generations. They appear to be discovering new kin all the time. The proverb therefore asserts an important characteristic of most kinship systems; viz that theoretically, there is no limit to the number of persons who may have kinship ties with one. Society sets limits, just as lack of genealogical evidence and personal interest may play a role in the mapping out of an individual's kinship universe.

The proverb is recalled when it is suddenly realised that persons who seem so far apart have a kinship connection.

113. **Nupuga bia nye daane mo se ba wone ba daane nye**
Full siblings may resemble each other closely but their hearts are not identical.
Commentary: *Nupuga bia* are issues from the same womb. They are therefore potentially full siblings. They certainly are thought to resemble one another as they share witchcraft traits. They also may resemble their parents and one another physically. The proverb remarks that these resemblances may not extend to their individual characters and temperaments. Two individuals who are siblings or close kin and might even resemble physically may yet exhibit remarkable differences in character and temperament. The message of the proverb is that appearance can be deceptive. One cannot therefore rely solely on one's acquaintance of a person's character to assess the personality of that individual's siblings and kin. What Radcliffe-Brown (1950) referred to as unity of the sibling group is not alien to Kasena. Siblings may be substitutable in certain ritual conditions such as leviratic marriages, ritual fosterage of children between some consecutive siblings (*boore*) etc but Kasena show by proverbs like this one that individuality is recognised.

114. **Ba ná jege n nubu kologo ba vei tega n ba ye gɛɛ mo**
When your kin's head is going down your neck bends side wards
When your kin is being put down you feel it
Commentary: The *nubu*, literally, mother's child, refers to kin and this can include agnatic kin as well as utrine relations.
  In Kasena wrestling, the winner is the person who is able to throw his opponent down. It is a definitive win when the opponent's occiput hits the ground. The proverb observes that when a kin is being thrown onto the ground other kin who are observing the match feel and act as if they too were about to lose the match. Although the contest or fight may not concern the kin, they are nevertheless inclined to feel their kin's loss is their own and to want to intervene on behalf of their losing kin.
  The point of the proverb is that kin cannot help but sympathise and empathise with one another in the face of external opposition.

115. **Kania ba to nɔn-doa sɔŋɔ ne**
Old women do die in one man's compound
Commentary: It is a truism that death beckons the aged and Kasena have a saying that "death is inevitable for those born of woman" (*Ba na loge nabiinu to ko laam daare toom no*). Death spares no lineage where there

are aged peoples. The point of the proverb is that death may seem to strike at certain lineages more often than others but this should not mean that those that experience death less frequently are spared.

Painful as the news of death is the death of an old person is often a moment of both sorrow and joy. People are sorry that death has taken away a loved one. Old people who are perceived as of the grand parental generation have an easy going relationship with younger folk, particularly, with their grandchildren or people of that generation and they are sorely missed when they die. At the same time an extremely old person who can no longer fend for himself or herself begins to be perceived as a nuisance, especially if he or she has been bedridden for a long time and no longer is able to control when and where to defecate.

In spite of the ambivalence that characterizes the passing away of the aged, death at a ripe old age is perceived as a victory of man over death and a dignified entry into the hereafter. Death on such occasions ushers in a period of celebration for the kin of the deceased, especially the deceased's grandchildren who use the occasion to exhibit themselves as the embodiment of the achievement of the deceased. Such deaths are also a time for friends and well-wishers to exhibit solidarity with the bereaved and this can take the form of invitations to homes for entertainment. Thus the occasion of death in this case becomes a special moment for members of the deceased person's joint family.

The message of the proverb is that misfortune and good fortune are not the monopoly of particular individuals, just as the death of an old lady is not exclusive to particular homes and families. Just as members of society must not remain aloof when an individual experiences personal hardships, the individual should not also personalise good or bad fortune.

116. Ko ywona mo tei fɔ-n-daŋe-da
Harmonious relations account for generosity
Commentary: The proverb, as a sentence, is ambivalent. It can mean that when food happens to be tasty people request for more of it. In the same vein when personal relations are good people are generous and considerate to one another. The point is that generosity can be explained and accounted for. It is premised on good relations rather than on compulsion. Therefore those who wish to benefit from the kindness of others must themselves exhibit kindness to their neighbours. One good turn deserves another. As another Kasena proverb reiterates, "those who are inclined to share what they have, share things with similar minded people", #155, *Adidaane de Adidaane mo di daane*. Generosity begets generosity.

117. Kukura ba done ka bu ka yi kua

A dog never inflicts bone-deep wounds on its young

Commentary: Mother dog may have reason to be angry with its puppy and to discipline it but never inflicts deep wounds on its young one such that harm could result.

The message of the proverb is that kin do fall out occasionally but even when they quarrel or fight there is the understanding that the conflict will not be allowed to get out of hand; it is circumscribed by norms and should never be allowed to lead to permanent and irreparable damage. This proverb is cited as advice to kin who fall out; it is directed particularly at those who wield power over others and can influence their prospects for the worse. Parents and those in *loco parentis* are an example. They are closer to the ancestors and they could use ritual power to destroy their dependent. They are expected to discipline their children and wards when they go wrong or show signs of disobedience but the penalty should be reasonable and not cause lasting damage.

118. To se n dwoŋi to mo kukura kwɛɛra

When dogs play they take turns to fall for each other

When dogs play they fall by turns

Commentary: Like dogs at play reciprocity is an essential ingredient to life. Life involves a certain give and take and people must do the same if they wish to live harmoniously with their neighbours and kin. In citing this proverb, Kasena remark that it is necessary for them to behave as though they did not know they were being taken advantage of by their kin or neighbours. They maintain that partners must take turns to play clever and foolish. If two people play aces at the same time the game loses its character.

119. Kara ba gwooni ka tu vɔrɔ

A farm does not scorn its owner's hoe

Commentary: The *kara* is the farm made some distance away from the homestead, unlike the *kaduga*. The latter is close by and it is the land that usually surrounds the compound that is cut into the pieces that are designated as *kaduga*. While the *kaduga* is likely to be small in size as generations of kin dwelling in the same compound have parcelled and re-parcelled plots into smaller shares so that as many compound members as possible can have access to the land for farming purposes, a *kara* can be as large as the owner wishes since there is less demand for bush farms. The size of the *kara* is often limited by the ability of the owner to cultivate the plot. A person who for a good reason lacks the means to cultivate his or her *kaduga* farms may invite friends, kin or affines (i.e. in-laws) to help out. Keeping the *kaduga* properly cultivated is almost a religious duty. However, the owner of the *kara* cannot expect to enjoy labour provided by kin or agnates, where that farm is concerned, except that he himself is a member of a group of peers who undertake to assist each other on reciprocal basis by helping out on members' farms.

The proverb remarks that even though the *kara* farm may be large the effort exerted in its cultivation by its owner toiling away on it single handedly makes an impact in the long run. No effort is ever so meagre it has no effect in the long run. Little drops make an ocean.

120. **Banpeno tu mo vare varem pa wea bera**
It is the patient man who hoes till noon

Commentary: *Varem*, the use of the hoe to clear away weeds and pile up earth around the crop, is an arduous task that consumes much energy, especially when the sun gets hot. As the farmer hoes up the grass he must also shake the earth lose so that the grassroots will be exposed and stand the chance of drying up so that the grass will die. The job involves bending for long stretches of time and farmers often complain of waist pains as a result. The Kasena practice quite often is to start the task of hoeing a plot as early in the day as possible, perhaps at about 6 a.m in the morning when it is yet cool. The work may be discontinued at about noon time when the weather is too hot to continue work and the workers are themselves too tired and require rest and a snack of millet flour. Work may be resumed in the late afternoon at about 3 p.m when the heat of the sun appears to have declined somewhat. The phrase *wea bera*, which occurs in the proverb, does not refer to a precisely defined time of day but can be taken in this context to mean the period just after noon when the sun is overhead.

The point of the proverb is that it takes endurance and a lot of patience for a person to work continuously hoeing the farm till it is noon. This is true not only for farm work but also for any task for which rewarding results are expected.

121. **Ba ba lɔre pabu dɛdɛ**
It is not every day that the prince stands out from the crowd

Commentary: A prince is considered more wealthy than the average Kasena person because his father the chief has amassed wealth. His behaviour and his manner of dressing make the prince to stand out among his peers. The proverb is of the view that although a prince usually stands out nevertheless there are occasions when he is just like other people in his dressing. Availability of clothing means that he is in a position to change his apparel more frequently than his peers and this might have the effect of sometimes making it difficult to recognise him.

When the proverb is generalised it can imply that the days are not equal and there are times when a person who is skilled or outstanding in a particular domain just cannot find the form.

122. Pabu ba lwoori zele

A prince does not beg others for clothing

Commentary: This proverb is similar to # 121 above, as it also refers to the superior wealth and privilege of the chief and his immediate family. Another version of the same proverb goes as follows: *Luga mo we pɛ bu ba lwoori zele* (The partridge says a prince does not borrow clothing).

The word *zele*, in Kasem is polysemous. In its primary sense, it denotes weight or anything that is considerably heavy. It shares the same root as the verb *zeŋe*, 'to carry a heavy object'. In this proverb, however, *zele* refers to heavy clothing or garments, such as the heavy smocks that traditionally were the prized clothing of chiefs and the wealthy. These garments are made from strips of cotton cloth. In the past a person had to exchange a herd or two to be able to buy a decent smock. As few could afford the really expensive items it is no wonder that they should be treated as heirlooms to be kept in the family and used when necessary by members attending important public events.

The idea of one person borrowing clothing from another to adorn himself for public exhibition is familiar to Kasena. Friends did so as well as kin. A wealthy father's clothes could be used by his sons whenever they went abroad. The only exception was the first born son who had to maintain a ritual avoidance of the person of his father and the personal items of property belonging to the father while he lived. In fact this prohibition continues to hold until the final funeral rites of the deceased father have been held. Even today, people still occasionally borrow clothing from their friends and neighbours.

The proverb makes the point that while ordinary people might resort to borrowing clothing items from others the wealthy person does not need to do this. In their collective representations, the chief is supposed to be richer than the average person by far. The reality may be different from this ideal which is often depicted in the Kasena folktales. There, the abundance of the chief's wealth is suggested by the estimation of his possessions in units of hundred and thousands. Certainly, reports on the wealth accumulated by Pɛ Kwara of Navrongo at the time of his death bears testimony to this out[12].

The prince is often represented as a person of means whose social stature reflects his father's wealth and opulence. This again is a myth which is not borne out by the reality. Chiefs in the past were of course arch-polygynists who could boast of numerous children, some of whom were by no means close to their father and thus distant from the chief's privilege and wealth. Nevertheless, the differences between the idealised image of chieftaincy and its reality should not negate the fact that the chief's favourite child, *pɛ bu-chochɔkko* (lit. the spoilt child) did share in the material privileges of chieftaincy that accrued to the chief. Such a child (usually a son) would be too wealthy a person to need to borrow clothing from non-royals to wear[13].

The message of the proverb is that one does not carry coal to Newcastle.

123. Pɛ ná zaŋe o dwoŋi mo wó leiri

When one chief falls another replaces him

Commentary: A chief takes the best place and the place of honour in a gathering of his subjects. This status of eminence is highly coveted in Kasena society, although the office is vested in a segment of the chiefly lineage. Given that chiefs are highly polygynous there is no shortage of candidates to replace a chief when he is no more. The phrase *pɛ zaŋe* refers to the death of the chief.

Kasena chiefship traditionally did not carry much coercive authority among the Kasena however it carried prestige and has always been sought after and keenly contested for by those who are eligible for the office. Kasena remarks suggest that it is a prince's duty to his fathers and to his descendants to enter the field of competitors whenever the office becomes vacant. By his participation he asserts his kinship with past chiefs while at the same time staking the right of his male offspring to enter the contest in future and be elected chiefs. Technically, it has been said, the failure to enter the contest for a vacant chiefship debars a prince's sons from contesting for it in future. For these reasons mothers have usually entered even their babies for the contest knowing fully well that such children did not stand a chance in the least.

The point of the proverb is that like chieftaincy so with all desirable offices and statuses: when there is a vacancy there will be no shortage of candidates and incumbents. An incumbent must therefore guard his or her office jealously against encroachment. He or she should behave in ways that show s appreciation and respect for the office. A similar proverb would be the saying that "If a dog declines a bone another dog will not fail to seize it" (*Kukura ná vae kua ka dwoŋ wó kwei mo*).

124. Diga ywei ná pere ba wó leiri ywei mo

If the main support pillar is broken it will have to be replaced

Commentary: The *ywei*, of which the Kasena riddle remarks, "oh my friend, Shortie, how strong you are!" is a stout wooden support that holds other cross beams in place before mud can be piled on to thatch the hut and build the platform characteristic of the typical Kasena hut. The *ywei* usually has a fork on which the cross beams rest. When one of the arms of the fork break the pillar no longer holds the beams securely. The entire superstructure then becomes insecure and risky necessitating its replace as the whole structure is in danger of collapsing.

The message of the proverb then is that when the bulwark becomes ineffective it must be replaced by another. Nobody is thus indispensable but when those occupying strategic positions become ineffectual or incapable of performing their duties they must be replaced to guarantee security.

125. Pɛ náʼ zo gaao o wóʼ dom kunnu mo

If a chief goes to the bush he will have to eat the seeds of the baobab
Commentary: A Kasena chief is relatively a wealthy person, at least in Kasena eyes. He benefits in many ways from the gifts that members of the community make to him in expectation of his support and for the ritual services that he performs for the well-being of the community. In former times, he exacted a kind of death duty from his wealthier subjects, the lineage heads. They in turn recouped their losses on the chief's death by not cooperating with the chief's family over the performance of some of the rites associated with his death, as entries in the White Fathers' diaries showed on the occasion of the death of chief Kwara in the second decade of the Twentieth Century. The chief's compound is easily the biggest in the community. His wives in the past were many and so were his children, all of which were signs of wealth as traditionally understood by Kasena and their neighbours.

Although ordinary people went from time to time into the bushlands for farming or some other related purpose, the chief rarely visited the wilderness except, perhaps to carry out some rite, as some of the fetish shrines are located in the bushlands. His office prevented a chief from engaging in active work. There is a belief that if the chief were to be allowed to do manual work the community would be afflicted with famine. People from the local communities therefore took turns to work on the chief's farms. This was not considered compulsory service; it was perceived in the context of reciprocities. It was not only the chief who benefitted in this way, clan-settlement heads, earthpriests and others in the community also benefitted from the labour provided by youth in their communities, although to a lesser extent. In return for the labour expended the workers were entertained to a feast.

Kunnu are the seeds of the fruit of the baobab tree, Adansonia Digitata. They were used as food only when there was severe famine and food shortage. The seeds are hard to crack and it required painstaking effort to process them into edible food; under normal circumstances nobody should be found eating *kunnu* which is perceived as inferior food. The association made between the bush and *kunnu* in this proverb suggests the hardships that people faced in the past when they went deep into the bush for hunting or for some other purpose. Except for the professional hunter, individuals rarely ventured deep into the wilderness. When hunting parties did so they took practical as well as ritual precautions. They would usually carry flour and a little water as the physical exertion of the long march made people to tire too soon and to get thirsty and hungry, as any (*pepara*) ritual hunt participant would affirm[15]. It is not unusual for people to lose their way temporarily and spend more time in the bush than had been planned. When food runs out in the bush people live off the land, eating whatever comes their way. This can include fruits and nuts that are in season. The proverb observes that although a chief is a special person if he should do what others do and visit the bush he would be subjected to the same hardships and would have to adopt the same coping strategies.

The point is that whatever the status of a person may be if he or she should find himself in changed circumstances he would have to suffer the same hardships like less privileged people and may have to adopt the same strategies for coping.

126. Pɛ liri kuru wo nabwonu kara ne mo
The roots that provide the chief's medicinal needs are located in the pauper's farm

Commentary: Kasena traditional medical resources were many and varied, including roots and herbs found in the settlement but more often in the surrounding bush lands where people have their farms. The chief is a powerful person who may sometimes feel that he does not need the pauper. However, he may just find that the roots of the specific plant he needs for the preparation of his medications are not on his own farms but in that of a nobody. He would then have to swallow his pride and seek permission from this nobody to be able to dig for the roots. The question is whether, as chief he could not have fetched the roots without permission. If the farm did not have crops growing on it the chief would need no permit to dig up the farm. Public opinion, however, would not have favoured a chief who destroyed another person's farm without his permission, especially if it were under cultivation.

The message of this proverb is that even the powerful need their less powerful neighbours. People should, regardless of their station in life, learn to respect their inferiors for there might come a day when the person we do not respect becomes the 'corner stone'. Kasena summarize these sentiments in the phrase "nobody knows tomorrow", (*nabiinu yeiri jwa*). A great man may fall while a nonentity might rise to become a key figure in society.

127. **Choa tu mo yei ka pipirim**
It is the hunch-back who knows how to manage his or her handicap
Commentary: The *choa* in Kasem is the part of the back close to the shoulders. The *choa tu* is a person who presents a hunch-back, an unusual deformation. Kasena theory about this physical deformity attributes most cases to the killing of a bush buck known as *pɔnɔ* in Kasem. A person's failure to receive a portion of the meat of this antelope, results, in Kasena belief, in the physical condition in question.

Hunters are expected to avoid the *pɔnɔ* as much as they can but occasionally someone kills it by mistake. In that case the meat of the antelope should be distributed to all kin of the killer. Those kin who fail, for whatever reason, to taste the meat develop a hump on the back side, according to the beliefs.

Observing the hunch-back it becomes clear that the individual would have problems managing the condition especially when in bed. It is hard for the non-affected to imagine how the affected person is able to cope practically with the handicap and to carry on with life like others. It might be wondered how such a person copes at bedtimes: does he lie on his face, on his back side, on his sides?. Most people lie either on their backside or on the left or right side, depending on which is convenient. These doubts notwithstanding, everybody knows that the hunch-back does cope with life.

The point of the proverb is that, as in the case of the hunch-back who has through experience learnt to cope with the handicap, so with every individual who has to live with special problems.

128. **Jeŋa ba jege ye ka vane ni**
The hand does not refuse the mouth
If the hand has food it will not refuse to supply the needy mouth
Commentary: The hand and the mouth, though different members of the body nevertheless collaborate and give mutual support to one another. The hand, if it has the means will not fail to provide for the mouth since its failure to give to the mouth results in starvation for the mouth, the hand and the rest of the body too.

Where people are associated intimately as in the case of close kin, mutual support is a guarantee. A parent will not refuse the needy child; if he fails to provide for the wants of the needy offspring, it may be that the means are lacking. It is for this reason that Kasena say, if your sibling is on the diospyros mespilifornis tree (*kekanɔ*) you will not fail to eat ripe fruits see proverb # 109 and if your mother is in the compound where the final funeral rites are been held you will not fail to eat bean cakes, see # 108. The reference here echoes what Durkheim (1947) has described as mechanical solidarity and the division of labour knitting together members of society.

129. Lulwei ŋɔne ná zuri o we de jei mo

When a blindman's sore no longer pains he says it has healed
Commentary: The proverb emphasises the importance of sight without which realistic diagnosis can be impeded. Not all sores give pain all the time and occasionally sores may give no pain at all yet the healing process has not come to completion. A visual inspection of the ulcer may be necessary to confirm that healing in this case has or has not taken place. The blind person may have a more developed tactile sense but this is not adequate in all cases as vision is sometimes necessary to complement feeling. Both scar and sore, as lesions have a physical manifestation and can be felt. However, they become indistinguishable in the absence of pain. What beats the blindman is his complacency facilitated by his loss of vision. Because he cannot see the lesion he is only to willing to conclude that absence of pain implies a cure.

The proverb makes the point that human beings tend to be shortsighted in their manner of dealing with their problems. They mistake a temporary respite for a permanent resolution of problems, perhaps because they are too optimistic or indolent and unready to face the truth or feel disinclined to the idea that they must galvanise extra resources needed in the search for a more permanent solution. In this respect they seem to behave like the blind.

The proverb is quoted at those who are shorted sight or naive enough to accept the status quo when worse could be in store. The ungrateful are also rebuked by quoting this proverb at them. They obtain assistance to the resolution of their problems and with the preliminary signs of relief they think they no longer require help and proceed to ignore their benefactors. In so doing they fail to realise that they might some day stand in need of help and might have to appeal to the benefactor they did not acknowledge.

130. Naao ná jaane n kwo n ná nɛ ko beinnu n duri mo

If a buffalo has gored your father to death you take to flight at the sight of its dung

Commentary: The word *naao* in this context is ambiguous. It usually means a cow. In some contexts the buffalo can also be referred to by the same term although it is more appropriate to call the latter *ga-naao* (bush cow). The buffalo which is considered a vicious and dangerous animal among Kasena has been known to gore people to death. We can therefore conclude that *naao* in this context refers more to the buffalo than to the domesticated cow.

The proverb remarks that when a person has been killed by a buffalo the victim's child develops an inordinate fear of this animal such that even the sight of the animal's excrement sends shivers down the spine of the deceased's child and compels him or her to take to flight. This author has not enough experience of wildlife to appreciate any difference between the excrements of the domestic cow and the wild buffalo but the point of the proverb could be that whatever the source of the suffering that has come a person's way even harmless and innocuous signs or reminders of the suffering generate fear and compel people to adopt avoidance behaviours.

It is believed that people take after their parents and that the father's destiny is bequeathed to the child. The proverb thus attempts to account for the irrational fears that people exhibit in the knowledge that a particular misfortune that once befell a parent or close kin might befall the child too. It is cited to justify the fear and the extra precaution that those who have been 'bitten once' take to prevent a repeat of the tragedy. In some respects this proverb recalls # 5 which remarks that "when the son of I-have-experienced-trouble takes his rests his weapons are on hand" (*Anɛcham bu sage de chwoŋa*).

131. Jazene sane jagwia ye jagwia sane jazene mo
The right washes the left and the left washes the right
The left-right symbolism that has been described by structural anthropologists like Needham (1967) and many others is applicable to Kasena representations. The right is the clean hand to be used in eating, giving and receiving and for performing various important social functions while the left is the "dirty" or unclean hand fit for ablutions and the handling and cleaning of human waste products and excretions. The right hand must be kept clean and should be washed before meals are taken. Nevertheless, in spite of the opposition between left and right, washing the right requires the involvement of the left. In the end, as the right is washed the left benefits vicariously.

The proverb remarks on the need for collaboration and mutual support even between individuals or among group members in spite their individual differences and capabilities.

132. **Bokɔ ná wo de sɔŋɔ o bu jwa wó de sɔŋɔ**

If the daughter does not destroy the family some day her child will do this

Commentary: The patrilinearity of Kasena society implies that daughters (*bokwa* or *kadikwa*) will marry out and go to live with their husbands in the latter's clan-settlements where their children will be born and grow up. A daughter and her children have literally no place in her father's clan-settlement. They are welcome to visit for a while and during the period of their stay, they are entitled to be treated as privileged persons accorded liberties not normally allowed agnates.

Among some of the privileges enjoyed by the clan daughter and her children are the following. They are not subject to attack by witchcraft emanating from the mother's kin; the visiting daughter is entitled to be addressed as "husband" by her brother's wives and "father" by her brother's children. She can in fact discipline her nieces and nephews more or less like their biological or sociological father. A measure of the clan daughter's power is her right to claim a niece as a maid servant and to marry her out to her own favourite, usually her husband's agnate. Her son, referred to as "our daughter's' child" (*bokɔ bu*), can take poultry belonging to the mother's agnates without permission. He or she has a right to claim a foreleg or wing when an animal has been killed in sacrificial offering. He or she can and is expected to mediate in quarrels and can, if need be, impose a settlement. A man is often called upon to act as marriage mediator (*yiɲinu*) in new marriages involving the mother's kin and his own patrilineal kin.

Some of these privileges, especially the license to seize poultry, are supportable where the daughter and her children are on short visits but when they become permanent fixtures they can become also a nuisance and a source of instability, especially as they are not subject to the normal sanctions that apply to agnates.

There are conditions under which a married daughter might return to her parents with her children. This can happen if her marriage is on the rocks or her husband has died and his agnates are not making life easy for her and her children. Her children could themselves decide that they would be better off living with their maternal kin and therefore decide to settle in their mother's clan-settlement when life with their own agnates becomes intolerable. It is when such permanent settlement takes place that Kasena begin to worry that all is not going to be well. The problem centers on the fact that the sister's child cannot be refused permission to stay yet the normal societal sanctions would not apply wholly to him. He can therefore become a disruptive force in the local community. Kasena believe in fact that the lineage ancestors themselves would be partial to the sister's child and would direct their benevolence (surely, a limited good) to such a person with the result that the good luck of the lineage is diverted from the rightful beneficiaries.

Kasena seek to protect themselves by adopting several measures in this case. Although the returned sister and her children cannot be refused accommodation they would be encouraged to set up their own homestead independently on land provided within the clan-settlement of the mother. This ensures that the sister and her children do not interfere unduly in the domestic affairs of her brothers. It also distances the sister's children from the lineage gods and ancestors who share their 'daughter's' maternal feelings and partiality to her children.

133. Ba ba mae gwia ba bere nabera sɔŋɔ
One does not point to the mother's home with the left hand
Commentary: The left is the inferior hand in the dual symbolic opposition between left and right, as we have pointed out above in # 129. This is the hand that is used to perform defecatory acts such as cleaning the anus or holding the penis to urinate. Things must not therefore be given or received with the left. Food cannot be eaten with the left; in fact it is a taboo to hold a calabash with the left while drinking from it[16]. It is considered a sign of disrespect, if not an outright insult, to use the left hand to point to a person or an object of some importance and in the case of the mother's clan-settlement it would constitute gross disrespect and ingratitude to use the left to point to it.

The mother's clan-settlement is equated with the mother herself to whom people in this culture feel they owe life. A person does not usually live in the mother's parents' village but in times of difficulties one is entitled to seek refuge there, as Okwonkwo did in Chinua Achebe's **Things Fall Apart**. The mother's natal family are usually more indulgent than one's agnates and are expected to come to a person's assistance in times of trouble. The first item of property that a person receives in life is from the mother's father or the mother's brothers. This is usually a chicken given with their blessings and the expectation that it would some day generate wealth and prosperity for the sister's child.

134. Chwoa yalei kɔe nakwe tampɔgɔ
Two thighs break the elder's bag
Commentary: A respectable man is expected to carry a bag in which he keeps his pipe and snuff and other tittle tattle. It is in this bag that he will carry gifts made to him on his rounds. It may be a leather bag or one made of string. In the division of the meat of an animal or a fowl slaughtered in sacrifice at a ritual, custom allocates a thigh to the most elderly person or

senior man of the lineage or segment of the lineage holding the sacrifice. If the victim is a fowl the meat is cooked on the spot and eaten but a slaughtered animal is cut up and a portion of the meat is cooked for the prestations to the ancestors and deities while the rest of the raw meat may be shared out to be taken home. Once home the elder is expected in turn to share out the meat among those under his immediate jurisdiction.

The proverb observes that only one thigh goes to the senior and no more. He cannot claim both thighs as the next most senior person is entitled to take the other thigh. It would be a dangerous example for an elder to set by claiming more than his share. The living may not immediately stop him from doing as he wishes but the ancestors who are the final arbiters would not fail to punish the greedy and inconsiderate elder. He could find that his "bag" has "burst".

The proverb is a warning to the powerful who are greedy and a reminder that they cannot abuse the privilege due to them on account of their seniority and the authority vested in them.

135. Zuŋa chwei gwori nakwe
The thigh of the puny bird embarrasses the elder

Commentary: Customarily, the elder's allotted share of a sacrificed fowl or animal is the thigh, as we have seen asserted in # 134. This is a good chunk of the carcass, especially where we are talking about a big animal like the cow. This proverb remarks that the rule is the rule. If a puny bird happens to have been used as sacrificial victim (this rarely happens in real life) then the elder should take his thigh as custom stipulates. An elder may feel then that the thigh in this case is too small to bother about. However, he must not refuse the share since it is a ritual injunction that stipulates what his share should be.

The recommendation here is that rules are rules, just as the law is the law: Just as a rule might favour a person in one set of circumstance, it might equally be unfavourable on another occasion. Opportunistic application of the norm or deviations therefrom are not to be encouraged. Accepting the rule only when it is in one's interest to do so or amending and bending the rule to favour oneself as circumstances change in reprehensible from the point of view of this proverb.

136. Nɔn-kwea ba sae sa-punnu wone
An elderly person does not dance in the blossoming bean crop

Commentary: The bean is a creeping plant that spreads out on the ground before it produces its flowers and later its seeds. Children may not appreciate that the flowers eventually produce the seeds and so can be forgiven for walking on the flowers. However, a mature person cannot be excused for doing the same thing since he is aware that he or she is destroying a valuable crop.

The point of the proverb is that culpability cannot be measured by the same yardstick since experiences, circumstances and motives may differ from case to case. Ignorance of the law may not be an excuse but fore knowledge and awareness aggravate the crime. Accidental breeches of the law are not as serious as willful and deliberate violations of the law.

137. N ná lage n fage kania, n wó fage ka de ka nagwɛ mo
If you are dressing up the old woman you do not leave out her feet

Commentary: The reference here is to the preparation of the old woman's corpse for burial. The preparation of the corpse must include her feet too since her body includes her feet. The message of this proverb is that consistency is a better policy; it is better to drink deep or taste not. If it is alright to perform a task then the job should be carried out as fully as possible. It can be said that the proverb reminds us of the saying that "a stone pebble mixed with beans gets to lick the butter" (kandwɛ dɛ swooni ŋwaane de laŋe nuga).

138. Wolon-nyeno ke o tete mo
The wicked person harms him-/herself
Commentary: The wolon-nyeno is a bad person. The expression means literally, one whose stomach is hot. The stomach in Kasena perceptions is the seat of the emotions. Having a "warm stomach" implies that one is unwilling to part with property or share with others what belongs to oneself. This springs from an evil disposition. Thus, such a person is not only stingy and selfish but also one who would not hesitate to harm others.

The point of the proverb is that the person with this sort of disposition is his own enemy for he harms himself in the long run. His malice can backfire on himself. Moreover, once it is known that a person has such a negative temperament and attitude others will not show kindness to him in his or her moment of need. After all, reciprocity is the rule of life. Nobody is an island.

139. Kalia ná gɛ mia ŋwa ka we mia nyɔna
When monkey cannot get the mia fruit it says the fruit is sour
Commentary: The monkey eats the mia fruit produced by Ximenia Americana which is known to be sour in taste. It is a fruit that human observers are not too sure why the monkey eats at all. Is it a question of a shortage of alternatives or one of genuine pleasure in eating this sour fruit? The proverb concludes that perhaps it is the former. The monkey

consoles itself with the observation that the *mia* fruit is sour when it is unavailable to the monkey. "Sour grapes!", as one might say in English.

The proverb is used as criticism for insincerity on the part of those who are only too ready to disparage those things that other people are able to have but which happen to be beyond the reach of the hypocrite.

140. Kukura ná vae kua kadwoŋi wó kwei mo

If one dog refuses a bone another will not hesitate to take it

Commentary: Kasena believe that their dogs relish bones. In any case, the bone that the master cannot chew becomes the dogs' fare. Meat has never at anytime been so plentiful as to make it possible for a master to feed meat to a dog. As dogs are accustomed to and love bones it is unlikely that a dog would see a bone and refuse to take it. Dogs are expected to compete viciously for bones left for them. Thus, should one dog refuse or reject a bone, other dogs that happen to be around would only be thankful for having been spared the need to fight.

The proverb seems to say that resources that are in limited supply engender competition among needy people and that in this context it is unwise to try to be finicky or choosy or to hesitate to take advantage of an opportunity, perhaps out of pride. A limited good will not remain available for long so that an individual can coming back for it in his or her own time. It would be a mistake to hesitate in such a circumstance. Any delay in taking advantage of a bonanza may translate into a wastage of an opportunity. This is perhaps an antithesis of the saying that another good fish will still issue forth from the ocean bed.

141. Ba ba gaale ni ba pae dedwoŋi

One does not pass a mouth to give to another mouth

Commentary: Where there are several expectant mouths one should not bypass any mouth to give a drink to another. Water is customarily served in one large calabash for a small group of visitors rather then in several calabashes. It is the rule among Kasena that when water is served in this manner to a group the person nearest the server drinks first before passing the calabash to the next person. Seniority does not necessarily count in this case.

The point of this proverb is that where several persons are longing for something that they are all equally entitled to have, one must not play favourites without good cause. Depending on the situation, the nearest should have priority. The nearest is thus the dearest, as it is said in English.

142.   Yi ba jege bwoŋa

The eye does not commit adultery

Commentary: *Bwoɲa* is the ritual impurity that is committed when a person engages in illicit sexual intercourse. Thus *bwoɲa* may be compared to adultery and although it may be translated as such in English, *bwoɲa* is not adultery pure and simple. It is in some sense a violation of the sexual rights of others, especially the sexual rights of relatives. A wife endangers the health and well-being of her husband when she engages in sex with another, especially relatives of the husband. Unmarried women do not however commit *bwoɲa*, although unmarried men do so when they take a woman who continues to be married to another to bed. For Kasena, *bwoɲa* is not committed in any other way except through physical intercourse. It cannot be committed through thought, desire and merely lusting after a person of the opposite sex; so long as the couple have not engaged in a physical sexual relationship no *bwoɲa* has been committed. Members of the opposite sex may exchange sexual jokes and innuendo and even touch or wrestle without this being seen as anything sexual. Thus, it is a Kasena truism that the eye cannot commit *bwoɲa*.

This proverb seems to be asserting a criterion for culpability which perhaps is different from what Judeo-Christian theology teaches. For Kasena, lust does not amount to criminal act. Perhaps, this is due to the fact the lust does not amount to a usurpation of anybody's sexual right or any other rights. However, we must juxtapose this interpretation with the general view that to harbour ill-will or bad thoughts (*boboŋ-lɔŋɔ*)is as dangerous as the perpetration of the evil deed or the offence itself.

143. Veiru yia ye wulaa mo se ya ba nae

A stranger stares but s/he does not see much

Commentary: It is considered an insult to describe a person's eyes by ideophone *wulaa* or by adjectives such as *wula, wala*. In either case reference is being made to the appearance of the eyes, which in this case seem to pop out. The *veiru* is a stranger from another area or village. The reference here is to the new comer who is confronted with novelty and finds it hard to conceal his or her curiosity about events, things or people and their relationships.

The proverb remarks that a stranger may appear to observe or show interest in everything that goes on in the host community however he or she may not always comprehend the significance and meaning of the events that transpire. It is only through a prolonged residence in a new community and education about that community, its norms, its past history etc that a new comer eventually gets an insight into another culture. A stranger may therefore be forgiven for not showing adequate appreciation of the host culture.

This proverb is often cited as an excuse for a stranger's lapses and failure to observe certain events, protocol and behaviours considered as appropriate. It amounts to a statement about the modes by which culture is transmitted through the processes of acculturation and enculturation both of which take time to achieve their effect.

144. Nabwona balei nu swogo ba maɲe diga ne

Two paupers will not fail to get out the ritual pots of their deceased mother

Commentary: The *swogo* is basically a private pot maintained by a Kasena woman. In it she would store things that she considers important to her being as a woman. She might keep pieces of meat there against a rainy day when visitors might descend upon the family and she might then be expected to defend her reputation as a woman by providing a good meal to them. In this respect, the *swogo* compares with the bow and arrows of a man. They each symbolise a person and his or her gender. Appropriately, the first born child of the parent's sex must never look into these private objects while the parent lives. Fittingly they are destroyed at the climax of a person's final funeral celebration. This destruction is the mode by which these important markers of personhood are conveyed to the deceased who requires them in the hereafter.

The symbolic significance of the *swogo* is emphasised at a woman final funeral rite when it must be symbolically destroyed after it has been brought out and taken to the cross roads leading to her natal clan-settlement. This requires a show of solidarity by the women folk of the lineage who may take contributions of condiments and soup ingredients to enhance the appearance of the *swogo*. At a stage the *swogo* is taken to the compound of the person who acted as mediator in the making of her marriage and then is returned as the funeral celebration nears its climax. It is met by women bearing funeral foods and a performance is staged at the meeting point. It is almost as though the deceased woman were being brought home again as a young bride. Some time later the contents of the *swogo* will be enumerated. Thereafter the womenfolk collectively convey the *swogo* to its place of destruction. There, it is broken into pieces after they have performed the necessary rituals. All this goes to show the importance of the *swogo* to Kasena which in some respects embodies the person.

The point of the proverb is that if a pauper is determined to celebrate her mother's final funeral rites there is nothing to prevent him or her from accomplishing it. What may be lacking is the prestige that the participation of a large group provides, as would most certainly be the case where the children of the deceased woman were wealthy and influential.

The proverb expresses the view that poverty and indigence are not obstacles to the realisation of ambitions. Also in ritual situations, it is the symbolism of the act that counts rather than physical quantities and frills.

145. Nabwonu nu ba jege birakɔga

The ineffectual person's mother does not have a backyard for a garden

Commentary: The mother's rights are often championed by her children, particularly her sons, where the father happens not to be alive. As agnates, sons can defend their mother's rights and her claims to lineage resources. In a society like that of the Kasena which is patrilineal and virilocal, a woman who joins the lineage of her husband at marriage remains a de facto outsider. It is for this reason that the lot of the childless woman was not one to be envied.

As a rule it is the right of every woman to claim the space just behind her rooms for her private use. There she might grow minor crops such as vegetables for domestic use. Her husband can defend her right to this space should others encroach on it. In the absence of a husband, her children should defend that right.

The point of the proverb is that a person who lacks substance and respect within the lineage may not be able to assert his rights against greedy agnates. As power derives from seniority within the lineage the pauper in this case is the female child or a son who is yet a minor. Competition within the lineage is a fact of life.

The proverb is drawing attention to the plight of the poor and the disempowered in society; they are sometimes denied their basic rights by more powerful neighbours.

146. Boboŋa keim ba nyɔne yera

The flesh does not say no to the desires of the heart

Where there is a will there is a way

Commentary: What the heart is set on there is always a way. The body will respond to the desires of the heart without considerations of fatigue. The proverb serves as a comment or a cynical observation on human behaviour. Individuals have a tendency to show reluctance when it comes to exerting themselves over things that are perceived to be of lesser personal importance to them or of insufficient perceived benefit. The contrary might be the case where the individual has personal interest at stake or perceives a personal gain. In this case, a person is willing to exert himself or herself and might go the extra mile in order to accomplish the beneficial task.

147. **Kabaa ná sε ŋwana ka wó sε veiŋa mo**
Once the slave consents to having a rope round his neck he must also agree to march
Commentary: A slave did not enjoy the rights that were due to citizens. Although it would have been prohibited to put a rope round a free person's neck and drag that person like livestock even for a joke, a slave could be so treated if it was felt that this was necessary to ensure that the slave did not bolt. The proverb remarks that a slave is entitled to put up a resistance, especially when being removed by a new master to another country but he must look for the right opportunity to make his escape. Once a slave has allowed a rope to be tied round his neck he must also realise the futility of physical resistance. The slave master holding the rope can always squeeze it tight as a means of coercing the recalcitrant slave.

The point of the proverb is that it does not make sense to cede power to one's enemy or adversary and then turn round to resist without the benefit of a weapon. Submission may be the best option for those who find that circumstances leave them no other option.

148. **Serekwε gwε ye kalwoŋo ni mo**
The hedgehog walks majestically while the eagle watches
Commentary: The hedgehog does not run away from danger posed by predators; it trusts its spikes to keep the enemy at bay. This works against the hawk which can only watch as the hedgehog, potential meat though it be, moves away majestically.

The proverb captures the scenario in which paradoxically what is longed for is so near yet so far beyond reach. This proverb makes an interesting contrast with the Kasena saying that "the sighting of the tortoise is as good as its capture", see proverb # 6, *Kanyambwoga nam mo ka kweeim.* Both hedgehog and tortoise have protection against certain predators: the former depends on its spikes and the latter recoils into its hard shell, which is perceived to be so hard that in folktales where animals are tricked into piling on each other to get to the sky, it is on the tortoise that all else pile. However, none has protection against man.

This proverb is often used as comment on events. It remarks on the paradoxical situation in which opportunities seem to be within grasp and yet unattainable.

149. **Fenfee gare kanweim**
To have a little is better than not to have anything at all
Commentary: Another version of the proverb reads as follows: **Taalem gare kateiga**. (A little broth is better than none). In Kasena culinary

tradition, *gole*, the thick stiff porridge that is their staple food, is usually accompanied by *dwoa*, broth made from a mixture of vegetables, spices, salt, groundnut powder or ground millet etc. Without broth, this thick porridge is almost tasteless to the Kasena palate. *Taalem* refers to having to eat stiff porridge with just a little broth but *kateiga* means stiff porridge served without the accompanying broth.

The proverb is clear as it stands. A little portion is better than nothing. "Half a loaf is better than nothing" is a common saying in English that has its analogues in many other African languages.

150. **Ba zeŋe gweeru ba vei pesɔŋɔ ye pesɔŋɔ bia daa bwea ?**
When the leopard is being carried to the chief's compound the chief's children do not ask what it is

Commentary: The leopard is a dangerous and an uncommon animal which many would hear about, especially in folktales and hunters' yarns, but would never see. It rarely visits villages and can only be sighted in the bushlands far from the settlements. The mystique surrounding the leopard has not failed to spawn yarns. One peculiar characteristic of the animal, as presented in folktales, is its tendency to lick its claws as though sharpening them prior to making an attack on its prey. It is believed also to feed on ants and to be most dangerous when found doing this because it is said to that the leopard reasons that a dandy should not be caught eating insects.

Kasena remarks suggest that the leopard was not easy to kill nor is it considered ritually safe to kill it, as sometimes deities masquerade as leopards. Thus, it is just the sort of thing the spoilt and inquisitive children of the chief's palace would ask about if it were being taken dead to the chief's palace. Ethnographic accounts show that in some traditional African communities the leopard was identified with royalty and hunters were either forbidden to kill it or if they did so had to send the slaughtered leopard or its skin to the chief's palace where its skin would serve as one of the emblems of high office. See for example Vansina (1962:327) on allegiance tribute and the surrender of the parts of certain animals and Bradbury's (1957) account of Benin and Edo perceptions of the leopard. Kasena hunters did not seem to have been bound by any such requirement. However, those who kill such game (including the big animals like lions, elephants, bush cows) have to be ritually cleansed to protect them from the spirit of the slain beast. These rites were performed by ritual specialists and not necessarily by the chief. However, traditionally hunters might, as a sign of courtesy, send a thigh of big game to the head chief in whose area of jurisdiction the animal was slaughtered.

The proverb is a rhetorical question which makes the point that children need not be overly impatient since their curiosity would be requited as soon as the beast arrives at its destination. The proverb is used as a mild rebuke to those who have not the least patience and tend to jump the gun. It is almost as if to say that adults who cannot control their curiosity are like children; they ought to know better. An analogue of this proverb is # 263 which remarks that the sound *korekore* does not remain in the hole (*Korekore ba maɲe bɔɔne ne*).

151 **Ba ba mae kasogo ba maŋe de ye de tiga**

One does not use the millet stalk to measure the python when the python is before one.

Commentary: The millet stalk served as a measuring rod for Kasena in traditional times. Unlike a stick it was easy to carry and to manipulate for measurement.

The python is considered to be an extremely long reptile; from the descriptions of the reptile one might suppose that it was really several times as long as the living creature really is. Unlike other snakes it is the subject of myth and it features prominently in the rituals of some clans that regard it as totemic. It is said to visit homes to welcome new members of the lineage when births occur or members of the lineage take wives. In that case it poses no danger to people. It would on such occasions, it is said, enter the innermost chambers where it remains for the duration of the visit. For the duration of the visit light must not be taken inside the chamber in which the totemic python makes its temporary abode in the compound. On its departure food is got ready for a send-off that is not too dissimilar to the send-off given to a married daughter who is returning to her husband after a visit.

However, the python is not a taboo or totemic animal for all Kasena clans and some clans hunt it for food. Accounts suggest that it is a difficult reptile to kill, as it can kill a man by twisting itself around the careless hunter and squeeze the life out of him. The strategy used by those who are adept at hunting the python lies in searching for its head and hitting it. In the wild, when the reptile is at rest, it is said to coil itself into several piles in the grass and it becomes difficult to locate the coil in which the head is hidden.

The proverb seems to imply the folly of trying to stretch out a python in order to ascertain its length. No body in his right mind would attempt to measure a snake by this means. However, in the folktale in which Nase, the trickster, trapped the cobra successfully, the feat was made possible by deluding cobra into thinking that there had been an argument about its true length with the trickster arguing that cobra was not as long as people had imagined. To prove to Nase that cobra was really as long as people imagined, cobra agreed to lining itself against a millet stalk and to be tied to the stalk to facilitate measurement. The folktale shows the folly of allowing itself to be trapped by being measured in this way. Measurement was unnecessary given that the cobra was already stretched out in its full length.

The proverb remarks that once we have the object it is pointless to subject it to measurement, since no new knowledge is thereby gained. For this proverb then, seeing is believing and what you see is what you get. Exactitude is not always called for so long as the physical evidence is available. In societies like the Kasena qualitative evidence seemed as satisfactory as quantitative data.

152. Tontoŋa zuri naga mo se ka ba zuri bochɔŋɔ

Delegation does not afford absolute satisfaction, it only saves the master the physical exertion of personally executing the job

Commentary: The Kasena word, *tontoŋa* is to be distinguished from *totoŋa* "work". It derives from the verb *toŋe* "to send" or "to work" and means a task which another has been delegated to go and perform. Literally, the proverb translates as "delegation of tasks cools the legs but does not cool the heart". When a heart is cool, a person is at peace with himself and the world. He enjoys satisfaction that can be compared to the draft of cold water offered to a person who has been walking in the hot sun.

The proverb deplores the manner in which agents carry out their assignments and observes that those who delegate to others can never receive total satisfaction for the performance of the task entrusted to the agent. It notes that delegation of tasks is nevertheless a necessity. It frees the sender from the physical toil of carrying out the task personally. Those who must delegate tasks to others must not however be surprised when there are lapses in the performance of the tasks so assigned. It is better to carry out the task personal rather than entrust its execution to others. The sender need not, for that reason be too critical of the subordinate when he or she fails to live up to full expectation. This proverbs recalls # 146 above which suggests that where there is personal interest work becomes a pleasant experience. For the agent the degree of commitment may be low which accounts for the failure on the part of the agent to exert himself or herself fully. After all, the agent's interest in the job assigned to him or her is perceived to be secondary. Parents often quote this proverb at their children when they go on an errand which they do not carry out to the complete satisfaction of their parents.

153. Ba ba toŋe bu bile

One does not send a child twice

Commentary: This proverb is more like a comment than a proverb since its application is more or less literal and its projection range is not as wide as to allow for its application to numerous other situations and circumstances, as would be expected of most Kasena proverbs.

It means that children do not have the discretionary approach that is expected of an adult. Children tend to interpret instructions rather literally with the result that they often exceed the requirements. Whereas an adult employing his or her discretion might not carry out the instructions fully thus making the sender feel, as in # 152 above, less satisfied, in the case of the child the expectations of the sender are likely to be exceeded, which may not be fully satisfying. It becomes then a problem that is not one of too little being done by the messenger or agent but too much having been executed.

The proverb therefore offers the suggestion that when a child or a minor is being entrusted with the execution of an errand care should be taken to make the instructions as explicit as possible.

153. N ná jege wiiru bukɔ n daa ba kua kua?

It does not imply that if you are married to hyena's daughter you are thereby barred from tasting a bone

Commentary: The hyena in Kasena perceptions is a despicable animal. It is cowardly and has despicable habits such as visiting homes and catching smaller livestock and occasionally humans. It is believed to eat carrion and to have an insatiable appetite for meat. Its greed is remarkable in its encounter with other animals in folktales.

A wife's father is entitled to make demands of the daughter's husband. These include bridewealth demands usually settled in livestock and other goods. The wife's father might also request that his daughter's husband spend a couple of days hoeing on his compound farms. In the past this was not a request that the son-in-law was in a position to refuse as persistent refusal of such requests could lead to eventual withdrawal of the married daughter. Traditionally the wife's parent could make or break a marriage. The wife's father is entitled to withdraw his daughter if the son-in-law fails to satisfy the wife's father's sundry demands. Though even difficult fathers-in law cannot nullify a fully constituted marriage they can recall and detain the married daughter under the slightest pretext thus bringing about temporary conjugal separation. This power of the wife's parent is alluded to in this proverb.

The proverb is a rhetorical question which states that being married to a hyena's daughter should not imply that the son-in-law should pass over all bones to the father-in-law, if he is to be allowed to keep his wife. The point of the proverb is that being indebted to another does not mean you lose your liberty or freedom of action, especially in those domains where there is potential conflict of interest.

154. Kapwogo diga toe tipwoŋa ne mo
It is in the dry season that the hut of the dirty woman falls
Commentary: Traditionally people used mud to build their compounds and many still do. These structures did not withstand persistent rainfall lasting several days, as is typical of August weather in Kasena land. The dry season however is rain free and this is the time when people repaired their houses or built new ones. In Kasena thought, the *kapwogo* is that woman who does not keep herself or her surroundings neat. Her opposite is the *kayoro*. A *kapwogo* not only is unkempt but also a poor cook. She is not much respected by other women. The proverb points out that the rooms of the *kapwogo* are not only in danger of collapsing during the wet months but also her carelessness would be enough to destroy them even in the dry season.

The point of the proverb is that carelessness engenders gratuitous accidents and calamities which are otherwise easily avoidable.

155. Adidaane de Adidaane mo di daane
Mr. I-eat-with-others and Mr. I-eat-with-others eat together
Those who are predisposed to share associate fruitfully
Commentary: As pointed out in the previous chapter this proverb is ambiguous. It can refer to marriage relations or to the sharing of meals. The verb *di* in the Kasem language refers primarily to eating and the consumption of food. It has also the extended meaning of marriage and witchcraft behaviour among its other connotations. The ambiguity is further exacerbated by the fact that it is possible to have a collocation of three different values of *di* or any combination or permutation of them such as ABC AAA, BBB, CCC, ABB, ACC, BCC etc where A is consumption of food, B is wife-taking, and C is consumption of another human being's soul. The act of a man taking a wife is described as *ka-diri* (lit. Eating a wife) while *ban-zore* (lit. Entering a man) describes the act of a woman taking a husband. This suggests the view that between the couple marriage is not a reciprocal relationship to Kasena. However where two groups that are not forbidden by the rule of exogamy from intermarrying are concerned, it is possible to describe their relationship in terms of the phrase *di daane*. Thus the phrase *Adidaane de Adidaane mo di daane* can mean 'those who intermarry do intermarry or do share food and consumables'. In other words, the knowledge that intermarriage is possible encourages marriage.

Those who eat together or have their meals in common will enjoy sharing meals together. In Kasena homes it is customary to share meals. Meals can either be exchanged between the various eating units or else women and children pool their meals and eat from common plates and bowls. This in itself is an indication of intimate relationship. Solidarity or kinship distance may account for the amount of sharing that is in evidence. Reciprocity and the willingness to reciprocate nurtures the culture of sharing. Between co-wives there is no obligation to share meals and a pair who have decided to share meals may at some point discontinue when it is suspected that fairness is not maintained. For example, one wife may cook food in limited quantity which is eaten in secret without sharing it with the other. The discovery of this may incline the other partner to retaliate and eventually cumulative retaliations leads to a discontinuation of the sharing relationship. Thus openness is a necessary requirement for sharing.

The point of the proverb is that it takes two willing parties to share. It takes two to tango, as the English saying goes.

156. Kafoo lunluŋu mo jiri jiru
It is the shadow of the coward that becomes the monster
A coward fears his own shadow
Commentary: The *jiru* among Kasena is a creature with the appearance of a black cat that can cause harm to people at night. It is believed to be some witch who has transformed into this 'were-cat', so to speak. The fear of *jiru* is enormous among Kasena and sometimes deters people from leaving home at night. In any Kasena community, reported encounters with the *jiru* at night can be expected. While not denying the existence of were-cats the proverb expresses the belief that certain reports of were-animals are attributable to the figment of the imagination. For a coward every black thing, including the coward's own shadow, is a monster because the mind is predisposed to seeing dangers everywhere including where none exist.
Diffidence breeds non-existent problems for people.

157. Kanvwogili mo lore tuu
It is the puny frog that begets the elephant
Commentary: The *kanvwogili* is a puny frog which contrasts with the great size of the elephant. Kasena generally believe that like begets like, hence the saying that "The baby elephant does not worry about become obese, what is of concern is time and long ife", see proverb # 100 above. It would therefore be a miracle for the tiny frog to beget the elephant, nor do Kasena really believe that this is physically possible. Nevertheless

miracles do happen. The point being articulated by this proverb is that the laws of nature are inscrutable. Paradox is part of experience and the unexpected can sometimes happen. In the case of human reproductivity, children are not always expected to resemble their parents, particularly the father, since paternity is sometimes ascribed to the mother's legal husband and not necessarily to the man who is biologically responsible for the birth of the child.

Great things have small beginnings. A puny parent may have children who are much bigger physically, just as the poor apparently inconsequential parent may beget children who achieve great things in this traditionally egalitarian society.

158. Nabiina nia goe chana

The words that issue from the human mouth can kill the moon

Commentary: Fortes' (1987: 172) remarks show that Tallensi have a concept of the evil mouth rather than the evil eye. Among Kasena it is certainly possible not only to talk of the evil eye but also the evil mouth. Excessive talk or comment about a person or an event is believed by the Kasena to be dangerous and harmful. Words are known to have a power of their own such that curses and certain incantations can cause harm or changes in the immediate environment. The remark that the human mouth can "kill" the moon or cause it to disappear from the night sky is an exaggeration meant to create an effect. Among Kasena there are 'masters of the rain' who are believed to control it; but the moon affects people's lives and livelihoods less and so for that reason there has not been an evolution of moon specialists. However, the point of this proverb is that the words that issue forth from the human mouth can be so powerful as to affect even the moon, if they were directed at it. How much easier then the fortunes of man!. Thus, the proverb on the one hand warns people against talking excessively about others and on the other, it admonishes the individual against giving cause to the public to comment negatively about one or one's affairs.

159. Nabiinu faro mo o dono

A man's friends ones are also his worst enemies

Commentary: The *faro* is the person who supports you and is eager to do you good, that is to say, your well wisher. A person's *dono* is his or her enemy who wishes him or her nothing but harm. Here then we have a paradox similar to proverb #157 above. The words *faro* and *dono* are antonyms; one denies the other.

The proverb is open to several interpretations. It could mean that friendship and enmity are two sides of the same coin which explains the ease with which a person can mistake his enemies for friends and his friends for enemies since the human being is such an inscrutable complexity. Clever enemies might just as well pass themselves off as friends. A friend tells the truth which may be unpleasant and it may thus convey the impression of ill-will; by contrast, enemies speak ill of a person but praise him to his face, thus appearing to be well wishers.

The warning here then would be to beware the Greeks and their gifts. Alternatively, the proverb observes that one cannot protect oneself against one's friends who would know one's secrets. They can exploit that knowledge to one's disadvantage when they decide to betray one's trust. Friends today, enemies tomorrow. These are motifs that are explored in Kasena folktales. In one such tale, the hunter who killed a buffalo leaving its baby was nearly destroyed by that creature when it transformed itself into a beauty and married the best marksman in the village. The hunter, the best marksman in the village, was tricked into disclosing his stock of magical tricks and he was just about to tell the last one when his mother stopped him. At the right moment the beautiful and trusted 'wife' assumed its true colours and would have killed the hunter but for the fact that he was able to change himself into an object he had not disclosed to his beloved 'wife'. Kasena conclude this tale by saying that it illustrates the wisdom of not disclosing all secrets to a wife.

160. Zaane mo jiri lorem
It is well-intentioned acts that become evil acts

Commentary: A well-intentioned act can be misinterpreted by others as an evil act. Similarly, kindness can have the opposite effect: it might as well be repaid by an evil deed. One good deed does not always deserve another nor is it always reciprocated. The point is that our acts and actions are open to a variety of interpretations. Related to this is the saying that "If you use a razor to shave a person's hair he might some day use broken potsherd to shave yours. (N ná mɛ fanchoa n fane nɔɔno yuu o jwa ma kanchua o fane n yuu). This saying refers to human ingratitude its shallowness and the unwillingness to reciprocate good gestures.

161. Sara ye voro
The mat is the best soothsayer

Commentary: The voro is an important ritual figure in the religious life of the Kasena people who traditionally have depended so much on their ancestors for their survival. The voro provides the means for communication between the living and their gods and ancestors. He is a ritual functionary and mediator between his divinity and the society. More appropriately, he is an instrument. By the manipulation of ritual objects the divinity discloses the otherwise unknown to a client thus enabling the performance of those rites that would restore harmony with the spirit forces. In this respect, the Kasena concept of soothsayer is comparable to that of their neighbours the Sisala. Mendonsa (1978:35) describes the Sisala diviner as having a passive function; in Mendonsa's words, "His role is somewhat mechanical and he is not expected to be a seer or a psychologist".

The Kasena *voro* is not endowed with special powers of prognosis, although there is no shortage of individuals these days claiming to be able to see into the future. The latter are the *vor-sampwori*, people who combine prophetic vision with the application of routine soothsaying procedures. A true *sampwora* (prophet) does not have to be a *voro* or soothsayer, he has prophetic talents which enable him to foresee and foretell the future and to advise his clients and society as a whole on actions to be taken to avert disasters. In the case of soothsaying, the seance involves the manipulation of objects and icons which serve as signs. The client may assign his own meanings to the individual icons in the soothsayer's bag. Thus a certain constellation of signs may communicate a message which the client understands but the *voro* might not know. It is therefore up to the individual to make meaning of the patterns manifest at the consultation taking into account pertinent private experiences. This calls for a certain pragmatism on the part of the client as well as the exercise of common sense. In a sense, it boils down to the client advising himself. As we have seen in a previous proverb, after a soothsayer has foretold the auspices it remains for the client 'to make sense of his statements' (*Voro ná voge-m n vo n wone*) and to take the final decisions on what actions would be necessary.

The Kasena 'bed' is their mat made from giant grass on which they spend the night. The dead are conveyed to the grave for burial in such a mat. When a distant visitor calls he or she is taken inside the compound and a mat is spread out in one of the huts for the visitor to sit on. The mat is thus an important practical and ritual object among Kasena people. In the case of the above proverb mat refers to sleep and peaceful repose and the enriched cogitation that takes place when the mind is not distracted by extraneous events.

The proverb remarks that the mat is like the soothsayer. People get the necessary quietude and peace of mind at night to think things over and take rational decisions, when they are in bed resting. '*N peini n boɲe n ni*' (Sleep over it) is a common remark among Kasena. They also dream about their affairs and thus gain better insights to things that affect their lives. Kasena, like many African peoples believe in dreams and have standard explications for their dreams. They accept that not everybody's dreams are true prognosis of events to come but certain people's dreams are valid indicators of future events. The comparison between serene thought and the disclosures at the *vogo* is perhaps apt. It is as if to say that explanations of life's events and problems sought through consultations with the *voro* could also have been arrived at by cogitation.

The proverb is thus advising against hasty decisions where much is at stake and where execution of the wrong decision can result in future regrets. The lapse of time and the opportunity of second thought are here being upheld.

162. Ba ba mae nabeiŋo ba dole naao
One does not use cow dung to drive away the cow
Commentary: Cattle are not put in a ranch in Kasena society. The cattle rove freely in the dry season when there are no crops that are in danger of being destroyed by domestic livestock. In the wet season, when crops are growing Kasena herd their cattle. Even then, there is always the danger of cattle straying and eating up crops. People drive away cattle from their farms by means of stones and throwing sticks. The point of the proverb is that it is of no use to employ cattle dung as missiles against a cow. Firstly, this is the cow's product and it cannot be expected to have any deterrence value, as far as the cow is concerned. Secondly, dried cow dung is light and will not hurt a cow to the same extent as a stone or a throwing stick would. However, Kasena sometimes mix cow dung with water to be used in sprinkling over crops to prevent cattle eating the crops. The smell of the mixture is such as would stop the cattle from eating the crop. Perhaps, in this respect, cow dung is the missile to chase away a cow.

The general point of this proverb is that you do not carry coal to Newcastle. For deterrence purposes, the unfamiliar carries more weight than the familiar, the *déjà vue*.

163. Kwɛɛra kandwɛ mo kaare yuu
It is the stone cast in play that breaks the skull
Commentary: Children sometimes like to play by casting stones at one another. Expertise at stone throwing is valued in this culture since the stone serves as a ready tool. This is dangerous play however, as accidents happen resulting in the children themselves or others in the vicinity getting hurt. Children are thus advised to desist from the practice.

The proverb makes the point that harm results from dangerous behaviours. Potentially dangerous behaviour can degenerate into something sinister unless checked. The proverb does not always have to refer to dangerous activity alone, it may also apply to behaviour, acts, utterances that begin as a joke but end up as something serious. A joke can develop into serious business. An utterance that was initially meant to be only a joke can cause offense and precipitate a quarrel or fight. In the same way, a love affair that was meant to be platonic might develop into a full blown relation that is forbidden. When things take a turn for the worst in such circumstances it is *setana* ('Satans') that are blamed. Thus, people must be careful about the things that they do for a joke, they should guard their behaviour and utterances.

164. **Zula ba bam bwora**
Courtesy does not make a person to throw out
Commentary: The concept of *zula* refers to courtesy, respect and kindness towards others. It is considered good to show courtesy and respect for others, especially when they happen to be older or senior people. The phrase *bam bwori* refers to the nausea that makes a person want to throw out. Nausea thus results in a diminution in body fluids and vicariously diminution in being.

The point of the proverb is that one's stature and honour in society do not diminish as one shows respect to others. This serves as a reassurance for those who are polite by nature and inclined to show respect and consideration to others, even when it is realised that respectful behaviour can be misinterpreted to be a sign of weakness or fear.

165. **Ni ba ŋɔɔne ye dedwoŋi chem**
When one mouth talks the other is compelled to respond
Commentary: It takes two parties to start and maintain a verbal exchange. People feel the urge to respond to what they hear said by others. The party listening might respond by uttering the words that would corroborate what the interlocutor says, even if their own private feelings are different, or they could express a contrary opinion. The first strategy is a mark of politeness but the latter is confrontational and might lead to further argument and possibly to a quarrel.

The proverb is providing an explanation to verbal behaviour and the social and interpersonal problems that sometimes result from the difficulty of maintaining silence. It can be cited as an excuse for saying something that has unintended consequences or as a defense for the failure to maintain silence where silence would appear to be the best policy.

166. **N na di nasia ye n ba di ka yukwolo?**
You eat the puny rabbit why not also its skull
Commentary: In Kasena folktale culture, the trickster is Nasia, the brier

rabbit. The rabbit is not rich in meat, being after all a puny animal. Like most other wild animals there are certain clans that taboo the meat of the rabbit. There have been reports of clans that strangely enough prohibit their members on ritual grounds from consumption of the meat from certain parts of certain animals. For example there is a clan whose members may eat the rest of the mud fish but not its head. This is one taboo which members of clans that do not have such a prohibition are wont to regard as absurd and ridiculous. Opportunistic as taboos like this one may seem to the observer, after all the head of the mud fish is boney with little meat, they are usually well motivated, as all Kasena taboos seem to be. See Rattray (1932) for a description of origins of some of Kasena taboos and their totemic beliefs.

The proverb appears to be poking fun at apparently ridiculous ritual practices. It maintains that you either prohibit the eating of the entire carcass or you don't. Not to eat the skull of the puny rabbit, where flesh is scanty anyway smacks of opportunism. The message of the proverb is that if something has to be done it must be done fully and thoroughly. Half measures are not the best way to do things. The goose must be sauced like the gander.

167. Bonaga we siu wo gwooni logo logo

The donkey says there is nothing wrong with resting wherever you happen to find yourself

Commentary: Kasena say in another proverb that (*bona-bweɔ ba keeiri ko dwoŋ teo ne*) i.e one male donkey does not bray in another's territory. The two proverbs do not contrast however. A donkey's stubborn disposition inclines it to stop wherever it feels inclined to do so. It may not be alright, however, to bray anywhere since this is an assertive act symbolising aggressive intention or a challenge to the rights of others, whereas taking a rest anywhere has not that meaning.

The proverb says here that it is understandable to heed to the call of nature whenever it becomes necessary to do so, since nature cannot be cheated. When exhausted the body must be allowed to rest to recover its strength. The satisfaction of physical and material needs and requirement is in order so long as the rights of others are not violated in the process. Similar to this saying is another which states that the Mossi is of the view that "You can't spurn rest" (*Beillu we siu ba gwona*).

168. Teena naao gare ko gore

The cow you hope to get is better than the cow you kill

Commentary: A more literal translation of the above proverb would be something like, "the expected cow is better than the killing of the expected cow". The implication is that if one were presented with two choices, a slaughtered cow on the one hand and the promise of a cow in the future on the other, it would make more sense to choose the promise than the carcass.

A cow is not meant to be slaughtered without very good cause, in the Kasena way of thinking. It is a treasure for the lineage, the living, the dead and the future generations. Under desperate conditions it is livestock that would be sold out to generate the cash necessary to meet pressing needs; a cow may also be exchanged for food for the starving family. Ancestral rites could occasionally compel the sacrifice of cow but even here it is an old decrepit cow or bull that will be killed rather than a productive cow. Killing a cow just for food was regarded (and still is perceived) as a waste of resources.

The proverb remarks that just as the cow you expect to have in future is better than the pleasure of eating its carcass now so are hope and expectations against future benefits to be preferred to instant but fleeting enjoyment. Investment is preferable to immediate consumption of value.

169. Boa we n ná maane woŋo ni ne jana ba n momwa toga
The sand lizard says to be forewarned is to be forearmed
The sand lizard says if you have been forewarned blood does not issue from your nostrils

Commentary: The big sand lizard is game among the Kasena. It provides them with meat and also killing it is a way to getting rid of a pest since it feeds on chicken. People set traps for it and kill it. Nevertheless sand lizard is regarded as a smart and difficult game to kill. It is big, strong and a fast runner. It can only be taken unawares and killed, especially as it has a sharp sense of hearing. In Kasem, to say that a person 'has the ears of the *boa* lizard' is to imply that the one's sense of hearing is excellent.

The proverb urges emulation of the sand lizard which seem to be ready for eventualities. The proverb maintains that it the careless and those who allow themselves to be overtaken by events who often suffer hardships. To be forewarned is to be forearmed.

170. Kalia we n yi ná luna n wó paŋe n gwoŋi mo
The monkey says if your eye is lodged in a deep socket you should give yourself a head start (in the mourning rites).

Commentary: For Kasena the appropriate way to exhibit grief is to shed tears and to wail out aloud. At an in-law's funeral the son-in-law is expected to show his grief openly, even if tears do not come spontaneously.

Monkeys resemble humans in their appearance and ways. Kasena remark also that they have deep set eyes. The proverb carries this analogy further by considering the possibility of monkeys having to exhibit forced grief through shedding tears like humans and it goes on to remark that if monkeys were so compelled it would be necessary to have an early start if the tears are to run down the cheeks for all to see.

The point of the proverb is that there is sometimes the need to preempt one's handicaps and inadequacies and to take precautionary measures well in advance rather than wait like other better endowed individuals until it is too late in the day. In some respects, this proverb bears resemblances to # 167 above. Both advise that people should preempt situations and adopt appropriate protective measures.

171. **Pitono we valo wo o teiŋa ne mo**
    The antelope says the waist makes a farmer
Commentary: Kasena agriculture (*varem*) centres around hoe cultivation. The hoe (*vɔrɔ*) has a metal blade and a short curved stick handle. Using it involves bending down to turn the earth and remove the weeds. Thus a good farmer is one who is capable of bending down for long periods. A sound waist is thus essential to a successful farmer. This sounds more like a saying than a standard proverb. It is cited in commentaries that reflect on farming; it lacks therefore the wide application to numerous situations expected of Kasena proverbs.

172. **N ná ba lage chuchuru bore bora n pa ko se ko zo gaao**
    If you feel no love for the *chuchuru* infant, at least give its due before losing it to the wilderness.
Commentary: The *chuchuru* is not considered human and in the past if a child was diagnosed to be a *chuchuru* it was disposed off instantly because of the perceived danger that it posed to the parents and the immediate family. It is said to dislike siblings and would either kill off such siblings or make its parents infertile, to avoid the eventuality of siblings being born. For a Kasena person, no sensible person would wish that he or she did not have siblings since these are one's guarantee of support in one's dealings with the world. To this day, the person who has no siblings is jokingly called *chuchuru*. The *chuchuru* is believed to be capable of harming the economic prospects of the family into which it has been born. See 204 below for further discussion of the Kasena concept of *chuchuru*.

Kasena distinguished between two kinds of *chuchuru*. The *chuchur-ywoŋo*, the harmless (lit. Good *chuchuru*) and the evil *chuchuru*, also known as *chuchur-balɔrɔ* or *chuchur-bɔŋɔ*. The evil *chuchuru* is believed to kill off its parents inevitably. A harmless *chuchuru* may not cause such damage but it is not believed to bring any good to its family either. It might die early but if it lives and grows to adulthood it gives no service to its family or lineage. The harmless *chuchuru* would have anti-social behaviour. It will make no friends and will never marry and have children of its own like normal persons. It is commonly believed that some day such a *chuchuru* will leave home and community for the wilderness where it truly belongs. The phrase *ko zo gaao* (it enters the wilderness) refers to this eventual outcome.

The Kasena position was that a harmless *chuchuru* need not be destroyed and that events should be allowed to run their course. Such a child was not likely to enjoy the affections of its parents and family but it would not be deprived of food. The above proverb refers to this. It maintains that while parents of the harmless *chuchuru* cannot be expected to lavish affection on it, nevertheless it should have its due. Parents continue to have obligations to it until it abandons home and returns to its true home in the wilderness.

The proverb is distinguishing between affectionate behaviour and obligations. The point is that affection alone cannot determine the discharge of duties and obligations to others. Lack of affection should not therefore negate duty or cancel obligations owed to others.

173. **Zwoni we baaro ba to o para ne**
    The rabbit says a man should not die by his outer perimeter wall
Commentary: The little rabbit is known to be rather difficult to trap or kill, a fact which perhaps explains the selection of this creature to serve as the trickster in Kasena folktales. It lives in the bramble bushes and any disturbance of the dry leaves sends a message of danger and then the animal is off. Thus it does not die where it lives (by its house wall, so to speak).

The proverb is a comment on the Kasena concept of *baare*, translatable as "bravery", which is derived from the word *baaro* (male). Its meaning can be said to encompass the Kasena ideals on manhood: courage, bravery, ability to endure pain and capacity to exhibit physical aggression when called upon to do so.

Certain types of death among the Kasena are regarded as disgraceful and inauspicious in some unclear way. Usually nobody is denied a proper burial on account of the manner of his or her death. It is the expectation, however that a person will die in the arms of his kin. He should be given a draught of water before he passes away. Where a person has died alone the custom is to perform the rite of "*ba dole ba kwei*" (lit. they throw and take) before the corpse can be prepared for normal mortuary rites. This is performed by the burial specialist who would be informed of the event and called upon to perform the rite. It seems that people dying in the wilderness or in the battle front were not so treated, however.

A person should die in his hut and not just by the perimeter wall. If he has been able to labour up to the perimeter wall he might as well summon up courage to get in before he passes away. No special rites are known to be performed for such a person who has died at the immediate precincts of the compound.

The message of the proverb is that a person should have the inner reserves of energy necessary for the final hurdle.

174. Zuŋa we dedo mo kwei omo chechare dem se balei ba kwea
    Bird says it is the lone individual who robs her nest and not two
Commentary: Young children like to rob birds of their eggs and young ones and this becomes particularly feasible in the rainy season when certain species of small bird make their nests on the stalks of early millet and guinea corn growing in the compound farms. When children notice these nests and their eggs they pay daily visits till the time that the eggs have hatched and the young birds have developed wings.

There is the belief among Kasena children that human teeth should not be exposed during these visits because the mother bird on its return would discover that human predators had paid a visit and would then move its nests elsewhere, out of harm's way.

Kasena children seek to rear young birds taken from the their nest till they are able to fly. For certain song birds children might build cages from millet stalks in which to keep the bird for exhibition to other children. The desire by young children to rear birds would seem to be an attempt at imitating their elders whom they have observed to rear poultry and livestock. In fact, a child learns poultry and husbandry practices both overtly and covertly beginning from early infancy when a good mother's brother or the maternal grandparent would make the child a gift of a hen on his first visit to the mother's family. This fowl, which comes with the blessings of the grandparents, is expected to increase with time and to serve as the capital that will generate the wealth of the child in future. The hen, in this case, would be reared by the child's parents until the child is old enough to assume responsibility for the fowls.

The meaning of this proverb is however obscure to this researcher. It is not immediately clear why it has to be a single individual that robs a bird of its eggs and not two. A possible explanation might lie in the belief that teeth should not be exposed. If two were to visit a nest simultaneously, conversation would be unavoidable and with it, the human teeth would be exposed and the enterprise would be ruined.

Implied in this proverb is that certain tasks are best performed by the individual alone rather than in the company of others. Too many cooks spoil the broth, one might say. Thus this proverb would seem to contradict the saying that power resides in numbers (*Zurigaluu mo tei dam*), see # 75 above. However, from another perspective, the contradiction would be apparent rather than real. While team effort may be required for certain types of jobs such as those that require exertion of physical energy or collective strategising, there are also those tasks which demand stealth and meticulousness and for which personal attention is the best way out.

175.   **Ajaŋwe yandei yare nɔɔno**
Excessive quest for glory wrecks a person
Commentary: The phrase *Ajaŋwe yandei* refers to the situation in which a particular individual features repeatedly as the subject of discussion. Literally, this proverb can be translated as "So-and-so-again breaks a person". Here, *Ajaŋwe* serves as the proxy for any personal name while *yandei* conveys the significance of repeated action.

The proverb at first sight might seem paradoxical since it is not always a bad thing to have fame, as is attested by personal names such as *Ayerezange* (my name has spread throughout the world), *Adiyere* (I have captured name or fame), *Ayerewora* (My people know my name), *Ayerewojei* (my name has not disappeared), just to mention a few of such names which suggest the significance of achieving and maintaining fame. The proverb however, refers to notoriety resulting from behaviour that is not socially sanctioned. Furthermore the proverb implies that while nobody is perfect, it is unacceptable for a person to turn deaf ears to the complaints of others regarding personal excesses. There is a belief that incorrigibility eventually invites the attention of the witches who are thought to be forever on the search for the pretexts that would cover up or justify the bewitching of others. In a society which, in the past, was not accustomed to the operation of a police force, beliefs like these were important instruments for maintaining social order.

In an egalitarian society such as that of the Kasena and their neighbours there was little room for individuals to rise above the generality and controlling mechanisms existed that curbed excesses, especially for uncommon acts or behaviours not justified by status or station. Traditionally, the person born poor or of average means who suddenly acquired wealth was suspected to have entered into some unnatural contractual agreement with a powerful river god such as Kukula at the Kayoro chiefdom. The latter would make its human client rich and be in turn rewarded by the sacrifice of the beneficiary's kin. See Austin (1961) for references to the role of Kukula in the quest for wealth and Dittmer (1961) for a tale on one such contract with a river God.

The point is that although people may relish publicity it becomes a bad thing when the same person is always in the news. As a previous proverb asserts, human mouths can harm a person. There is here a suggestion that evil can flow out of the human mouth because the ill that issues from human utterance has the potential to entitle the agents of evil: the dwarfs, the divinities, the witches etc to act against a man. Even the divinities can be jealous of the happiness of man. Beliefs like these of course account for secrecy and the unwillingness to show off.

176.   **Bu-veila koe ka nyena**
        The roving child is older than its parent
Commentary: The roving child who has seen the world is older than his father. This seems a paradoxical statement to make. However, ageing in this context refers to the acquisition of wisdom and experience. Superior wisdom and seniority in age are synonymous as ageing, in Kasena perceptions, goes with increase in experience.

In traditional times it seems to have been the position that one who had lived many years would have experienced life in its various dimensions and this must be enriching for the experience of such an individual. Thus, parents must to them, be naturally more experienced than their children. The former have lived for many more years and they have seen and experienced life as lived by the senior and deceased generations. Knowledge and wisdom are after all perceived as transmissible by oral tradition from generation to generation. This notwithstanding, Kasena concede that there are other ways of acquiring experience and knowledge and this is suggested by the above proverb since wisdom can also be transmitted horizontally through interactions with others, including strangers. Thus, a person may also gain knowledge and experience by visiting places and learning from new experiences. It is in this respect that itinerant child who has been abroad can be said to be older than the parent.

Implied in the proverb is the warning that people should not equate knowledge and experience solely with maturation in chronological age. An older person must not therefore adopt a dogmatic position *vis a vis* those who are his or her juniors. The senior can also learn from the junior. As one other proverb states, wisdom is not like the *cheilima* fruit which resembles garden eggs; for wisdom does not grow inside the stomachs of elders and the aged.

This proverb seems to be one of the more recent proverbs. The reason is to be found in the fact that in former times, particularly in the pre-colonial past, leaving home and journeying to distant places was risky and therefore not common. Secondly, older people, because of their breadth of acquaintanceship which was due to affinal and amity ties spread throughout the chiefdoms, had an enhanced pretext to travel abroad more often. However, with the Pax Britannica and the demand for the labour of youth, it became possible for some younger persons to travel outside the district to other districts and especially to southern Ghana. Thus they were exposed to other ways of life and learned new ideas from their experiences.

The proverb is often quoted in admiration of the wisdom which younger people, because of their exposure to the wider world, have come to acquire.

177a.   **Sea ni pɛɛla**
      Sea yi pɛɛla
      Baked bean bread has had more than its complement of cooking potash

177b.   **Na yi nyeŋo**
      Water has got to the crocodile

Commentary: *Sea* is a kind of traditional salt or potash with acidic taste. It is obtained from the ashes of burnt millet stalks. As an ingredient used in the preparation of traditional Kasena foods, sea is essential, even when table salt happens to be available. It is needed to soften cooked vegetables or make food taste less sour. It is an essential ingredient in the preparation of bean bread, *pɛɛla*, a favourite item on the menu.

Quite apart from the application of two different metaphors in the two sets of proverbs above, they still differ in meaning. In 177a, where two versions are differentiated by the choice between the verbs *yi* and *ni* there is a slight difference in meaning. The verb *ni*, ordinarily means 'to hear' while the verb *yi* implies 'to reach the expected level'. In the version with the verb *ni*, the salt has been more than enough while the version with the verb *yi*, suggests that the quantity of salt added is adequate and no more would be required for the item of food under preparation.

The proverbs in question all affirm that a necessary ingredient or catalyst should not be introduced in quantities that far exceed the amount required for the desired effect to be realised. The same idea is expressed in the saying *na yi nyeŋo* (water has got to the crocodile). The crocodile is an amphibian but it spends much more of its life in the water than on dry land. Water is a necessity for a crocodile especially as rivers and ponds dry up in the late dry season. The provision of water must be a great blessing and welcome news to the crocodile faced with dwindling water resources. However, when there is too much water and hardly any dry land, water ceases to be a good thing anymore.

This item in some respects resembles more a saying or *sinseira* than a proverb. It echoes other proverbs such the statement that if you pine for the elephant it will walk on your tender crop of millet, see # 78, and if you pray for the rain it destroy the hours of labour expended on plastering your masonry, see # 79 above. It finds application in commentary on situations in which a desired ingredient exists in excess. In this case not only will a limited good be taken for granted it becomes a nuisance.

178a.   **Piseeru tilei tɔge daane te ba ŋwane bwolim ŋwaane mo**
It is because of mutual assistance in the removal of ropes around their necks that two geese keep each other's company.

178b   **Bone tɔge daane de ba ŋwane bwolim ŋwaane mo**
It is because of mutual assistance in the removal of ropes around their necks that two goats keep each other's company

Commentary: 178a and 178b are two versions of the same proverb. It is the practice sometimes to tether two animals like goats or sheep to each other with a common string or rope. The idea is to make movement difficult and therefore prevent the animals from going astray or leaving the vicinity of the owner's compound. However, this researcher has not come up with a satisfactory explanation for the remark on restraining two geese by putting a rope around their necks. It is more usual to tie fowls or domestic birds by their legs. This is described by the Kasem verb, *dageme*, the use of a string to tether both legs of a fowl to restrain movement.

The proverb is used to underscore the limitations to freedom of action that two parties that are connected by a joint interest which neither wish to jeopardise by a separation experience. This seems to apply in the case of marriage and family life. Women are known to remain married to a man in spite of gross conjugal disagreements because of fears that a separation would also mean separation from the woman's children. Children remain with their father and his family when their parents separate. The mother may only take away infants dependent on her for breast milk, but even these will have to be returned when they are weaned.

179.   **Dedɛɛro mo tɔge mwanno yiga**
It is the wealthy man who is followed by those who perform the *mwanno* dance

Commentary: Drummers perform for a variety of reasons one of which is economic. Dancers and spectators reward the performers for their show. Drummers when out performing seek a patron in anyone perceived to be rich and generous who is likely to reward them for their performance. A measure of their artistic success lies in the size of the crowd attracted to their performance, the generosity of the crowd and the kind of patronage they are able to attract. When out at a public gathering or the market performing, drummers also seek out eligible individuals capable of rewarding them. They know the wealthy and powerful by his reputation and his garb. Once a patron is identified, the drummers might constitute themselves into an entourage to follow the patron about in the market place or at the public function. They are rewarded by the patron with money and millet beer. For the *nadunu* (wealthy person, lit. 'heavy person') the reward is the prestige that accrues from the fact that he has drummers following him. This in itself draws attention to him and advertises his social importance.

The *dedɛɛro* is a notable and powerful person, one who is wealthy and prosperous. It is such a person who stands out in this egalitarian society whom the drummers court. Song are composed in his praises. He in turn is expected to reward the drummers for the honour they confer. Musical artists are also fair weather friends who might also turn on a niggardly patron and compose songs that do not flatter his image.

The point of the proverb is that it is those who know they can afford it who advertise their presence before those searching for patronage. Privileges and prerogatives have their price which those who crave for attention must pay.

180.	**Lela mo kwei bu-kaane nyeene**
It is the fast hand that receives the daughter-in-law's afterbirth
Commentary: The afterbirth is given special ritual significance among the Kasena and will not usually be disposed off haphazardly. A wife is expected to give birth to her children in the husband's compound. The husband's mother who is naturally anxious for a grandchild is also eager to be the first to catch the afterbirth at the moment of childbirth. The proverb states that if the husband's mother wishes to be first to catch the afterbirth she must be fast at it since the moment of its exit is not so easily timed. The early bird, so to speak, catches the worm. The antithesis of this proverb is the one that states that "childbirth cannot be rushed" (*Lelala bu ba lora*).

181.	**Tete veiru mo gwi otete**
It is the night visitor who turns himself away
Commentary: It is the nocturnal visitor who dismisses himself. Night time is not usually the best time to visit, except in the case of suitors who are after the hand of a girl. Even then, they should not arrive when people have all gone to bed. There is of course no fix time for bedtime but most people would be happily in bed or "in mat" by ten o' clock in the evening unless, there is good reason for staying awake beyond this time. The

evening meal is taken between 7 p.m. and 8 p.m, after which people prepare to sleep. The compound head barricades the main entrance before going to bed and opens it in the morning. Thus, the late night visitor might find no one awake to respond to greetings or offer welcome. It is the custom on arriving at a compound to hail the occupants with the phrase *a biseim* and wait for the response, *a zaane-m* or *a zaaba* that would indicate that one is welcome. Until his greeting have been responded to a visitor should not enter a compound that is not his own. Moreover, the late night visitor will find the entrance barricaded and he may have no option but to leave.

The point of the proverb is that those who knowingly break the norms may have to suffer the consequences of their own actions. Norms and institutions have their own inbuilt punitive sanctions.

182. **Doa kantɔgɔ we vwei ni ne mo**
The debate about the likelihood of rain falling takes place by the entrance to the windscreen

Commentary: The Kasena windscreen is a makeshift dwelling structure made in the bush farm or in the clan-settlement. Those who are building a new compound in the settlement are required to leave the old compound and live in one such windscreen until their first rooms are ready for occupancy. It is a ritual requirement for the founder of the new compound and his senior wife to live in such a structure for as long as it takes. The *vwei* is a conical-shaped structure made from millet stalks or grass and straw. It is made in such a way that it guarantees privacy and provides shelter from the elements: sun, wind and rain. For these reasons its entrance is through a small opening.

Talk about the rain is a daily occupation among the Kasena in the wet season or when the sowing season is at hand, perhaps because rain is never a certainty among Kasena and neighbouring people. The thick clouds may gather menacingly in the eastern horizon yet it might not rain. On the other hand, the weather might not show signs of an impending storm and yet rain might fall unexpectedly. Arguments about whether it will or will not rain are not therefore unusual among people who have reason to be anxious about rain.

Those who wish to engage in these arguments about the weather should at least be where they can observe the sky and be guided by the signs. Being inside the windscreen is not the right place. On the other hand, the proverb is advising that those who have reason to argue about the rain, perhaps because there are signs of rain on the horizon, should do well to stay by their windscreens or homes so that should it begin to rain they would have shelter. In some respects the proverb echoes # 240 which says 'if the thought of your dear one comes into your head save some of your meal for him or her but if the thought of your enemy comes to mind string your bow'.

The point of the proverb is either that it is better to explore the evidence rather than have recourse to baseless guess work, where the opportunity for verification exists, or that given grounds for suspicion that an event might be imminent, better be prepared for the eventuality.

183.   **Divana ba chɔge sɔŋɔ**
Refusal to share your meals does not destroy the lineage
Commentary: Lineages occupying single compound can differ as to their span and genealogical depth. There is at one extreme end the compound which is occupied by a man and his wife and children, a simple conjugal family, while at the other end of the spectrum we have large lineages whose members dwell together and trace their descent ties to some great grandfather or even further back in genealogical time. In the latter case, group solidarity may not be too strong and members may not share meals. In fact it becomes impracticable for a large group of kin to share meals.

What makes for lineage unity is not necessarily the sharing of meals, which is more or less a function of interpersonal ties between the womenfolk, i.e. the wives and mothers of lineage members. A lineage may therefore continue to stay in the same compound although its members do not share their bowls of cooked food with each other. In any case those who cook the food and share it are not agnates but the wives and mothers of agnates and these come from different natal lineages. Clan sisters married into the same lineage and dwelling in the same compound may establish reciprocal dish exchanges. What often undermines compound unity are the dictatorial inclinations of the compound or lineage head, sudden deaths blamed on witchcraft, basic conflicts and related issues.

The point of the proverb then is that lineage norms do not imply total harmony. Lineage ideology can accommodate a certain amount of personal difference and withstand mechanical difficulties and disharmony between individual lineage members.

184.   **Chira zundia ba gwoona**
The deceased do not bear grudges on account of the size of the dish set aside for them
Commentary: The term *chira* refers primarily to the ancestors but in this case it can also stands for the dead or the deceased. It is customary to have dishes in which to leave food for the dead, particularly the recently

deceased members of the lineage whose funerals are yet to be performed. These are viewed as still participating in the lives of the living. They are believed to visit home and to demand rights and privileges that were due them before death. It is the final funeral rite that severs the link and sends off the dead to the land of the ancestors. The requirement that the dead should be fed is met by leaving small quantities for them when people go to bed since they are believed to revisit home at this time. Such food will eventually be eaten by orphans, if there happen to be any in the compound as it is forbidden for those who have not lost their parents to eat such food. The Kasem verb for sacrifice or prestation to the spirit beings is *kaanem*, a word that implies that a token is used. People sometimes refer to a gift that is meagre as *kaanem*.

The point of the proverb is that what matters in the ritual context, and perhaps in other situations too, is the symbolism and the intention behind an action more than the question of quantities that are involved.

185. **Peini ba koe chwei, de dae vɔlɔ**
The penis is not older than the thigh, it does not suffer *vɔlɔ* illness
Commentary: Age implies precedence. *Vɔlɔ* is a disease which makes the penis elongated. As the penis and the thigh are part of the same body it is meaningless to establish a scale of precedence between them. This is in spite of the penis' reproductive role and its location somewhat above the thighs. The thigh compensates for this because it is longer than the penis since an elongated penis is abnormal. As we have shown in previous comparisons involving the parts of the body, the point in this proverb is an assertion to the effect that whatever the function of a particular part of the body or its characteristic it needs the support of the other parts. No part of the body is useless or indispensable.

Thus, in spite of individual differences a team is effective because of the contribution of its members, who in their own diverse ways, contribute to the success of the group.

186a. **Ywoori yia fii ba tae**
When the '*ywoori*' frog stares at you it becomes difficult to shoot it in the eye.
186b **Ba ba tae ywoori de yi ne**
One does not shoot the *ywoori* species of frog straight in the eye
Commentary: The *ywoori* species of frog has rather big protruding eyes that appear to stare without blinking. It is usually eaten and people, especially children, hunt it with catapults.

The point made by this proverb is that although there is no taboo against shooting and killing this frog nevertheless the way it stares at a person makes it difficult to harm it. Such a stare provokes sympathy.

The message of the proverb is that it is not human to look the victim in the face and yet fail to feel compassion for one's victim. Those who contemplate evil or harm against others carry out their designs out of sight and without their adversary's knowledge. As another Kasena proverb remarks, "one eye fears another eye" (*yi kɔre didwoŋi*).

187.   **Kukula ná tɔge yiga ko ná dage ka nabɔŋɔ ko ye ka tembaaro sɔŋɔ mo**
       When the short man is leading the way it has to be a delegation to his mother's brother's home or to his affines village

Commentary: When a party is on the move they walk in a file. All things being equal, a short person would not normally be required to lead the way for a group or a delegation that is going abroad or to another clan-settlement. The general rule is that you put your best foot first to gain the admiration of others. A short man is not perceived as a handsome specimen of *homo sapiens* among Kasena. For another thing, a short person slows the progress of the group as his paces are shorter. The exception to the convention that goes against placing a short person at the head of a team on the march comes about when the team is being led by the man lacking stature to either his in-law's village or to his mother's village. These are two places that have a special significance for the individual. Agnates and clan-settlement mates are expected to accompany a man to his wife's parents' village on formal occasions such as when the daughter's husband has been invited to come over and hoe up the farms or to mourn a deceased parent of the wife or her close kin. These are critical moments and its is felt that a person needs all the support he can muster from his agnates, neighbours and well-wishers. A good performance on such occasions redounds to the glory of the guest clan-settlement collectively and could mean a gift of a second wife, while a dismal performance can undermine a daughter's husband's standing with his affines, the wife's family, with the result that his in-laws might take a lukewarm attitude to the marriage. In the case of the sister's child, he is the best person to lead a delegation to the mother's natal village to discharge ritual obligations, because of his presumed familiarity with the place and the mother's people. Placing the sister's child at the head of the delegation makes him visible and serves as a reassurance to the wary villagers who, without such a signal could well have felt apprehensive and nervous. In the days of inter-clan hostilities, the sight of the sister's child was enough to prevent hostilities.

The point of the proverb is that it is normal for a group to feel that it ought to put its best foot first in order to create a positive first impression in external situations. Unusual events have rational explanations.

188. **Yiniga ná sɔge ka pwogo n yuu ne kwaane n peese ka n doge se ka ná zo n sɔŋɔ a ba-n wane ka n ja**
If poverty nests on your head try to get rid of it for, should it penetrate your house, you will be unable to get rid of it
Commentary: When a bird makes a nest its intention is to breed. Likewise poverty breeds poverty, thus compounding the situation. This makes it difficult to get rid of. For this reason, one should never allow poverty to get near. The *sɔŋɔ*, the compound homestead is a person's abode and his last refuge so it must be defended against the enemy. Kasena defend their compounds by means of a high wall. The enemy would have to climb that wall to be able to launch an attack with a bow and arrow. Not only is this not easily done, it allows the inmates time to defend themselves and their livestock.

Poverty is man's enemy; it is like a pestilence to him and he must try to keep it at arm's length. The proverb is referring to the vicious circle of poverty in which an incautious person can get sucked.

189. **Taalem gare kateiga**
It is better to have a little sauce for your food than no sauce at all
Commentary: The Kasena staple food, *gole* which is a kind of thick stiff porridge usually eaten with a vegetable sauce, is the common fare in many parts of the savannah zones of West Africa and beyond. Hausa call it *too*. The Eastern African version is *hugaale* which differs only slightly. *Taalem* is to eat a morsel of thick stiff porridge with too little sauce in the sauce bowl. The verb *tei*, on the other hand, implies eating stiff porridge without any accompanying sauce. From this verb has been derived the nominal *kateiga*. Ordinary *gole* is never considered nice when taken without the accompanying sauce. In fact, it is the sauce that gives it its pleasant taste. It is only *gol-nyɔne*, sour porridge (prepared from flour mixed with the dried fruit of baobab) that may be eaten without sauce because it tastes sweet-sour and therefore nice.

The point of this proverb then is that half a loaf is better than nothing at all.

190. **N yera ná zomma n ni silasia mo**
If you are lazy you watch the driver ants
Commentary: The phrase *N yera zomma* (body pains) refers to a reluctance to subject the body to any form of pain or hardship. A person who feels this way is also a lazy person since work involves exertion and

pain. The *silasia* species of big red ants are known to be industrious as they emerge from their hole in crowds to lift food for storage. Under normal circumstances no busy person will find time to watch these ants. In an economy which exemplified Durkheim's model of a mechanical division of labour everybody was a farmer and it was only at leisure periods that people did anything else. Adults did not get time for pass-times like nature study as their leisure hours were themselves taken up with sedentary subsidiary occupations. Games were sometimes played by youth and adults when there was not much to do. Their favourite game was *bia*, which was played with the help of dice. Kasena would query a person who was observed watching nature thus, 'is it that you are short of work to do?' (*n laam gɛ totoɲa mo na?*). Ants in particular were considered destructive and while people knew they did not have the means or the time to get rid of ants they would deride the observation of ants as a frivolous waste of time. The proverb exemplifies the paradox of the lazy busily observing the industrious.   One conclusion from this proverb then is that the lazy justify their laziness by finding a sinecure.

191.   **Ye tan bore mun-na bora ne mun-kikeila bora**
        Don't judge the flour water as if it were the flour balls
Commentary: In the Upper-east of Ghana, where the Kasena and their neighbours live, the customary afternoon snack was and still is in the traditional homes flour made from millet ground together with pepper. This is buttered before being mixed with cold water. Kasena call this *muni* (flour). They have several ways of preparing the snack, hence the proverb that "Every town with its own ways of making the *muni* snack" # 232 below. The phrase *bore bora* in Kasem means to adjudicate and show which of two parties has right or justice on its side. The snack usually contains the thick and frothy fluid that will be drunk first, the flour residue, and the rolls of flour (*mun-kikeili*). Some people drink the fluid and hand over the rest to children to eat. There is the belief that this fluid which for them is a mixture of water, millet juices and flour not only quenches thirst, it sustains the worker.

    The proverb makes the point that the fluid from the snack cannot be treated in the same as the flour balls. Two things that are different should not be judged by the same yard stick.

192.   **Ba lɔre lulwei o nu toom ne mo**
        It is at a blindman's mother's funeral that the extent of his handicap can be measured
Commentary: The mother's death is the occasion when the true character of a person and his or her worth can best be measured. The child becomes

the chief mourner on the parent's death and the public look up to the bereaved child to show the way in the performance of the crucial mortuary and funeral rites. It is realised that it is not every blind person whose handicap is immediately obvious to the onlooker especially those who are not close members of the family The eyes of some blind persons may seem normal to the casual observer. For such blind persons it is possible to disguise their handicap and this can be done by not exhibiting the defect publicly. However, at important public occasions where the individual is the principal actor the handicap becomes difficult, if not impossible, to conceal from the public.

The mother's mortuary rites are one such occasion when public attention focuses on the individual. Son's especially are expected to bury their parent. Not only must they authorise and execute some of the rites, they should supervise the grave-digging. They would be told by the grave diggers that the task is progressing and the bereaved should grease 'the mouths' of the diggers with beer and gin to encourage them to exert themselves. The bereaved child must also see to the reception of the mother's clan-settlement members and important visitors. His friends and well-wishers would also be around to condole with him and ameliorate his grief. The death of a parent is the busiest moment in a person's life. Only sleep grants a respite to the bereaved child, as another saying, # 66 above, suggests: "death does not know that my mother is dead".

The message of the proverb is that a clever person may disguise his shortcomings but then there are going to be occasions when it will be impossible to maintain the facade. The death of the mother is a crucial moment in a person's life when an individual's true worth is up for public scrutiny.

193.   **Ba ba lwo na nɔn-gwia yerane**
         Water is not deliberately poured on just anybody
Commentary: Water was never readily available in Kasena homes except perhaps in the wet or rainy season. Dousing a person with water was done either inadvertently, as in the maiden song, "*A lwogi na a ka-a bɔɔlo yerane twei na se-a seeiri ywoo*" (I mistakenly poured water on my boy friend; get me clean water to wash him down) or when it became necessary to do this. For example, if a person faints water may be thrown over him or her to revive him or her. In another context when a woman who has separated or divorced her husband returns to the husband's compound for whatever reason the ritual of dousing the estranged spouse with water is performed to symbolise her returned to her former husband. Outside these few occasions it is a personal affront to pour water on an individual without good cause.

Thus the message of the proverb is that unusual behaviour has its motives.

194.   **Pε ná jege de nɔɔno nayera pwooli-m jaŋa mo**
When you are on bad terms with the chief even the shepherds challenge you to a wrestling match
Commentary: The chief is a powerful personality in the chiefdom. All disputes that involve clans or individuals from unrelated clans are brought before the chief for adjudication. In colonial times the right of the chief's court to deal with customary cases was greatly reinforced by the encouragement of the colonial authorities. Chiefs like the Navro-Pio in fact had local police to help reinforce the decisions of the chief's court. Thus it stands to reason that if a person was on bad terms with the chief he could not expect the chief's protection should he have a case with anybody. Traditionally the chief dispensed impartial justice and occasionally even the emblem of his office, the *kwara*, was invoked in the process. However, since colonial times chiefs were known not only to be impartial but also vindictive.

Shepherd boys' favourite pastime was wrestling. They could not however, as minors engage adults in wrestling nor would any sensible adult have proposed a match to any but his own mates. A minor would be sanctioned for throwing any challenge to an adult, worst of the kind of challenge suggested in the proverb above to adults. It would be regarded as presumptuous and a gross sign of disrespect.

The point of the proverb is that the respect that children and minors owe to adults derives from the latter's good standing and good repute within the community. That respect can be questioned given the knowledge that a certain individual has ceased to enjoy the support of the community and its authorities. An observation of Kasena society would show that adults who are known to be simpletons, mentally deranged, or criminals are not sometimes accorded the respect that other *bona fide* members enjoy.

The message of this proverb then is that when a member of the community loses the protection of the community that individual becomes fair game and should expect to suffer indignities.

195.   **Noa na mae tei to ka ta mae konto mo**
The finger is what it is today what it was yesterday and will be tomorrow.
Commentary: The finger of an adult does not appear to grow longer or shorter. It retains the same size as far as the mature individual is concerned.
The point of this proverb is that it not everything that changes with time:

Certain things will change while certain others will not change. We must not therefore expect that with time everything will change.

196.   **Wε mo na swo wolo to o veiŋa ye ka yera mo**
        The person God has bestowed favour upon walks with a different style

Commentary: A person's manner of walking shows his confidence and self assurance. An important person such as the chief or the wealthy walks leisurely without any semblance of hurry. In the Kasem language this walk is described by the word *gwε*.

In Kasena view their *Wε*, God of the above, is the Almighty. He bestows the ultimate gift. As Kasena say, His gift is better than the gift made to a person by powerful humans like the chief. The person who enjoys the favour of God is different from other lesser mortals.

The point of the proverb is that luck and good fortune, which in Kasena eyes are attributable to God, account for the outstanding differences between persons in the same condition.

197.   **Ko yeini ko gwori mo pae bone tɔge de de bia**
        It is necessity that makes goats to join the company of their young

Commentary: This is one of those proverbs for which this researcher cannot pretend to have a satisfactory explanation. Goats graze together on the same fields. In the wet season when crops have to be protected a family's herd of goats are tethered in the same place to graze. The young goats are not usually tethered and they go where the older goats go. As the herd remains together the young males worry the females as trying to copulate with them and in the process constitute a nuisance to the mother goats. This, to the Kasena mind, is awkward behaviour as the billy seems not to respect the rules of incest. For Kasena, sexual relationship between persons of the opposite sex who happen to have a kinship tie between them is forbidden. The incest taboo is not limited to close kin but applies to distant kin as well. The explanation for the tolerance of the older goats must, from the point of view of the proverb, be that they lack an option in the matter. If goats had a choice as to where to graze in peace they might seek separation from the younger billy goats that are such a nuisance.

The message of the proverb is that people sometimes have to put up with behaviours from others that they do not like or do not condone with because they have no other choice in the matter.

198.   **Bone ba zoore wiira yaga**
        Goats do not attend a market established by hyenas

Commentary: The market from traditional times has been an important social and economic institution. It was also the channel of communication between affines, kin and friends who are separated by residence. Although it was often an individual or a chief who was responsible for a market's establishment and that individual claimed custodial rights to it and performed the necessary rites to the gods of the area where the market was located, nevertheless anybody including strangers, could attend a market and be sure of some protection. As a social institution, one of the market's functions was to provide a forum for entertainment; it is there that people indulge themselves. Drinking and drunkenness are not unusual in the market and often as the day wears on the atmosphere gets charged and market authorities have a hard time restoring order. Drunken men sometimes attempt to settle old scores leading to disorder and confusion.

In Kasena folktales, the goat and the hyena have always been 'enemies'. In reality hyenas find in the domesticated goat cheap prey. It would seem therefore unwise of and rash for a goat to knowingly visit a market where hyenas are in charge. After all hyenas were to establish a market, the objective would be to meet their needs; therefore goats that visit would be treated as commodities freely on offer. Goats would not do that as they are too smart for this. Comparatively, goats are perceived to be more danger-conscious than sheep. There is a saying that while the goat runs away from the road at the sight of an approaching vehicle the sheep remains to confront the vehicle over unreturned change from fares paid to the driver.

The message of the proverb is that nobody in his or her senses trusts his or her neck deliberately into a noose no matter the sincerity of the assurances about safety of doing this.

199   **Memena we n pwoa ná maŋe ya ba daga de n ta wó bere n baro**
The ant says even if your private parts are undeveloped for sex you will still show them to your husband

Commentary: The term *pwoa* here refer to the bosom and the female genitalia. As a puny creature, the ant cannot be said to have much by way of a genital organ. The proverb suggests that ants nevertheless copulate. Conjugal norms require that a wife should not be shy and should rather discuss her sexual problems and inadequacies with her husband. She may have a low estimation of her sexual attractiveness but she should not assume that her husband has no interest in her sexually. She should offer herself and leave to the husband the decision as to whether or not to have intercourse with her.

From the point of view of surface, as opposed to the underlying interpretation, the proverb seems to be based on real life marital problems, such as those brought about by the practice of clitoridectomy which until recently most Kasena maids had to go through prior to marriage. The operation sometimes leaves a scar in the genitalia and the vaginal orifice becomes too narrow thus making penetrative intercourse painful as a result. The proverb is asserting that a woman who finds herself in that predicament should not assume that her husband would not have sexual interest in her. Rather it is for the husband to experience the difficult and to take the decision on what to do to treat the condition. Traditionally even parents of brides did not sympathise with daughters who refused the husband the right of sexual access.

Sexual activity is the basis of marriage among the Kasena. This is not for the gratification of the physical act alone but more importantly, for the prospect of having issues to continue with the family line. In Kasena marriage life a wife cannot, without good reason, refuse to have sexual relations with her husband. A husband for his part has an obligation to sleep with his wife and to provide her with children. Failure to do so without good reason can result in a wife seeking separation and eventually remarriage and divorce. Women have been known to say "I did not marry him just for his food". Marriage thus transfers rights and privileges as well as obligations and duties. Marriage was essentially contractual arrangement binding on the spouses in the first place and their immediate kin as wife-takers and wife-givers.

The point of this proverb is that those who are associated as occupants of statuses in any social relationship, have duties and obligations as well as rights and privileges. Rights cannot continue to be claimed without discharging the corresponding obligations towards the correspondent partners. Those who cannot discharge their duties with respect to others must show cause for their inability. A person may feel that the quality of service due to a correspondent does not meet the expectation, that should not be an excuse for withholding the service unilaterally. The correspondent should be given the opportunity of sampling the service or product involved and granting an excuse from the obligation. It is for the correspondent to reject or accept the service and he or she should not be denied that right.

200.   Sɔŋɔ ba koe ko tu
        A house cannot be older than its founder
Commentary: This proverb at the literal level, has more than one explanation. It can mean that the compound house, as a mud and wattle structure, cannot be older than the compound head; or the lineage

members who dwell in the compound cannot be older that the person who has succeeded to the headship. Neither of these interpretations is wholly true.

The material used in building Kasena compound houses makes these structures prone to decay and collapse. The component dwelling units may fall in the wet season and may be rebuilt from time to time. With time a compound may be abandoned thus becoming a *didwoɲo* (ruins). The physical structure can remain in being for many decades. Thus it is not inconceivable for some compounds to be older than their current heads. On the other hand, the site that a compound occupies may have been selected by people who have long since died leaving their offspring to continue there. Secondly, on the question of seniority of the compound head *vis a vis* compound mates, it needs to be pointed out that in the customary norms of lineage succession, generation takes precedence over age in the establishment of seniority. It can happen that a chronologically younger person takes precedence over an older person because the former is of a senior generation. We can illustrate how this comes about thus. A man may take his first wife at the age of 18 years and begin to have children by her; then in his middle age he takes a younger wife who may be less than half his age and about the same age as his first child by the first wife. In his old age he might marry for the last time a girl who is about the age of his grand child. His children by all three wives would differ substantially in age and yet be of the same generation. Thus this man's youngest sons would be senior to his oldest grand children and take precedence over them although age wise the latter (the grandsons) could be older by far than the former, the youngest sons born to the most junior wife.

Thus for the proverb to make sense literally we must interpret the verb "*koe*" in terms of a system of ranking based on seniority, as socially defined. In this respect the proverb statement becomes true in the sense that the head of compound and lineage is senior than other agnates since seniority ascribes to a man the headship title. We are discounting female agnates who are expected to marry and to leave their natal family in order to live with their husbands and their children in another settlement. Females do not succeed to headships of compounds. Traditionally, it was by accident that females headed compounds.

The message of this proverb is that legitimate authority ought to be given its due in spite of the fact that there may be other bases for contesting rights.

201.   **Nampɔle daane jaŋa mo**
The *Nampɔle* ritual delays the wrestling match

Commentary: A wrestling match is aimed at ranking individuals by their strength and wrestling skills. The wrestlers would throw their arms around each other and begin to wrestle. Head butting was allowed. The contestants might tackle or trip each under or do whatever is necessary to put the opponent down and pin him or her to the ground. Boxing or kicking was not allowed.

Before the wrestling starts combatants might size each other. One party might engage in brow beating preliminary rituals to score a psychological advantage over the rival wrestler. So long as the adversary refuses to be deterred by the gimmick these preliminary rituals can only be a mere waste of time on the part of the wrestlers.

The message of the proverb is that where the opportunity exits it is best to put the issue to the test than to indulge in preliminaries that merely whet the appetite but settle nothing.

202. **Bone twɛ daane mo de ba ŋɔne maa milimi daane**
It is because goats have been tethered too close to each other that their ropes get entangled

Commentary: Goats as smaller livestock are tethered in a field together in the same area to make it easy for them to be moved to new pastures when the goats appear to have exhausted the grass in a particular location. The danger is however that when goats happen to be placed in such a way that they are near to each other their ropes can get entangled. When this happens they have to be freed soon or else they end up strangling each other. For the goat owner himself the entanglement can pose difficulties when attempts are made to release the goats from their ordeal.

The proverb advises that those who do not get along have the option to move away from each other's way and they should do so. Conflict brews between people when they happen to share the same limited space.

203. **Keira ná gwori ni de wo maa gwori yia mo**
If the mouth cannot respond to overwhelming emotions, then it will delegate the eyes to do so.

Commentary: Wailing and shedding of tears are customary outlets for grief. Wailing may be undignified for certain adults, especially men; however, where grief cannot take the form of loud wailing, rather than suppress it, it should take the form of weeping and shedding of tears which draws less public attention to the individual.

The proverb shows that alternatives are always available to those who find one type of behaviour inappropriate or out of place.

204.   **Nɔɔno ba zoore o kwei odwoŋi sɔŋɔ chuchuru**
A man cannot enter another's compound to dispatch its *"chuchuru"* child

Commentary: The *chuchuru* child is not only traditionally undesirable but one that is believed to pose dangers to its kin. It is believed to be a manifestation of wild spirits that masquerade as humans in order to be able to prosecute their wicked and malicious designs on man. Traditionally, such a child must be got rid of, as soon as possible. A child must first of all be confirmed as a *chuchuru* by diagnosis before action can be taken. Even before the formal diagnosis, those around the child would have noticed signs of its non-humanness. The *chuchuru* as a neonate may exhibit congenital deformations. It is said that these types of children do things that normal babies could not be expected to do. It is also believed that people in the compound notice unusual phenomena in their surroundings which they might eventually attribute to the doings of the *chuchuru* child. For example, a lactating cow in the compound might not produce milk in the expected quantities when milked because the *chuchuru* child would have gone out when nobody was about and milked the cow for its own needs.

Traditionally, Kasena took the stance that a *chuchuru* should be got rid of or destroyed before it played havoc on its parents and family. A specialist called *chuchur-kweeinu* was invited in to dispatch the infant because it was felt that the job entailed considerable risk for non-specialists. The corpse of such a child was buried in the bush where it is believed 'to belong'.

The proverb hints that the issue of a *chuchuru* is a sensitive one to be handled with tact by those who are not immediate members of the child's family since there are no incontrovertible evidence that a child is definitely a *chuchuru*. Thus, no outsider can take the lead in the disposal of another person's child on the suspicion that it is a *chuchuru*. The decision is for the immediate family who stand to lose or gain by the decision to take. They might perhaps seek the support of outside specialists including soothsayers, in arriving at a decision and in the performance of the necessary rites.

The message of the proverb is that there are certain sensitive issues that only the inner group, as the "we" group, might deal with. Others should not be oblivious of this fact.

205.   **Kaane ba go de o gwoni de yuu**
A woman does not slaughter a python and sever its head

Commentary: Women and men have their duties specified by norms that reinforced a division of labour along the lines of sex. Today this division of labour is less strict than in the past. Traditionally, men would bear arms but women could not and did not. However, women did accompany their men to the battlefield where they were in charge of the war medicines and provided water for the thirsty fighting men. Equally important was the ululation they cried out as they shouted words of encouragement to their menfolk. Like warfare, hunting was and still is reserved for men. Men who were about to embark on a hunting trip were expected to avoid female company (i.e. sexual activity) prior to the event.

Killing a python was considered a difficult task, as discussed in Proverb #151 above and it was not expected that women would be able to perform such a feat. Killing and severing the head of the game or its tail is a demonstration of prowess. The proverb observes that if a woman were to succeed in such a perilous task she should be modest about it and should not boast too much about her prowess by going to the extent of cutting off the python's head to serve as a trophy. Most Kasena women would call a man over to kill a snake rather than attempt to kill it themselves. When Kasena describe a woman as a 'he-woman' (ka-bea) they are not paying her a tribute just as when a man is described as a 'she-man' (ba-kana) or an effeminate man they are saying something derogatory. A husband who abuses his wife is not encouraged by his kin and there have been occasions when women who were fed up have proved to their husbands that they were physically stronger. The lineage treats such events as domestic matters and does not rush to the husband's support. However, if a wife carried this too far the lineage would have to intervene.

The proverb is about roles and associated expectations and excesses. The message of the proverb is that behaviours are role bound and though there would be occasions when individuals may find it necessary to exceed the role expectations, they must not make a habit of it as this might seem a usurpation or reversal of status and roles customarily ascribed. Rights and privileges as well as duties and obligations associated with acknowledged or institutionalised roles and statuses should be safeguarded to ensure that some role bearers are not unduly embarrassed or appear to be put on the spot by openly or covertly challenging them or usurping their roles and statuses and thus making them lose face publicly.

206.   **Kaane kuri mo lona se o ni ba lona**
        A woman's bottom may be warm but her mouth is not warm
Commentary: A warm mouth is one which is quick to speak out and speaks out of turn. This has never been seen as a compliment by Kasena. A hot bottom on the other hand is seen to be one that is productive in the reproductive sense.

Men in traditional Kasena society kept their own counsel. Though they did not always exclude women from their meetings they did not willingly discuss weighty matters concerning the lineage in their wives' presence. Old women were exempted, perhaps because as mothers their loyalties cannot be questioned. The wisdom of excluding wives from such discussions and secrets is illustrated and reinforced through folktales such as the one about the hunter and his new wife. The latter was a beautiful young woman only in appearance but in reality a buffalo seeking revenge on a hunter who had killed its mother when it was only a young calf.

The loyalties of non-agnatic women in the past were suspect given the fact that marriages were unstable and women not only divorced frequently they also remarried men from rival clans. An estranged or separated wife could not be married by a man from her former husband's clan-settlement nor could any other man whose lineage maintains clanship ties with the erstwhile husband's lineage. Should that eventuality arise the former husband's lineage head would appeal to the authorities of the allied lineage in question and the new husband would be told to let the woman go.

If women happened to be around when men held their discussions they were expected to remain silent. Wives could not volunteer comments and suggestions until called upon to make a contribution. Women were moreover considered to be less experienced than their menfolks in worldly matters since they did not venture out as often as men. Those women who unwisely commented on issues that were before their menfolks were usually silenced by quoting this proverb at them.

207.   **Lwooru ba jege lwo-dedɛɛro**
There are no rich beggars
(A beggar has no choice)
Commentary: People begged for favours from others because their choices were limited. Their chances of getting what they are requesting depended on their manner of making the request and their ability to persuade the person being appealed to that they lacked an alternative source of help. This was a necessary strategy in a more or less egalitarian society. A beggar cannot therefore behave like a person of means. For one thing, the beggar should not be seen to dictate to his beneficiaries or to insist on specified quantities or quality of the thing being asked for. She or he must be content with whatever is provided, as one proverb has it, 'one does not sound the gift hoe', see # 97 above. A demanding beggar is one who is choosy.

208.   **N ná beeiri pa n na pa**
If you search for "*pa*" you will find "*pa*"

(If you search for trouble your will find it)
Commentary: The word "*pa*" in this context is an ideophone which refers to the sound made when a smack to the face is administered. The proverb makes the point that trouble is never too far off; those who seek it will not fail to get it. In some respects, this proverb echoes the saying that if you look forward to seeing the elephant it will destroy your tender crop of millet, see # 79 above.

209.   **Chichwoŋa tiina ŋɔɔne diga tiina wo-dɛɛro**
Outsiders' remarks about family events do not always reflect what obtains inside the home
Commentary: The word *chichwoŋa* is a derivative in this context from the phrase "*ka che chwoŋa ne*" (to meet on the path, or stop people on the path for conversation). It refers to outsiders who meet and need something to talk about and end up gossiping about events that have been reported to have occurred in the compounds of others. Kasena recognise that gossiping is inevitable, they say, food may be short and will not therefore go the rounds but rumours do circulate, see # 84 above.
    The point of the proverb is that what is said in the gossip often is a gross misrepresentation of the facts.

210.   **Sawea ná ba tɔɔre-m, ja ka naga**
If rumour happens to be close at hand get hold of its leg
Commentary: If rumour were animate and it happened to be close to you it would be wise to get hold of it rather than allow it to escape. That is to say, it is wiser to investigate and verify the truth than to take rumours at their face value. This proverb and # 209 above are relatable as they reinforce each other.

211.   **Nakeimnyeno mo twe pɛ**
It is the talebearer who insults the chief
Commentary: The chief, as the most powerful person in the community, was the source of favours. He also wielded a set of punitive sanctions which made it unwise for even the elders of clan-settlements to be in his bad books. There is therefore no shortage of stooges vying for the chief's favours by doing him real or questionable favours including peddling rumours of plots against the chief. There could also be those who might seek to use the power of the chief against those they did not like. The *nakeimnyeno*, or the *ke-ba-daane nɔɔno* (bring them into a confrontation) as the literal meanings of these derivatives suggest, is a person who knocks heads together. He does so by bearing tales. Kasena accept that a

chief, as the most outstanding personality in the chiefdom, must be the talk of the polity. He is criticised by his supporters and detractors alike. He should not however bear grudges. Nevertheless, like any human being it pains to know that all that is said about him is not complimentary. The proverb asserts that the person who repeats the insults that are supposed to have been uttered by his subjects is ultimately, the cause of the chief's pains and for that reason he or she is the one who insults the chief vicariously. The negative comments relayed to the chief thus confirm his suspicions which hitherto had been unproven and therefore cause anguish to chief. Thus, it can be said that it is the talebearer who insults the chief and not his potential detractors.

The proverb warns that the intentions of talebearers are suspect and they are as guilty as the detractors, if not more so.

212.   **N zɔ-niiri dwoi n yi-nɛɛre**
What you hear is of greater worth than what you see
Commentary: This is a twist of the saying that seeing is believing. The proverb's message is perhaps that negative reports have a greater impact than what is seen and observed in real life. In another respect this proverb serves as a rebuke to those who relish hearsay and rate it over visual evidence.

213.   **Ko wi kabeila ne gare ko wi zonkɔgɔ ne**
It is better to use the sauce bowl in the chore of blowing away chaff from grain than to use the old calabash bowl
Commentary: The verb *wi* refers to the use of mouth air to blow away chaff from grain. This is done to millet that has been roasted and the grain subsequently pulled out with the bare hands or by means of a sling. The grain that falls into the receptacle usually contains some husk and chaff. Blowing the husk away by mouth makes the grain safer to eat. The process takes place inside the *zonkɔgɔ* "old calabash bowl" and rarely in the vessel in which sauce is served, the *kabeila* which is not only heaver but much more fragile being made of clay.

The proverb implies that there is more dignity in using the sauce bowl than the old calabash bowl. The former is deeper and less likely to allow the grain in the vessel to spill or get blown away. While the sauce bowl is much more treasured and is kept within the compound, the old calabash bowl may be used for any chore and might be eventually discarded.

The proverb would be appropriate as advise on the desirability of maintaining privacy in the trashing out of family and related issues. No good results when family conflicts are publicised or dealt with in the public. However, should one party resist attempts at settlement within the privacy of the home and lineage, then, the proverb implies, there can be no other option than to expose the issues and adopt more uncouth means of managing the disputes that might be at issue.

214.   **Ba ba lɔ sɔŋɔ ba ti dɛ dedwe**
        A house is not built to completion in a day
Commentary: A compound house begins when the founder and his most senior wife leave their previous compound and pitching a shelter screen in a plot allotted to them and ritually prepared for the new homestead. Building of the first huts then begins. More and more huts are added as time goes by and the membership of the family increases as children grow and marry. As old huts fall off in the rainy season newer additions are made in the dry season. A compound should continue to grow until it reaches its maximum size. This can takes a century or more and then it begins to decline as former members find it necessary to leave. The state of relations between compound members and the carrying capacity of the land around which serves as the farmland are important factors. The proverb is literally true as far as building a compound the Kasena way is concerned. It is however used to advise that it takes time to accomplish things. Its analogue in English would be the proverb which states that Rome was not built in a day.

215.   **Pɛɛre ye nachwɛ mo woloŋo maa ye nabia**
        The gift is a cow while meanness is a bull
Commentary: The heifer holds hope for its owner in a society which practises animal husbandry; when reared it will some day generate a herd for its owner. Whenever it calves milk will be available for its owners. A bull was not useless piece of property but it did not hold the same expectations. It could be sold in times of need or killed in ancestral sacrifice where the meat would have to be widely shared among agnates and others who might happen to be present at the occasion. A cow was valued more in bridewealth prestations. Today, bullocks have a new use as traction animals to draw ploughs which are a recent introduction dating back to the 1940s. In some respects, a bull benefits those with cows to be seeded, however the bull's owner has no stake in the animals that are the progeny of his bull.

The gift, in the short run, implies property alienation while its opposite, stinginess means that personal wealth is conserved in the short run. Economically, it would seem that the latter rather than the former is the better strategy for accumulation of wealth. This apparent in the short run. The point of the proverb is that being close-fisted or not wishing to exhibit generosity may indeed ensure that property is not alienated but that such property may not generate much return in the long run.

In a society that in the past lacked the technology to store perishables for long periods the best strategy was to invest surplus value by redistribution. Kindness and generosity, as modes of redistribution and reciprocity are really investments that can generate a dividend in the future or in times of need as these modes obligate others to reciprocate in the future when there is need for assistance. A gift thus has incremental value.

216.   Wɛ pɛɛre gare pɛ pɛɛre

God's gift is better than the chief's present

Commentary: In Kasena thought, Baŋa Wɛ (God of the Above) who is higher than anything else was "the creator God" and the master of all. Even the activities of the powerful local gods, the *tangwana, jwona* (shrines), *liri* (medicinal agents) and ancestors and the mother earth are sanctioned by Baŋa Wɛ who is the author of human destiny. Kasena have a saying that "what God has not slaughtered the earth will not eat", refer to # 51 above.

A true gift is one that God bestows on a person. The gifts of the lesser gods such as the powerful Kukula were suspect since these are debts and traps that the gods set for greedy men with the view to exacting their price in human life. The chief is a powerful person who had much in his gift but he is also a creature of God and his gift means nothing unless it is sanctioned by God who is the giver of life, the greatest gift. The generosity of the chief, moreover, is not altruistic and he expects that those who have benefitted from his largess would be indebted to him for more than they have received.

This proverb is a religious statement reflecting Kasena conceptions of the greatness of God. The message of the proverb then is that mankind, no matter how powerful, cannot be compared to God.

217.   Paro jeŋa ye kukua mo jwoŋinu jeŋa maa ye gegalɔ

The giver's hand is short but the recipient's hand is long

Commentary: The concept of wealth is expressed in idioms involving the hand. A wealthy person's 'hand has things' (*o jeŋa jega*) while a poor person is one whose 'hand has not' (*o jeŋa ba jega*). The short hand therefore is that hand which does not stretch far enough to allow others to receive from it.

The proverb is a reflection of human behaviour. People are only too ready to receive presents but they are unwilling to make gifts to others except where that gift is seen as a kind of investment against the future. The point about the gift, as Macel Mauss (1960) and Sahlins (1970) suggested a long time ago, is that the character of the return gift, though in some sense obligatory, is ill-defined and left to the discretion of the person making a return gift. What counter gift will it be, when will it be made, how will it be made and in what quantities or form? The preemption of questions like these means that people are not always eager to give and they give out of an obligation. The point of this proverb is that true generosity is rare. The hand that doles out is a stiff hand that does so reluctantly while the receiving arm receives eagerly.

The proverb is applied to illustrate and comment on negative attitudes to the gift and gift-giving.

218.   **Ba sɛ nakwe-jwora ni kɔga yera ne mo**
        It is in retrospect that the wisdom of the puny elder's advice is recognised and acknowledged.

Commentary: There is a tendency to measure wisdom by looks and appearance and even by social stature and wealth. The *nakwe-jwora* is the puny old fellow who pales in insignificance by comparison with others, especially more youthful or personable people. His puny stature may make him look like an immature or inconsequential person. Senility is not culture specific and Kasena also know that as a person ages he or she grows senile and is prone to loss of acuity and alertness. Those who do not see beyond the characteristics of senility exhibited by the aged, especially in the puny aged are only too likely to ignore the advice of the puny fellow who lacks a commanding stature. The warning of the proverb is that society ignores such a person's advise at its cost. The mistake is realised only when it is too late. People come to recognise that they could have done better by taking his opinion more seriously. Similar to this proverb is the saying that the poor have no claim to the truth.

The message of the proverb is that advice should be taken on its merit no matter the personality of the giver or his appearance.

219.   **Ba ko bu-doa bɔɔne ye o tiina jei mo**
        The parents of the only child sit by as his grave is dug

Commentary: The lost of a youth is regarded as a painful misfortune for the community and the immediate family. For the parents it is a devastating blow and if it happens to be an only child who has died the sense of tragedy is almost complete. Under these circumstances, it is not unusual for the bereaved to be heard lamenting how unjust fate has been; they would wish that death had seized them instead of the youth. The death of an only child carries nullifies the hopes of the parents. There is a feeling that their security in old age and the expectation of immortality that only the survival of offspring can guarantee have disappeared.

Paradoxically, the death of an only child is associated with feelings of guilt in the community as it begins to be suspected that the parents have themselves had a hand in the death of the youth through their involvement in witchcraft dealings.

Kasena society deals with the tragedies of premature deaths by quick burials; often no grave is dug, rather an old one is opened for the interment of the corpse. The sight of the corpse maddens the child's parents. The distraught parents are likely, according to this proverb, to remain on standby even as the child's grave is being dug. It strikes this researcher that this behaviour is somewhat strange viz. bereaved parents standing by the grave of the only child. It seems to be at variance with actual behaviour. On can understand why it would be difficult to remove them from the corpse. What is more common behaviour is that dear ones show disbelief and an unwillingness to accept the fact; in extreme cases, distraught survivors have attempted suicide, an observation we find referred to in Cardinall (1921). In most cases, the dear ones would have to be forcibly removed from the compound to allow burial to proceed.

220.   **Ba ba yage yera ba pae bu**
One does not give unrestricted licence to the child
Commentary: A child, it is expected, would be treated with tenderness. It will not be called to account for its misdemeanors in the way that adults would. However, there is a limit beyond which this license should not be carried. A child also needs to be disciplined when it is wrong. This proverb is used to justify the need to make the child feel accountable for its actions. The literal meaning of the proverb is that if a child were to slap or beat an adult, the adult should not have to look on and allow the child, because of its age, to continue to exercise its physically aggressive behaviour, the body after all feels pain. As one proverb maintains, 'it may be alright to experiment but certainly not by beating or hurting others', see # 81. The adult would be in his or her right if he retaliated by hitting back. This proverb is invoked in circumstances similar this scenario.

221.   **Kukura ba ku kua ka pae ka dwoŋ**
A dog does not prepare a bone for another dog to take
Commentary: Dogs are observed to struggle and even to fight for food and meat especially. Traditionally, Kasena did not give flesh to their dogs, rather bones that people could not chew would be left to the dogs. Two dogs would fight over such a bone. Its is therefore inconceivable that one dog should expect that its fellow dog would chew the bone of contention to make it softer for the benefit of the other dog. Not even mother dog would do such a thing.

The point of the proverb is that in competitive situations, one does not stand idly by in the hope that one's competitors would voluntarily surrender what they have acquired through their sweat to a fellow competitor.

222.   **Lwooru ba lwoori o kɔne o dwoŋ**
A beggar does not beg in order to feed another beggar
Commentary: As one in need, a beggar is entitled to beg from others considered better off for handouts to meet his or her own immediate basic needs. It is because a beggar is perceived to be down on his luck and in need that donors show sympathy. Generosity is exhibited by those who feel their circumstances are relatively better than those of the beggar. A person cannot build his wealth by begging for alms and the beggar cannot beg for alms in order to be able to exhibit generosity to others, as if he or she were a wealthy person. It becomes even worse where one beggar must beg in order to keep another from starvation. Not only would the practicing beggar lose the sympathy of the donors it would not be possible for the two beggars to subsist on what only one of then brings in. After all, what a beggar receives is hardly adequate for himself or herself let alone another.

A beggar cannot thus expect that a fellow beggar would beg for alms for his or her benefit. If one beggar feels too big to beg for alms then he or she has no claim on the alms that another beggar has been able to attract. The proverb is not against a parent begging to feed himself or herself and a child. On the contrary, there is considerable sympathy for women who are compelled to beg to feed their child. This proverb is similar to # 222 above.

223.   **Nakwe jeŋa ba jujuga**
The elder's arm does not twist easily
Commentary: The proverb is using physical strength as its metaphor although ultimately, it is not physical capabilities that are at issue. Maturity is believed to go with age. Until a person has peaked physically, the older an individual gets the stronger his or her bones are expected to be. Thus, in some respects an older person's mature bones are stronger than those of a younger person. The analogy can be said to derive from experience. To those who eat local chicken, an old cockerel's bones are tougher and harder to crack with the teeth than those of a tender chicken. In another sense, the strength of the older person derives from the coping strategies he or she might have developed over time. This can account for a capacity to resist the twisting of his or her arm by a younger adversary.

The term "*nakwe*" in Kasem can refer to one who is older, even if he or she is older by a shade. It can also refer to a person who has achieved seniority and become acknowledged as an elder with an institutionalised role and authority derived from it. Succession to traditional offices such as elderships is based on seniority in age and generation.

The message of the proverb is that an elder may have grown frail with age but he or she still retains power, particularly ritual power based on custody of the ancestral shrines. Such a person is not easily coerced by younger persons who might have more physical vigor.

Compare this proverb and its interpretation to the Akan proverb: "If an elder has nothing, he has elbow", cited in Van der Geest (1996) with its twelve different interpretations.

224.   **Badeinu ba jege badein-yero**
There are no dignified bachelors
Commentary: A bachelor, *badeinu*, is one who has no wife. It may be that he cannot afford a wife due to poverty or for some other reason such as personal inadequacies. The fact that a man cannot have a wife is a serious indictment of his personality, from the Kasena point of view. To them, such a person is a failure in life. Is it that he has no kin and friends who will help him find a wife; does he treat women badly with the result that no woman would remain married to him; or it is that he is not man enough to attract women? Material poverty *per se* was never an acceptable explanation for a person's inability to find a wife, especially in a society where everybody is a farmer and dependent on hoe cultivation. It was laziness that was perceived to be the source of poverty or in the case of the physically handicapped, an inability to work and earn a living. This is not to deny the legendry case of the youth who would rather remain a bachelor than take a wife with a blemish, as illustrated in folktales such as that of Ayiying who claimed by a half-bodied goddess which at first taunted the unwilling husband but eventually transformed itself into a beauty to Ayiying's satisfaction. There was not much differentiation in such a society in the past, especially as land was available to all. Thus as Kasena say, even a poor but able-bodied man should find a wife: *Nabwonu mae o naga mo o swo o kaane* (It is by means of his exertions that a poor man finds a wife). Although a husband needs to have resources to be able to meet bridewealth and other demands made by wife-givers it is also accepted that a poor man's caring attitude and his concern for people can influence wife-givers to show consideration and not withdraw his wife on account of his inability to afford the bridewealth goods. Marriage is thus perceived as democratic.

The proverb is commenting specifically on marriage. The person who does not have a wife cannot be expected to maintain his dignity.

225.   **Kanware pae chuchwooru**
Hunger gives madness
Commentary: The English say a hungry man is an angry man; Kasena think that such a person is like a mad person. The pangs of hunger may make a person do irrational things that he or she might not normally do.

226   **Mɔle siseiŋa ba diini zwoŋo**
The cheap horse does not climb the hill
Commentary: A horse was valued for its speed and ability to carry its master over long distances. It was considered a relatively expensive item for Kasena thus making it the preserve of the wealthy and the princely. Unlike cattle, horses were not bred locally and those who needed them for prestigious reasons would have had to pay an exorbitant price for them from Moshie traders. Thus it would be surprising to find a horse selling at a low price. If such a commodity existed then it could mean only one thing, a horse that is no good as a horse. It was often the practice, to exchange many herds of cattle for one horse.
   The message of the proverb is that people should beware cheap things; they do not take a person far. Good things do not come cheap while cheap things are likely to be worthless.

227.   **Yeizura tu mo chɛ swoori**
It is the healthy who make new farms
Commentary: The making of a new farm from virgin land is a demanding task. A plot that is being farmed for the first time is usually hard ground to dig up using the traditional Kasena short hoe. It therefore takes a healthy person who has command of his full strength to do it. Even in those cases where it is possible to obtain labour from kin or affines, it still takes a healthy person to mobilise the labour. The farmer owner, as custom demands, should pay people visits in the homes to be able to make the request. These days bullock driven ploughs are available for those who have the bulls and the equipment or can afford to pay for the service. The point of the proverb then is that health is a prerequisite for success in life.
   There is abundant recognition of the importance of good health in the execution of engagements. Often a person replies to a request from another for labour or assistance with a phrase such as "If the morrow is good .." (*ka ná poore ka lamma..*).

228.   **Jawɔr-nyeno beinnu ba daga**
The faeces of the lazy person do not amount to much

Commentary: The quantity of faeces produced is a function of good feeding. Kasena often remark on the huge quantities of excreta that litter the valley bottoms as the early millet ripens and food becomes available again after the hunger months of April and May. The lazy person cannot feed himself well because he has not worked to produce an adequate supply of food. Good feeding and willingness to work hard go together as another Kasena saying points out, *tontoɲeno keila ba teiɲa* (the cheeks of the worker cannot be pressed). The worker engaged to carry out a job is entitled to food and entertainment from the 'master'.

The message of the proverb is that hard work and industry are the basis of prosperity and well-being.

229.   **Je-kora ba vei ni**
An empty hand does not feed the mouth
Commentary: The empty hand or in this case the 'dry hand' is the hand of the pauper. The hand feeds the mouth with food. Therefore the empty hand has nothing with which to feed the mouth. As another Kasena proverb has it, "the hand does not refuse to give to the needy mouth" (*Jeɲa ba jege ye vane ni*). See # 126 above.

230.   **Siseiɲa we dimeo gare disua**
The horse remarked that familiar pastures are better than lush pastures
Commentary: The horse may not a Kasena product but they have nonetheless a fair acquaintance with it and its eating habits. A prince usually keeps his horse at home where it is fed by his boys. The view that the horse is choosy as to what it eats stems from the special care that is lavished on it as a precious piece of property symbolising its owner's claim to wealth and prestige. While other domestic animals are taken out to eat whatever grass may be available, the horse is regularly fed with the best feed that can be obtained locally. The problem is that youth can be careless and when the feeding of an animal is entrusted into their care, it cannot be certain that they will always feed the animals well. Perhaps, if an animal were allowed to feed on its own it might at least obtain a bellyful. Nevertheless given a choice between freedom to rove about and face the uncertainties of life such as having to feed on whatever the land has to offer and suffer thirst as well as exposure to all manner of danger and hardship, the horse may yet opt for the comfort and security of the stable.

This proverb can be regarded as the Kasena analogue of the saying that the 'devil you know is better than the angel you do not know'. The message of the proverb is that considerations such as those of kinship, security and familiarity can outweigh immediate economic gain. In other words, value can also be measured in non-economic terms using parameters such as familiarity and security of tenure.

231.   **Kabaa ba nabɔŋɔ jega**
         The slave has no mother's family
Commentary: A slave has no kin. Implied in the literal statement is the view that those who have kin could never have been permitted to remain in slavery. Kasena did not institutionalise pawning or the enslavement of kin. A slave was therefore a person of foreign origin. Since his masters did not know his origins they could accept him as a kinless person and a slave. A slave can be said not to have a mother's lineage. A mother's lineage has an obligation, albeit moral rather than legal, to redeem the sister's child in his crisis moment. Thus, the fact that a slave remains in bondage can only imply that the mother's people are ineffectual or else they do not know his whereabouts and for that reason cannot attempt a rescue. Either way, the bottom line is that the slave lacks kin he can call kin.

The mother's brother and his lineage were expected to intervene when a man was in danger of losing his life or liberties. The mother's lineage meant a lot to a person, they provided refuge to the beleaguered daughter's child. This goes to confirm the saying that one must never exhibit disrespect for the mother's brother by using the left hand to point to the village of the mother's brother. Traditionally, the mother's lineage was expected to redeem their sister's son's wife if he stood in danger of losing her owing to his inability to find the means to settle bridewealth obligations. However, any livestock loaned out had to be repaid in due course. Given what the mother's family is willing to stake on behalf of the sister's child, it would have been out of character for the mother's family to fail to redeem the slave if they were capable of doing so.

The proverb's message is that kinship is a valuable asset in a person's life and his liberties and citizenship rights depend on it. Kinsfolk are expected to provide mutual support and failure to discharge their joint obligation to the one in need undermines the very foundations of kinship and the *raison d'être* of the kin group.

232.   **Teo ko mum-viri ko mum-viri**
         Every society has its way of making a flour snack
Commentary: Anybody may prepare millet flour snack, although this is more a chore for women than for adult men. There are many ways of making a snack from millet flour. A variety of grain crops may be used such as finger millet, early millet or sorghum. The millet may be boiled,

dried and then fried before being ground to make the flour that would be used in the snack. Alternatively, it could be roasted millet or raw millet that is processed for the purpose. The flour is usually knead with the hands while small quantities of water are added in stages until the right consistency is obtained. Finally water is poured in in such a way that it foams.

There is certainly room for variation in any of these stages. The point of the proverb is that there is not a fixed standard method of preparation of millet flour snacks. A visitor cannot therefore insist that the snack presented to him or her by the hosts should be made according to a particular formula.

The message of this proverb is that there are many alternative ways of doing things. A community or group may have its own favorite way of doing things and this should be understood. It is calling for tolerance since diversity is perceived as normal and not necessarily an aberration.

233.   N ná nɛ siseiŋa de ka ni gara, yage se ka taa kɛa se n yeiri ka
         na ke ka tu mɛ
         If you see a horse with its bridle let it go for you can't be certain
         where it left its owner

Commentary: A horse that has been harnessed is a horse that has been prepared for riding. However if it is found just roving about without its rider it must mean that there is something that is amiss. It would be unwise to claim it, for it cannot be lost property or property without owner. The latter would be a contradiction.

It is customary not to claim vagrant livestock without abundant proof that the livestock in question has no owner. Where there is evidence that a stray animal has no owner within the community or in the chiefdom and that nobody is likely to ever claim ownership, then and only then may the earthpriest claim it. Such an animal would be used in sacrifice to the earth and the gods. In the case of the harnessed horse there must be an owner nearby; more importantly, it might not be fit for riding which explains why it is not being ridden. It could be that you have met an untamed horse which has thrown off its master.

The lesson of the proverb is that it not every treasure trove that is worth having, especially if it happens to be an unusual trove. Cheap things may have an unpleasant sting about them.

234.   Manlaa we n ná diini twio n ji ko vɔɔ
         Chameleon says when on a tree assume the colour of its leaf
Commentary: The chameleon is a common sight in this savannah

ecological zone, especially in the wet season. It is notorious for its ability to camouflage itself by assuming the colour of its surroundings. Its ability to simulate a wide spectrum of colours has led to the rainbow being termed "the chameleon's bow". The capacity to change and blend colours is perceived as magical and explains the fear in which many people hold the creature. It also protects it from predators. Kasena do not seem to have an emic explanation for why or how the chameleon should camouflage itself. However, their folktales often depict the chameleon as a weak animal that is denied its rights by other parties. However, its magical powers soon come into play to enable it to get its own back.

The point of this proverb is that a wise person learns to adapt to circumstances for survival. We could paraphrase the proverb by the English proverb: "When in Rome do as the Romans do".

235.   **Ba ba yeigi yiru lɔɔ ne**
One does not buy a genet cat in the bag
Commentary: Market transactions usually take place between strangers. Traditionally, distribution of local produce was often by gift exchange and reciprocity. Of the market, Kasena have a saying that "The point of market transaction is to exploit fools" (*Ba zoore yaga jworru ŋwaane mo*).

The *yiru* equated with the fox by most literate Kasena, it is not exactly a fox but rather a genet cat. It is a kind of wild dog or feline that visits homes in the night and makes away with chicken. It is hunted down when opportunity exists because it is perceived as a nuisance. Secondly, though its meat is not a favourite item, there are no known taboos against eating the meat of *yiru*. However, it does not commonly feature as a commodity, dead or alive, in the market place; perhaps this is due to the fact that its is not easily caught.

The proverb is making the statement that if genet cats were an item of commodity sold in bags it would be wise to examine the goods before purchase. First and foremost because one can never trust any stranger who is selling to play fair. Genet cats are such a rare commodity a buyer could be conned into purchasing an animal that really is not a genet cat. Secondly, a genet cat is a smart animal which once let out of the bag would be impossible to get hold of. Finally, the very idea of buying things that one has not inspected smacks of naivete.

The message of the proverb then is that it does not pay to throw caution to the wind or to take things for granted in interpersonal relations, especially when dealing with those one does not know too well or in matters were assumptions can be dangerous.

236.   **Na ba duri gweeni**

Water does not flow in the opposite direction

Commentary: Rivers and streams in established channels flow in one direction and this is from a northerly direction southwards into the larger tributaries of the Volta river which eventually flow into the Gulf of Guinea. Kasena have names like Tono, Kukula etc for the stretches of the tributaries of the Volta that flow through their land. Until recently, they had apparently no notion where these tributaries ended although they knew that most of their rivers tended to flow southwards.

The term *gweeni* implies a leftward direction. The left stands for the unconventional or the usual. In this case, north also known as *kaseŋo jeŋa* (lit. the Kasena side) aligns with the left only because of the geographical inclination of the land which slows gently southwards.

The proverb makes the point that there are customary or accepted modes of doing things. It cannot therefore be expected that the wrong modes would be applied to the solution of problems. Similar to this proverb is another which maintains that "the hole through which the arrow penetrated in the way out", see # 98 above.

237.   **Chworo we o wó fo o tete ni mo se o baa fo o bu ni**

The hen says it would defend its own actions but it could not presume to profess the innocence of its chick.

Commentary: The phrase *fo ni* means to deny an accusation levelled for wrong doing. Poultry are notorious for the harm that they cause, particularly to millet sown on the farms. Mother hen is usually accompanied by its chicks as it moves about in search of food. The grain and the white ants that some poultry keepers provide their young fowls are rarely adequate and poultry are allowed to dig around for whatever food is available. Though mother hen might assist the chicks to forage it does not mean the chicks necessarily feed under the supervision of mother hen. Thus, mother hen could only be justified in defending itself against accusations for harm caused. Where its chick is concerned, it could not presume to deny such accusation since chicks feed independently of the mother hen.

The point of the proverb is that kinship does not entitle one person to rebut outright accusations levelled at another or to hold brief for another without good evidence. As Kasena say, siblings may bear facial resemblances but their dispositions are different, see # 113 above: *Nu puga bia nye daane mo se ba wo ba nye daane.* Each person must account for his or her actions personally. The danger in holding brief for a kinsman is that if it should result in oath swearing the sanctions for false oath-swearing would be visited on both kin.

This proverb is sometimes stated as *Chworo we o wó fo o tete ni mo se o baa fo o chichare ni* (The hen says it would defend its own actions but it could not presume to profess the innocence of its egg).

238.   **N ná boŋe n faro boboŋa di n daare n zege; n ná boŋe n sebannyeno boboŋa di n taŋa n zege**
If the thought of your dear one comes into your head save some of your meal for him or her but if the thought of your enemy comes to mind string your bow.
Commentary: The proverb is referring to this uncanny feeling or foreboding that each one of us gets from time to time about an impending visitation. The proverb advises that these feelings should not be dismissed, rather one should be prepared for any eventually that our thoughts happen to settle on.

In the past a person could be taken unawares by an enemy who had descended suddenly. This was particularly true in the days of the slavers. The latter mounted surprised attacks and those caught unawares were easy prey. The remedy for this was to live in a state of preparedness. A bow that is inaccessible and unstrung was of no use to its owner in times of sudden emergencies. In the same way, goodwill visitors did not always announce their visits as we found out in other Kasena proverbs. We are reminded of this in the Kasena saying, "a visitor forces his way in but does not force his way out" (*Veiru zoore de dam mo se o ba nwoŋi de dam*). If the visitor arrives in the day time food or a snack could be got ready but it was the nocturnal visitor who posed the biggest problem, especially if he or she arrived after the meals had been served and eaten. Kasena are aware of the impracticality of reserving food for emergencies, especially when household members have not had enough.

239.   **Veiru zoore de dam mo se o ba nwoŋi de dam**
A visitor forces his way in but does not force his way out
Commentary: The explanation of this proverb is straight forward. Visitors to the Kasena compound do not need to give prior warning before they come. In line with this attitude, a visitor is never hurried nor is he or she asked what his mission might be, as we find among Ghanaian Akan peoples. He or she can present his mission in his own time and this can only be done after the formal greeting rituals.

This proverb is quoted at the visitor who is insistent on leaving sooner than the hosts have had time to provide some form of entertainment. The Kasena view is that a visitor is, as it were, in the jurisdiction of his or her hosts and can be detained. The consent and permission of the members of the compound household are necessary before the guest can leave. A visitor can be detained where it has been decided that a meal should be prepared for that visitor.

The saying has practical significance in the case of the eligible but yet unmarried girl who, in the past, dared to visit her boyfriend's house. The old ladies would not fail to cause her detention by making a public or formal proclaim (by ululation and announcement from the roof-tops) of her marriage to a member of the host compound, even if this was not initially her intention or that of her boyfriend. This was not considered unprecedented behaviour and if the family of the girl should insist that she be returned, she would be returned in due course. Today, young women may visit their boyfriends in the latter's homes in safety, although occasionally the rule is invoked to the embarrassment of both boy and girl. In the same way, a woman who was once married to a member of the household and subsequently separated should not revisit unless she wished to be claimed anew. In the latter case, there is a rite that is performed to re-incorporate the divorcee. It involves pouring water over her.   The saying goes to illustrate or confirm another proverb which maintains that a male donkey cannot bray in territory owned by another male donkey, see # 55 above.

240.   **Veiru wo-maŋɔ mo o niwudiu**
What a visitor comes to find is his food
Commentary: As Kasena say, "A visitor forces his way in but does not force his way out", so remarks proverb # 239 above. A visitor does not always give prior warning before visiting. People are not required to warn their hosts about impending visits, except where the visit is a formal one, nor can a visitor be turned back under any circumstances. Kasena believe that it is God and the ancestors who bring guests and visitors. There are of course occasions when warnings are given prior to visits. One of these occasions concerns the formal visits that the new wife's "brothers" make to demand formally the bridewealth due them. Among the Kasena of Navrongo this is called the *gwoŋina*[17]. Similar but somewhat different is the *kayiri* found among the Paga Kasena. The *kayiri* in Paga follows almost immediately after the bridegroom has taken his wife home. No warning is given and, in fact, any agnate of the bride's might make this visit and demand a roasted fowl. The *gwoŋina* is however, more elaborate and is usually arranged before hand. Even then, the drama of hostility staged by the bride's "brothers" seems to suggest that perhaps in former times no warning was necessary.

As the visitor requires no prior appointment to visit, it means that the person on visit cannot predict what he or she will find in the compound he is visiting. Hence the statement that what a visitor finds is his luck and lot. He or she is hailed as the harbinger of good luck when the visit coincides with good news or an auspicious event in the host family such as child birth. If the visit coincides with a misfortune no blame is however put on the visitor but he or she might not obtain the hospitality that could have been provided. It also means that the visitor will have to exert himself or herself to be of some assistance to the host family in its hour of misfortune.

Kasena often look for signs that serve as prognostications of the outcomes of visits to places outside their clan-settlements. People occasionally turn back and change their minds about certain visits when the auspices seem not to be good or favourable. Some of the signs include hitting the foot against a stone or some other obstacle on the way. Hitting the left foot is good for a person whose succeeding junior sibling is male and vice versa.

The proverb is used to justify the invitation that must be extended to a visitor to share in the fortunes of the host family, especially its good fortune. For example, if the visitor arrives as the family has just slaughtered a fowl or an animal in sacrificial offering the meal that will be cooked will be served the visitor because it is believed that it is the recipient spirit agent that has conducted the visitor to the place of sacrifice to participate in the event.

241.   **Faŋa tu mo nɛ ye o ta o we ko ná tera n ni ne ko wo n tampɔgɔ ne**
        It has been said since the days of the ancestors that if it is not in your mouth it must be in your bag

Commentary: Traditionally, a visitor to another clan-settlement or village carries a bag. This is one of those proverbs with limited usage. It is quoted in the context of formal greetings at the visit of a stranger to the Kasena compound. It serves as entitlement for the prosecution of business. Among Kasena, it is unethical to prosecute business until the guests have been served with water. Thereafter the guests should allow a decent interval to elapse before they propose and eventually exchange formal greeting with the hosts. Only then may business be transacted. It is in exceptional cases where it does not forebode peace that business may be transacted prior to this.

The proverb refers to the two most important reasons why people normally make visits: to hold discussions and to make a presentation. The former issue from the mouth while prestations issue from the bag that a visitor carries.

242.   **Kandwɛ dɛ swooni ŋwaane de laŋe nuga**
It is on the bean's account that the stone pebble gets to taste butter

Commentary: Beans may be cooked fresh in the pod, this is not however the usual way of preparing beans for a meal. More often, after beans have been harvested they are dried and then later pounded and winnowed to extract the bean seeds. Thus bean seeds may regrettably contain stone pebbles, bits of pod and other impurities which are not always easily removed before the beans are cooked. A varieties of dishes can be made from beans. They may be cooked alone or mixed with other legumes or grain such as millet or hibiscus sabdariffa seed. In the preparation of *swopɔlɔ*, beans are cooked mixed with millet and or hibiscus seed; a seasoning of pounded groundnut is introduced at some point. To enhance the taste of the dishes made from beans it is customary that a quantity of butter is added.

Butter is an expensive culinary item which is not to be wasted. Certainly it cannot be wasted on stone pebbles yet paradoxically this is what sometimes happens. It is not in all dishes that housewives can afford to introduce butter and the bean is thus privileged. Though care is taken to remove all stone pebbles from grain and legumes before cooking, regrettably some remain and are cooked together with the grains. The unlucky person knows only too well how it feels when in eating a spoonful of beans the teeth chew grains of stone as well. The proverb is commenting on this feeling of horror when people chew stone pebbles; they curse when this. It would seem paradoxical that although some respectable dishes do not get to relish butter, stone should nevertheless enjoy a privilege allowed delicacies. This, however, is how things are.

The proverb is commenting on the paradoxes of life. Opportunism is a way of life. So long as associations are unavoidable and desegregation and disentanglements cannot always be effected, discrimination will not always be possible or feasible. Thus on account their associations and links the entitled and the ineligible could come in for the same treatment. Individual merit cannot always be isolated and made to serve as the basis for differential allocation of on benefits or punitive action. As another Kasena proverb remarks, if a lizard should hide behind a tree both will become legitimate targets although the hunter is really interested in only the lizard, see proverb # 50 above.

243.   **Nabwonu ba jaane o boŋo o diini o lei guŋu yuu**
A handicapped person does not tether his goat on a silk cotton tree

Commentary: It is customary to tether goats, and sometimes sheep too, though the latter are normally herded by shepherds, to prevent them from destroying the crops in the wet season. Leaves are occasionally fed to goats and sheep especially in the dry season when grass is scarce, but kapok leaves are not by any means a favourite item for fodder. It is more usual to lop off branches of acacia albida for livestock to eat in the dry season..

The silk cotton is about the tallest tree in this savannah ecological zone. A *nabwonu* may be a weakling but in this case it refers more to a person who is either physically handicapped or else senile and therefore incapable of doing the things that most able-bodied persons are capable of. Such a person cannot be expected to climb trees, least of all the tall huge kapok. The handicapped person should therefore be advised against tethering his goats where he or she could not easily untie them when necessary. When the skies have darkened and it becomes clear that the storm will break, people rush out to untie and bring their livestock into the shelter of the compound.

The proverb is employing hyperbole. It should not be understood that the proverb is in any way suggesting that Kasena tether their livestock on trees. The fact that they do not do this is explained by the reference of such behaviour in jokes that are meant to embarrass some kin groups. A joke used to teases the members of one of the clan-settlements in the Navrongo chiefdom recounts that once upon a time a man from their kin-group upon noticing how his goat loved the leaves of the fig tree, which is by no means a tall tree, decided to take the goat up the tree and tie it to one of the boughs to that it could have its fill of the leaves. It ended up strangling itself. The butt of the joke is that no one in his senses would take a goat up a tree to feed on leaves.

The point of the proverb is that a person should know his or her limitations and act accordingly rather than over reach himself and need being bailed out. Compare this to the proverb which says the handicapped person mounts his donkey while it is still lying on the ground, see # 88.

244.   **Swa dae cheilima ya leiri nakwa wone**
    Wisdom is not like the *cheilima* fruit growing inside the elder
Commentary: The *cheilima* fruits appears to grow well in the wet season and require less attention that other garden crops. In its season, it is found cheaply on the markets which attests to the ease with which it can be cultivated. However, it is not a particularly sweet fruit although some people seem to enjoy eating it.

Wisdom, in this proverb, is being compared to the cheap fruit which is easy to cultivate and is therefore easy to come by. Wisdom, the proverb warns, is not really like such a cheap fruit; it does not come easily, even to an old man or old woman, in spite of the established association of old age and wisdom in Kasena culture. Wisdom has to be cultivated through experience, instruction and learning , i.e. in the hard way. It cannot therefore be expected to show up in everybody who happens to be old. It is not ascribed like most age and generation linked statuses, but must be earned. It is for this reason that another proverb remarks on how a widely-travelled person is 'older' than his or her parents in wisdom and experience.

245.   **Ndwoŋ yi mɔɔ ndwoŋ yi kapere**
One neighbour's eye is ripe fig fruit but the other's is raw fig fruit
Commentary: The proverb is not to be understood as comparing two individuals who are neighbours to ego or self; rather, the reference is to ego and ego's neighbour or to the insider and the outsider. The proverb statement would seem to give the former, inaccurate impression to the listener.

The ripe fig fruit is considered good to eat. It is sweeter and moreover poses no known health problems unlike the raw fig fruit which does not have a pleasant taste and can result in abdominal upset for the person who has been rash enough to eat it in large quantities. The health dangers of the raw fig fruit are referred to in the proverb which says, "when the children consume raw fig fruits it is the stomachs of their elders which ache", see # 74 above. Another difference between the ripe and the raw fig fruits is that the ripe fruit is softer and breaks easily whereas the unripe fruit is hard.

The eye that is compared to the ripe fig fruit is considered delicate, and that is the eye of ego, whereas that the one belonging to alter is in this proverb compared to the raw fruit and needs no protection as it is not delicate.

The proverb is a criticism of self-centred human attitudes and behaviours. It shows that a selfish, self-seeking person considers whatever relates to himself or herself as deserving special treatment but the same person refuses to accord the similar or equal treatment to others and things that concern them.

246.   **Putana daa mo baa daare se twio wó di**
The skin on the belly may not remain but the tree top will be attained.
Commentary: The metaphor is taken from tree climbing. Quite often the tree climber makes bodily contact with the tree and in doing so the stomach may rub against the trunk as the climber tries to heave his body

up the tree. This mode of tree climbing can result in the skin of the belly lacerating. It is naturally painful, especially if the tree has a rough trunk.

This proverb is used to show determination on getting something done no matter the costs or the consequences.

247.   **Benaga ná lage ka de-m n ba nae ka zwa**
When a donkey is about to throw you off you do not see its ears
Commentary: The wise rider of the donkey looks for signs that the donkey intends to shake off its rider. One such sign is when it bends its head in readiness to shake itself of the rider. The ears are thus for a moment below eye level and seem hidden from view. Another interpretation might be that if the ears of the donkey remain visible its rider might be able to hold onto them and so save himself from a nasty fall.

This is a popular Kasem proverb that points out that when a misfortune is due the unlucky individual gets no prior warning when such warning would otherwise have enabled him or her to take the necessary precautions and thereby avoid the mishap. In fact misfortune is so inevitable that sometimes it strikes when it is least expected, as is the case where the butter melts in spite of the fact that it carried in the night and only the moon is visible, see proverb # 85 above.

248.   **Nayel-pepala lage ya tiina yiga mo**
The well curdled milk loves the sight of its owner
Commentary: Kasena consider fresh milk as not so good to eat. There are those who throw up on taking it. Fresh milk is however given to children, and occasionally to babies, especially if the mother is not sufficiently productive of milk to guarantee that the baby will be well nourished. Kasena generally love the milk that has been kept over night and has become sour and congealed in such a way that big lumps of curdled milk result. It has always been a delicacy especially those who did not have lactating cattle did not have it for consumption.

It is a truism that those who have herds of lactating cattle are also those who have sufficient milk they could keep long enough for it to curdle. In the traditional subsistence society those who had milk in abundance would redistribute it among family members and friends.

The proverb is here remarking on the fact that when a delicacy is in abundance, to those who have ready access it soon ceases to be a delicacy. They are not anxious to consume it, unlike their neighbours who crave for it. The wealthy can afford to accumulate value for the prestige attached, as scholars of the leisure class like Veblen (1970) have long affirmed. A comparable proverb in Kasem goes as follows: "*sabia lage ya tiina yiga mo*", Money loves to keep the company of those who own money in large quantities. Value attracts value.

249.   **Tuu na to tei to ba wó cha ko konto mo**
The way an elephant falls so will it be butchered.
Commentary: The elephant is regarded as the biggest possible animal known to the Kasena. Hunting it was a collective enterprise for them, involving ritual observances like abstention from sex for the duration of the hunt and the period running to it. Rituals were also conducted to purify and cleanse those who were involved in sexual misdemeanors, prior to embarking on the hunting of such a dangerous animal. Bows and arrows were not often enough to kill the beast immediately. It seemed arrow poison was not powerful enough to result in instant death. A mortally wounded elephant died after taking many shots and where it fell was often far from the place where it was first shot. Because of its size and also because it took the collective effort to kill it in the first place every member of society was entitled to cut as much of the meat as they needed.

The proverb remarks that the size of the slain elephant made it impossible to turn it over in the way that a smaller animal would be turned over to allow it to be skinned before the meat would be cut up. Thus the butchering of an elephant begins from the exposed side. It is after much of the accessible flesh has been removed that the meat on the flank on which the dead animal fell can be cut up.

The point of the proverb is that though there are rules for solving problems, yet there are other peculiar problems that demand the recourse to unorthodox methods suggested by the peculiarity of the circumstances. The nature of a problem suggests its solution. As another proverb remarks, the right way to extract an arrow lodged in a person is through the hole it made as it pierced through the flesh, see # 98 above.

250.   **Chibi-beira di fibɛ mo**
The absent chick eats male ants
Commentary: Kasena distinguish between several species of white ants: *fiu, fwoŋo, toa* and *kunkwio. Fiu* are the white ants that Kasena collect from their natural colonies in the bush to be fed to their poultry, particularly to young chicks. *Fiu* differs from *fwoŋo* in being brown while *fwoŋo* is pale. As the latter do not build colonies above ground they are usually cultivated or enticed into pots containing dried cow-dung, fruit of the baobab and the like where they collect in colonies to be harvested the following day.

The male members of *fiu* have sharp fangs that are a worry to chickens when chickens try to eat them. Fowls therefore avoid the males and eat only the females. Young chicks stay by the mother hen which fends for them but chicks can also be independent as proverb # 237 maintains: "The hen says it would defend its own actions but it could not presume to protest the innocence of its chick". Thus, a chick which happened to have ventured out of sight of its mother at the time the meal of white ants has been served will not be able to compete for the juicy female ants. On its return it will find that the left-overs are not even edible and it will have itself to blame for this.

The message of the proverb is that limited resources are distributed on the basis of first come, first served especially when is not considered necessary to allocate limited goods on the basis of a special criterion. Late comers take the worst, the left overs.

251.   **Badunu zi bugi tei, ko baa jeini gaa baŋa ne**
No matter how tired the big *Badunu* bird may happen to be it will never settle on a grass reed.

Commentary: The *badunu* (the horn bill?) is about the biggest wild bird in the imagination of the traditional Kasena who were not acquainted with the ostrich. In addition to its size this migratory bird is believed to make mince meat of snakes. A tired bird will perch somewhere convenient and safe to rest and to feed; this, for most birds, means tree-tops and on the ground. Smaller birds might settle on millet stalks and tall grass growing at the height of the rainy season. However, for bigger birds like the *badunu* and the predator birds, hawks and eagles, a reed of grass is out of the question since their weight will not be supported by one reed of grass, not even the elephant grass is stout enough to support the weight of a big bird.

The point of the proverb is that standards differ. One solution cannot be applied to all problems regardless of the situation and the circumstances. Human beings differ as to the their conditions and circumstances and as such, it cannot be expected that even under desperate conditions some well placed individuals could sink as low as other less advantaged individuals. There is a bottom line for everything.

252.   **N ná tage wε n ga n dae kasambɔlɔ**
If you target the sky and fail to score a hit you are not necessarily a lousy shot

Commentary: The *kasambɔlɔ* is the person who is hopeless with the bow and arrow. The term is an insult. Describing a person as *kasambɔlɔ* almost amounts to saying that that person is effeminate since in the troubled times of the past it was a man's duty to defend his community by bearing arms. Thus, boys learnt to shoot at tender ages and in their leisure hours they played competitive games shooting at a target. As recently as the late 1950s when this writer was first taken to Kasenaland as a child, groups of youths could be found in the dry season engaged in such games.

The term *wɛ* in this context refers to the sky, which in Kasena thought is limitless. They view heavenly bodies like the moon, sun, and stars as too distant to be within man's reach. Juxtaposed with this perception of a limitless heaven is the folk conception that with adequate means the sky and the heavens can be reached. These are not novel ideas spawned by the recent attempts to place humans in the heavenly bodies. Kasena mythology asserted the possibility of contact with the heavens. One example is the etiological tale which maintains that in their golden age the sky was near to earth and people cut and cooked it for their meal until one old woman decided to add local salt (potash) to the cooked sky which as a result revolved and withdrew from earth and man altogether. In one riddle, we are told about those cousins aiming and shooting at the sky as they lay on the backs.

The proverb makes the point that it is in order to aim for the sky and even if the ambitious one does not quite attain his or her objective, there still cannot be any shame in that. People should accept challenges even if there is no certainty that success will follow. Shame can only be felt where a person has failed to attain a modest goal, one that others in similar circumstances can easily accomplish.

As another Kasena proverb points out, see # 81 above, there is nothing wrong with making trials or experimentation so long as people are not hurt by it: *Ba ba mage ba ni mo se ba ke ba nia*. No disgrace attaches to failure where a person has set himself a difficult or impossible task.

253.   **Kali-doa mo chɔge kali-kɔgɔ yuu**
It is one bad monkey that brings disgrace upon the monkey troupe

Commentary: Wild monkeys are considered a nuisance among Kasena because of the destruction they wreak on crops cultivated in the bushlands. In fact it appears that the fear of this explains the reluctance of Kasena to cultivate the bushlands outside their settlements. They seemed not to have had any means of controlling these pests outside the application of ritual or magical devices which did not always work. The bad name that monkeys get collectively for destruction of crops is based on the harm that a particular troupe has caused to a particular farmer's crops. In the absence of evidence pointing to the particular animals involved all monkeys get the blame and incur the hostility of all farmers.

The message of the proverb is that when people are associated the opprobrium that results from one individual's doings is attributable to the group to which that individual belongs. Thus it becomes necessary for the group to sanction its members when they are seen to be doing anything that is wrong or unacceptable. A proverb remarks that if a lizard should hide behind a tree both will become targets.

254   **Fone wo nakwala ni ne**
        Fear can be found in the shallows
Commentary: This is a proverb taken from Howell (1994) and seems to be current in the Chiana chiefdom. The proverb is interpreted by Howell to mean that a person cannot always tell where in the river or pool is deep or shallow. These uncertainties therefore imply that a person must take care getting into water. She used this proverb to illustrate Kasena resistance of change in the past. *Naluŋa* is where the water in a river is deep as opposed to the *nakwala* which is shallow. As Kasena live in a dry ecological area many did not in the past learn to swim, except for those who cultivated bush farms and had to cross the bush rivers to get to their farms. The fear of water was therefore genuine. A Kasena proverb maintains that "There is no ladder inside water", *na wo ba jege nateini*. This is to say that a drowning person has nothing to hold onto in order to climb out to safety. If water is not so deep as to submerge a person it is generally, but not always, considered safe to wade in such water.

The proverb is saying that although it might be safe to wade in the *nakwala* shallow water nevertheless there are times when care must be taken. One can imagine the danger posed by floods; the swift currents of a shallow river can drown people who cannot cope with the current. Thus fear attaches to the unknown. The warning is that one should not underestimate potential danger sources, even if they appear to be innocuous. As another proverb remarks, if you underestimate a river, it will catch you (*N ná gwooni buga ka ja-m*).

255   **Ba ná wɔge nu bu wó di se ba ná wɔge bu nu baa di.**
        If they roast mother child would eat but if child were roasted mother would not eat
Commentary: Since cannibalism in the material sense rather than in the spiritual sense of witchcraft practice was beyond the imagination of the Kasena, whose practices and attitudes suggest that there was a considerable fear of the corpse, this proverb would seem to lack a literal base for interpretation. However, roasting here is a metaphor that can be said to represent death and the mortuary practices that are associated with death, such as the performance of the final funeral rites. In the Kasem

language, the final funeral, *lua* is 'burnt' (*fuli*) and this symbolically refers to the destruction of the critical items of personal property belonging to the deceased. In the case of a male, his bow and a token number of arrows are burnt publicly at an occasion which signals taking leave of the deceased. For a woman, it is her special utensils: calabashes, dishes and pots (her *swogo*) which is broken at the cross roads. These are events at which the surviving children, especially the firstborn child, play a critical role. Tradition calls upon the child at this moment to make prestations and utter a farewell pray to the deceased.

The proverb thus refers to the probability of children outliving their parents and celebrating their deceased mother's funeral with as much pomp and pageantry as their circumstances would allow or, in another idiom, "eating the burnt parent". This should involve an element of conspicuous consumption, (*lua dim*, literally, eating the funeral) expected by society. On the other hand, the mother as a parent is expected to mourn the child rather than celebrate a event which should never have occurred, the expectation being that parents will predecease their children.

In its extended meaning, the proverb shows that the parent-child tie is not based on reciprocity and that the parent's commitment to the child is deeper than that of the child to the parent, if the two types of commitment were a matter for comparison. A parent is expected to be willing to do more for a child than a child might be willing to do for the parent. It should be in the nature of the relationship that the parent should readily sacrifice and be willing to go to extra trouble on behalf of the child. In implied reference to this proverb, parents are wont to tell their children, albeit jocularly, to allow them an interim break or to humour their immediate desires in view of the long term inequality of such a relationship. This proverb is customarily quoted to clinch the point.

256.   **Kapaa ná cheiŋi buga nyeŋo ye dwei**
        When the cobra claims the pool the crocodile does not contest
Commentary: Though typically, it is the lion that is regarded as the king of the bush nevertheless there are some folktales in which the cobra is presented as the regal lord of beasts. Its majesty derives from its venomous poison. The masters of the waters are usually the crocodiles and the hippopotamus which though amphibians, spend much of their time in the rivers and pools. The crocodile in particular seems to conduct itself in such a way as to suggest that its is the master of the water environment. It lives off not only the fish in the water but also any livestock found in or near the banks of the rivers and lakes. Even humans who come close to its habitat are not spared. The myth of the crocodile's power is fueled by beliefs that the chief crocodile wears a red fez cap like

a human chief and some myths talk of the dual-headed crocodiles with two heads that strike in all directions. Nevertheless, the belief is that there is another master of the aquatic environment: the cobra which can also live in that environment and that it is only in the absence of the cobra that the crocodile reigns.

The proverbs is stating the point that power is unequally distributed in such a way as to establish an open-ended power hierarchy. Just as in the absence of the more powerful cobra the crocodile might carry on in a manner suggesting that it is the master of the waters, so do powerful individuals sometimes conduct themselves in ways that seem to indicate that they acknowledged no superior force or authority. The proverb is thus a comment and a critique of the use and misuse of power and authority.

This is one of those borderline utterances which may be classified as either a proverb or a saying.

257   **Si to de togo ne**
The pea has dropped into its shell
The Kasena pea is round and seems to fit neatly within its shell which is shaped like the seed. This utterance is not attributed to anyone person in particular nor is it ever attributed or associated with the wisdom of the ancestors. This makes it difficult to classify it as proverb or as a *sinseira*. It is perhaps closer to the *memaŋe* or proverb than to the *sinseira*. It is applied where two events seem to complement each other.

258   **Bobone tɔnno de wo yaga ne**
The skins of kids can also be found in the market place.
Comment: This comes through as a remark or observation and straddles the boundary between proverb and saying. Unlike a true proverb it cannot be attributed to the ancestors or men of old because this is clearly a very recent item. On the other hand, it does not have the true quality of a Kasena saying. It is played neither with the objective of drawing laughter nor is it attributed to any known person.

Traditionally a slaughtered goat was skinned to allow its flesh to be cut up and cooked as meat. The skin was dried in the sun and later worked into a shape suitable for use in the making of products like bags or capes for male use. Goat skins were not commercial items traditionally and they appear to have entered the market only recently with the introduction of abattoirs and the sale of meat in the market place. An inspection of the meat market in the big towns of Navrongo, Paga and Chiana will reveal a display of a variety of skins taken from slaughtered domestic animals. The dried skins are themselves commodities to be purchased by tanners and leather specialists from the area as well as from the neighbouring

Frafra communities that have developed a speciality in tanning.

The proverb's observation is an accurate reflection of the contemporary Kasena market where a variety of animal skins of various sizes and shapes including those for old as well as young animals can, contrary to expectation, be found on display. In other words, it is not only the mature billy goats that are slaughtered but also the kids too. The proverb is directed at youth, who sometimes behave as thought their youthfulness conferred temporary immunity against death. Ultimately, death is no respecter of age.

People must sacrifice to their ancestors and divinities to secure their own lives against calamities and hazards. Tender billy goats (*bebala*) may be more expendable than older ones (*bobɔlɔ*), the former are yet to put on flesh and fat and may do so if spared and if they survive disease. The owner of the tender billy has hopes for it. Thus, it is with misgivings that a man kills his tender goat and he does so because there is no alternative. In a sense, the proverb is also commenting on attitudes to life. It seems to argue that there is no pleasure in the taking of life, even if it is an animal that is being killed, but conditions necessitate killing. Wanton killing is deplored and a normal Kasena family would not slaughter an animal for food. In addition to sacrificed animals the category of livestock that would be killed includes the animal that has been wounded and is not considered likely to live and killing to prepare a meal for a group of important guests.

259.   **Swɛ lwoori bagua**
The ripe shea fruit has preceded the raw shea fruit
Commentary: The sheanut tree, butyrospermum parkii, is a wild fruit tree that plays an important role in the domestic economy of the Kasena-Nankana and related peoples in the savannah regions of Ghana. It produces fruit in May-June just as the food shortages attain their peak. The fruits are green and the ripened fruit (*swɛ*) is sweet and soft to the touch while the unripened fruit (*bagua*) is hard and can sometimes be caustic to the taste. The ripe fruit is expected to fall with a little breeze. The crop is usually harvested by climbing the tree and shaking its boughs to make the ripened fruit detach and fall off. Though there is a greater likelihood that the ripe fruit will yield to wind or the shaking of the tree, experience shows that sometimes the unripened fruit also drops, particularly when the tree is subjected to a violent shake or when the wind is gusty.

The proverb, like # 258 above, comments on the fact that death is no respecter of age as death does not spare children, younger adults or the aged.

260.   **Boŋo kolo ná lɔɔre to mo lɔe kambi**
It is the goat that treads with care that breaks the pots
Commentary: Traditional Kasena kept their livestock within the compound for safety. Within it space was provided in the middle of the compound to serve as the kraal (*nabwoo*). Between the kraal and the dwelling units was a low wall over which the occupants of the compound would climb over to enter the human living areas. Though the low wall or *gengaŋa* was essentially a barrier which was meant to keep the livestock out, goats might sometimes jump over it and enter the dwelling units.

Goats, unlike other domestic livestock are fond of poking their heads into pots and utensils in the hope of finding water or left-over meals. They may enter the living quarters and rummage through the kitchen pots and pans. Occasionally pottery are broken in the process. Not all goats indulge in this but some particular goats develop the habit for invading the living spaces; it is however, tempting to think that the active goat is the culprit all the time. The proverb sets the record straight by pointing out that even the goat which does not appear to exhibit the stereotypical aggressive characteristics might also cause the damage and the damage in this case might be greater as onlookers might watch out for it.

The proverb is cautioning people to beware the hypocrites, the wolves in sheep clothing who profess to be the saints that they are not.

261   **Nɔɔno ná tera sɔŋɔ ne n boŋo lore bebale mo**
The goat belonging to the absentee produces only males
Commentary: People do leave livestock with their kin and friends to breed and care for on their behalf. The absentee owner might show up several years later and seek an account for his investment. There are several reasons for this practice, including the opportunity to have a better breed of males cross one's she-goats, ewes or cows in the expectation that the resultant breed would make an improve the herd. For his labour in caring and breeding the livestock, the care-taker may dispose of whatever milk is produced, in the case of cattle, as well as the meat of the livestock that dies, so long as the skin of the dead animal has been preserved to be exhibited to the owner. The owner of the herd that has come into being might reward the care-taker by gift of a goat or two, if he was pleased with the result. The matter is entirely in his hands to act as he sees fit. The care-taker, for his part, has no legal title to any of the goats in his care or compensation for his labour. Thus, it can happen that a thoughtless herd owner fails to reward or compensate the care-taker.

The proverb observes that human beings being what they are, sometimes the caretaker out of greedy or envy or preempting a raw deal from the herd owner might keep some of the herd for himself with the explanation that the animal left in his care had not been as productive as might have been supposed. He might explain that the litter have tended to die or the mother goat, ewe or cow left in his care produced mainly male issues.

The point of this proverb is that the affairs of the absentee never prosper to the degree that the absentee expected. Either care-takers are negligent or they pull one off on the absentee. A similar saying maintains that "Delegation does not afford absolute satisfaction, it only saves the sender the physical exertion that would have been involved", see # 152 above.

262   **Boŋo keira de wiiru keira maŋe daane**
The cry of the goat and the cry of the hyena have coincided
Commentary: The goat and the hyena are two animals that are often compared and contrasted. The howling of the hyena is a familiar sound to Kasena in former times. Parents and baby-sitters still attempt to reproduce the *buuwuii* cry of the hyena in order to frighten and silence crying children. Hyenas are believed to visit the settlements at night with the expectation of catching a stray goat for supper. The cry of the goat and the howling of the hyena are believed to be different from one another. Where a hyena is a goat has no business being, as a saying suggests: "goats do not attend markets set up by hyenas", see # 198 above. Be that as it may, the unlikely and the unexpected sometimes happen and the proverb is drawing attention to this fact.

In some respects the coincidence of the hyena's howl and the goat's cry would suggest that something serious is amiss, perhaps the hyena is attacking the goat. This is to be expected, but at times it just happens that two events that are usually connected or related just happen to co-occur by accident. This proverb is quoted to draw attention to the concurrence of likely or unlikely events without a causal explanation.

263   **Korekore ba maŋe bɔɔne ne**
Korekore does not remain in the hole
Commentary: The ideophone, *korekore* is a true onomatopoeia in that it echoes dry sound such as will be heard if dry leaves were disturbed. The ideophone is synonymous with *sogesoge*. For every case where such a sound is heard, it can be assumed that there is a cause since the sound is the result of some disturbance. It is presumed that to be curious is natural and those who notice the *korekore* sound would wish to know what caused it. In the past safety might depend on such knowledge. Dangerous animals and reptiles or even one's enemies may be in hiding nearby and it might be that the sound *korekore* is precursor to an attack. On the other hand, the sound in question could be caused by game, a small mammal that would furnish protein.

The statement of the proverb implies that when the strange sound, *korekore* is heard it suggests that the thing causing that noise has bestirred itself and must be about to leave its hole. The best thing to do then would be to exercise patience and wait for the outcome. At least the observer would then be prepared for the eventualities: attack or flight, as the case might be. The impatient individual, especially a naive child, might be inclined to thrust his hand into the hole to find out what is there. It would be foolish to assume that the creature is a harmless rat or other mammal since the creature could just as well be a dangerous snake or reptile in which case it would be unwise to thrust one's hand into the hole in the hope of catching the creature.

264. **Dedɛɛro chene wae vwio**
The arrow of the powerful prevails against the wind
Commentary: The concept of power is synonymous. Taken from the literal perspective, the *dedɛɛro* in this context refers to the man who is endowed with great physical strength. Thus the class of *dedɛɛro* includes the chiefs, the clan-settlement elders and the wealthy. It is not to be understood in the absolute sense since inequalities exist also between individuals as occupants of statuses in the community. Power can be democratic.

The proverb is remarking that the individual who is physically strong is able to shoot the arrow further than weaker men. The power behind his arrow is such that it will not be deflected by the wind and will achieve greater penetration.

The point behind the proverb is that people are not equal and their capabilities too differ. Just as the force of the wind is expected to deflect arrows but certain arrows may still resist it, so do exceptions occur in social relations. The rules and norms of society do not therefore have the same degree of compulsion on all. Some members, because of their relative privileged position, may be exceptions to the rule. It is in this respect that this proverb is quoted to show that inequalities exist in life.

265. **Jwoŋi n pa a nu ba chamma**
Take it for mother is not a difficult task
A thing becomes difficult because it is hard to accomplish, is a source of personal inconvenience to those involved, especially the third party or the intermediary who becomes the messenger. Naturally, people like to receive gifts, especially those that do not place irksome obligations but sometimes what is being conveyed has a sting in its tail. The proverb is referring to the intermediary or the second person. The argument is that the go-between or the intermediary is not to blame when things go wrong.

The extent of his or her culpability is limited to his or her mediatory or messengerial. He or she cannot be responsible for the content of the load that he or she carries to another, the third person.

The phrase *a nu*, in this context, can refer to any woman in *loco parentis*. It can be the mother of the first or second person. This may be the biological mother, the husband's mother, or the step-mother. The 'mother' would usually live in the same compound as the 'son'. Though a woman is not obliged to cook for her married sons the latter's wives are required to send a plate or bowl of food to the mother-in-law whenever they cook. Thus people are expected to maintain daily contact with their mothers. It is for this reason that taking a message on behalf of the mother is not, from the proverb's point of view, a difficult task.

The proverb is played when it becomes necessary for person being requested to take the message to show the person giving the message that he or she cannot be responsible for the contents of the message and their effect on the ultimate recipient and or the giver himself or herself. The messenger, in this case, suspects that the message being entrusted to him or her is not one that would be well received.

266.   **N ná tei yi, n ba de fula**
If you own the eye, you cannot blow on it
Commentary: Put differently, this proverb is saying that a person who finds that a speck of dust or extraneous substance has dropped in his or her eye cannot extract the offending object by blowing on his own eye. The affected can only appeal to others for assistance in the removal of the object.

The point of the proverb is that no one is an island. Though self interest may compel those who suffer to exert themselves to seek relief, nevertheless, there are those cases where the healer's art is ineffective where his own ailments are at issue. A similar point is contained in the riddle which wonders how it is that the son of the soothsayer should surfer death despite the fact that the rest of society acknowledges its dependence on the soothsayer for its material and spiritual well-being: **Voro na voa, o bu to we bε.** In his hour of need, the soothsayer must seek the assistance of a colleague soothsayer.

CHAPTER FOUR

Interpretation of the Sinseira (Sayings)

Introduction:

The approached adopted above in Chapter Three for the interpretation of the proverb, *faŋatu memaŋe*, will be employed here too for the interpretation of the *sinseira* (singular) and *sinseiri* (plural), the catchy sayings of the Kasena which provoke for them so much laughter. As we have suggested above, the borderline between the two genres is not a sharply defined one. This is also illustrated by the use of the term *sinseira* to describe the proverb. See, for example, Wedjong (1969). Many of the items presented in that publication under the name of *sinseiri* are in fact proverbs. As in chapter three, the items presented here are not listed in any order of priority nor is any criterion used to determine which items come first or last. If anything, it is the order in which the items were collected that accounts for the order of discussion.

1   **Zem mo zem nabara wiiru**
    Today is today, the river hyena
    The hyena remarks that today is his day of reckoning.
    Commentary: This is a remark attributed to a hapless hyena bemoaning its bad luck when confronted on its journey home, to the wilderness, by a flooded river. It must brave the floods or risk being discovered and killed in the day time.
    The hyena is one of the most despised of wild animals, among Kasena. In folk-tales, it takes the butt end of the jokes. It is not only greedy but stupid and is easily outwitted by the trickster. Nevertheless, it is one of the few animals that is classified grammatically into the human nominal

gender of *wom* and *bam*; see Awedoba (1997) for a discussion of the meaning of genders in the Kasem language. Its gender classification may seem rather unusual. One explanation for its inclusion in the human gender may perhaps be due to the fact that in some ways it exhibits human qualities. Certain cases of mental illness are attributable to encounters with the hyena and can only be treated traditionally by ritual means, often necessitating initiation into the soothsayer's cult and the making of a shrine dedicated to the spirit of the hyena. Doubtless to say that unlike most other mammals that are considered good to eat, the hyena is not usually regarded as good enough and would not be killed for its meat.

Though scavengers, hyenas were wont to visit human settlements in search of food. They would come at night to take smaller livestock when most people would have retired and gone to asleep. As the wild bush where the hyena lives is often separated from the settlement by a river, its journey home meant crossing a stream or river at fordable points or where the river stretch was dry. After its hunt it must however return to the bush land before the break of day to avoid detection and certain death. An unlucky hyena might arrive at the banks of the river to find that its channel is swollen and the way home is barred. Then it would be out of luck unless it was able to find a hiding place. Kasena must have come across many such stranded hyena in the past to motivate the saying.

This saying is used to capture the condition of helplessness in which a person who never suspected trouble finds himself or herself. Life is a gamble and people must take reasonable risks, like the hyena which finds it necessary to visit human settlements to seek food when life in the wild yields inadequate support. Experience has taught the hyena that it is fairly safe to hunt around villages close to the bushlands. Nevertheless there is the occasional hazard that risk takers are prone to. As Ghanaians are wont to say in Pidgin English, *"every day fo tiefman and one day fo masta"* (The thief may be in luck most of the time but there is the one occasion when the property owner too is in luck).

2.   **A pa se ko taa ye-m se n vo Bola se-m ba?**
     Wish it were you having to go to Bolgatanga and return.
Commentary: "Bola" is the Kasem version of the place name Bolgatanga, the administrative capital of the Upper East Region which is about 18 miles southeast of Navrongo town.

Some mischievous driver of a commercial vehicle once played a prank on the person to whom this statement is attributed. As he mounted a vehicle to clean it for a pittance its driver took off for Bolgatanga where he eventually deposited the author of the statement who then had to make the return journey on foot as he had not a penny on his person. The above statement was first uttered on its originator's return to Navrongo, when some acquaintance jokingly enquired about the journey to Bolgatanga. If we may paraphase this statement, we could put it thus: "Don't ask me about the experience; if you had to go all the way from Navrongo to Bolgatanga and then have to walk back, you would not find it much fun."

His statement has become a catchy phrase for a number reasons, especially as it evoked the ridiculousness of the situation and at the same time sympathy for the author's plight. After all he was made to suffer for no other crime on his part than that he mounted a commercial vehicle without its driver's permission. On the other hand, at the time of the event, Bolgatanga was only 30 minutes away and it cost only one shilling and six pence in lorry fare, which was within the means of the average person.

The author of the saying in question lived off the market in Navrongo. He did not farm for himself like most self respecting people. Rather, he would perform odd jobs for the drivers of the commercial vehicles that carried passengers and freight between Bolgatanga and Navrongo, including sweeping the floor of the vehicles and helping to load and unload them. Needless to say this behaviour did not always earn respect for those who would rather live off the market in this way, especially if they were not too young for this kind of adventurous life. The statement was probably first uttered in the early 1960s. The author of the statement to most Kasena would seem to be no more than a tramp. Today, the "Bori" boys are a powerfully organised group with political clout to boost.

An 18 mile walk in the 1950s and early 1960s was not an extraordinary event. It was not unusual in those days to see Mossi traders and their donkey caravans walking through Navrongo down to Kumasi in southern Ghana, covering a distance of over 600 miles in the process. However, for many traditional Kasena in those days, Bolgatanga was still a foreign place. The local Frafra people of Bolgatanga belong to a different ethnic group and speak a language which is not only different from Kasem, the main language of Navrongo, but lacks mutual intelligibility with it. Although the people of Navrongo have social relations with the neighbouring Nankane-speaking people whose language is similar to Frafra, very few social ties have knit Navrongo and Bolgatanga until recently. Before pax Britannica, people rarely ventured outside their chiefdoms. Even the construction of a motorable road and the availability of public motorized transport does not date beyond the 1940s. Consequently, Bolgatanga has remained a foreign place to most Navrongo people until recently. It was an adventure for the individual to whom the remark attributed.

3.   **Deeim konto, dɔɔm konto, Amena sɔŋɔ dae baŋa**
     Last year it was like this, this year no difference. Why, there stands
     Amena's compound!

Commentary: The statement may be paraphrased thus: "I was caught in
this mishap last year and now the same is happening to me. I shall ensure
that the misfortune does not recur this time. After all, Amena's compound
is not too far off for me to seek refuge there". It is recounted that the
author of the statement, a man from the Chiana chiefdom which lies about
15 miles to the west of Navrongo, frequently went out early at dawn to
fetch ripened sheanut fruits that would have dropped from the trees
throughout the night. One day, as he went from tree to tree he was
attacked by a hyena, which might have perhaps mistaken the originator of
the statement, as he bent over to collect fruit, for an animal and pounced
on him. He fought off the hyena but not after it had inflicted wounds on
him. Sometime later, he was out at night when he heard the howling of a
hyena nearby. He immediately made for the nearest compound where he
explained his predicament, clinching it with the memorable phrase in
question, to his listeners amusement.

   Deeim stands for last year or last season and *dɔɔm* for the current
season or year. It would seem that traditionally a season was counted as
a year, *bene*, among Kasena. The wet season, *yadɛ* and the dry season,
tepwoŋa, (lit. the white earth) are contrasted in Kasena thought such that
the earth is said "to enter", as the wet season succeeds the dry which in
turn is said "to emerge" as the wet season sets in. In line with the counting
of seasons as years, traditional people estimate their ages by seasons so
that a 50 year old might describe himself or herself as 100 years old, as
they sometimes do when called upon at modern courts to disclose their
ages. Occasionally, *deeim* might stand for the indefinite past while *dɔɔm*
stands for the immediate past or the current moment.

   The popularity of the statement in question derives its aesthetic quality
and appeal yet again from the plight of its author. There is sympathy for
the originator who was not only once attacked by the hyenas but was
nearly attacked again, events of rare occurrence, since hyenas are not
believed to attack able bodied people. However, side by side with the
sympathy felt is the implied criticism of a man who acts out of character.
While women are traditionally expected to forage for shea nuts, the main
source of the domestic supply of butter, it is unbecoming for a man to go
foraging for fruits before day break.

   This saying has over the years become more or less like a proverb as it
is quoted to illustrate that a person in his senses takes precautions to
ensure that a previous misfortune does not afflict him or her in the same
way. In other words, once bitten twice shy or as Kasena will put it, *naao*

ná jaane n kwo, n ná nɛ ko beinnu n duri mo (if a bull has killed your father you run when you see its faeces), see proverb # 130 above.

4. Pedea, Angola
Courage, as Angola would have it

Commentary: This is a popular saying whose history is for the moment unknown to this investigator but we can imagine the circumstances in which it was popularised. Its origin is attributed to a man called Angola who may have uttered this single word in his moment of trial. The word *pedea* (courage) is an abstract noun derived from the words *puga*, "stomach" and the adjective, *-deɔ*, "strong". The word means courage, determination or endurance. Its synonym is *wodeɔ* which has a similar derivational structure: *wo*, "stomach" and *-deɔ*. This goes to illustrate the perception of the stomach as the seat of courage.

These then are words of self encourage and fortification for a man who may have been at his wits end.

5. Beilim we siu ba gwoona
The Mossiman says you can't underestimate a respite

Commentary: This saying is clearly one of those that may pass for either a saying or a proverb and can and often is used as the latter.

The word *beilim*, which is derived by elipsis from *beillu*, is the Kasem word for Mossi person or any native speaker of the Moore language. Members of this large ethnic group have also been known as *gwala*, a term which also means slave raider. Although the archetypal slavers for the Kasena-Nankana were the Zamberma, a band of free booters described by Holden (1965) as having come originally from Niger, and their Kasen-fra allies who devastated the societies of the upper east and the Sisala district of the Upper West, Mossi princes and their armies seem to have raided peoples like the Kasena to the south of Moshie country long before the Zamberma raids in the dying days of the 19th century, just before the British made their presence felt in this area.

Mossi were known not only for their slave raiding activities but also for their trade. They sent down caravans to international markets like Salaga and Kimtampo where they exchanged Savannah products for kola nuts and other forest products. Peoples like the Kasena through whose territories the caravans had to pass sometimes played host to them but they were not above treating Moshie traders as fair game and robbing caravans. This kind of "disruptive" behaviour by the so called acephalous peoples of the Voltaic zone attracted the attention of the British who had a keen interest in the trade and led first to reprisal attacks and then to the stationing of a post in Navrongo in 1906 to check the predatory activities of the people.

The saying in question is not attributed to a particular Mossiman; there is no special basis for even saying that any Mossi man actually uttered this statement. Assuming that historically a certain Mossi did make this remark, as a non-Kasena there would still be no need to identify particular Mossi by name, unless such a person had been a long term residents in the area where the saying is current. It is plausible to assume that the statement is based on an observation of the habits of Mossi traders who were only too ready to rest where necessary and also to accept whatever hospitality is offered by strangers, the local people. This behaviour is contrary to conventional Kasena attitudes which incline towards distrust for aliens and alien lands, which to this day are still referred to collectively as Gɔlɔ.

The saying seems to exhibit a realisation that a tired person in need of rest must take it wherever and whenever the opportunity presents. In later years when conditions in the northern parts of Ghana stabilised after the British occupation of the area some enterprising Kasena men would join Mossi caravans on their way to southern Ghanaian markets where they would sell livestock.

6. **N ná jaane ŋweeno n tula ni o we omo ya maa vei Kayaa yaga mo**
    If you catch a thief trying to climb down your granary he will say he was on his way to Kayaa market

Commentary: The Kasena granary is a structure shaped like a cone, cleft at the top narrow edge. It is usually located in the enclosed inner space within the compound homestead which serves as a kraal for the domestic livestock. Standing about six high a wooden ladder is necessary if a person is to get into it. The *tula* (granary) serves as the food store where the main staples, usually millet, are stored for the season. Although the cultivation of millet is a joint undertaking which involves the collaboration of all able-bodied members of the domestic group, the male head of the group owns the granary. He alone may enter the granary to fetch grain for the women to cook. Women are not usually allowed to descend the granary, not even if they were household heads. A man's first born son is forbidden to look inside the granary of the father until his funeral rites have been fully carried out and succession has taken place. One of the symbolic rites of a father's final funeral celebration involves the first born son taking grain from his deceased father's granary. Until then only the deceased's most junior son might take grain from the granary. He enjoys this right as the proxy of the deceased.

It is not expected that a thief would steal grain from another's granary in view of the ritual restrictions and sanctions associated with a person's granary, where his soul is even believed to rest during his life time. A man's junior sons, more than anybody else, might possibly contemplate such a thing.

There is clearly no relationship between going to Kayaa market and getting into the granary. It therefore becomes absurd to give former as explanation for latter. The point of the saying is that there can be no excuse for attempting to steal grain from the barn. However, if a thief were to be caught in that act, he would nevertheless have an explanation as all thieves do, no matter how far fetched or preposterous such an explanation or excuse might sound. The point is to say something rather than admit to such an act against the father.

It seems that this would be a saying more common in Paga, the border chiefdom, than in the chiefdoms further south. Kayaa is a small Kasena chiefdom in present day Burkina Faso. It is not noted for its market which as small chiefdoms go cannot be expected to have an exciting market. Traditional rural Kasena markets held in the evenings. This was convenient for the villagers as it did not interrupt farming and other chores. Visiting a market of this kind cannot therefore serve as a very unsatisfactory excuse for ones crimes or lapses.

7. **Boboŋa biseim**
   Greetings made in the imagination

Commentary: *Biseim*, in the Kasem language refers to greetings offered by a visitor. It is customary for the person who is visiting another compound, one that is different from his or her own, even if it is within the same village, to utter the word "*biseim*" on getting to the yard of the compound. The in-mates or anybody who happen to be around are expected to accept the greeting by uttering the reply "*dé zaanem*" in the singular, or "*dé zaaba*" in the plural (we welcome you). The word *biseim* may also be used to mean something like "excuse me". This second usage may feature in the context where a household member enters the room in which visitors are made welcome. In this case it serves to notify the guest and to apologize for the intrusion on the guest's privacy.

Biseim implies an encounter between two parties in which the "addressor" is the arriving party. The saying draws attention to the fact that a person can only proffer compliments of the *biseim* type to another by first making a visit to that person's home or where the interlocutor happens to be located. Two people who live in the same house do not normally greet each other by proffering *biseim*. As *biseim* is only meaningful when associated with outward behaviour, therefore, *biseim* cannot derive from intentions alone. The value of *biseim* lies in the act of visiting which carries considerable weight among Kasena people, as it is a display of concern for the party being visited. This theme of the visitor placing the visited in his debt reverberates in other spheres of their social etiquette and in their concepts. The social capital generated also becomes the basis for making requests, as *wara*, (greetings) and *peiga* (asking about a person's health) exemplify. *Wɛ warem* (lit. Greeting God) is a religious act based on greeting God; request for labour takes the form of visiting the homes and "greeting" the individuals whose labour is being requested as in the concept of *vala warem*. The same can be said of the procedures for seeking curative help or *liri warem* (lit. greeting the divinity behind the medicine or its agent, the healer). Courtesy visits to in-laws, condolence with the bereaved or display of sympathy and solidarity are expressed in the idiom of *peiga daanem* (lit. Doing the sleep).

A behaviour is described as **Boboŋa biseim**, (Greeting made in the imagination) when intentions are not backed by deeds or action or when actions are not motivated by genuine interest in manifest objectives. It serves therefore as criticism of half-hearted attempts at doing good.

8. **Lam we gwoŋo ne, Asutaane**
   Beauty is in the grave

Commentary: The Kasem word *yibeeili* means grave or tomb. Although this is not strictly a taboo term several euphemisms nevertheless exist for it which include *bɔɔne* (hole) and *gwoŋo* (a hole or depression). Asutaane is an individual noted for this remark. He is critical of the excessive concern that some people exhibit for facial appearance or the beauty of the human body. His point is that there is more to beauty than external appearance. The universal preoccupation with physical appearance has the result that people seem not to realise that death will come to all and sundry one day and then what was once perceived as aesthetically pleasing would be reduced to rot. It is to say that death is the ultimate leveler leveling the hierarchies that man establishes. A beautiful person will die and be buried and like all corpses the forces of nature will take over and reduce beauty and ugliness, to the base material from which all human beings were made. What then is the use and the fuss!

There is perhaps a strain of Christian philosophy here, and Asutaane was a catholic. Nevertheless, it must be remarked that the traditional Kasena burial practice itself insists on leveling. The burial outfit is more or less standard, just as the construction of the grave must conform with the traditional norm. A loin cloth to girt a man's private parts and a girdle for a woman is more or less sufficient. The ancestors, it is believed are resentful of changes to burial norms.

There is a myth that a person of slave origin was once buried together with his bow and arrow. This was new, as the weapons are usually heirlooms. In the case of the slave, it was said that he had no one to inherit his property so it was considered appropriate that he should take along with him his weapons, the symbol of his manhood. But the ancestors visited calamity on the living for the violation of custom. From the Kasena point of view, there is equality of all people in their mortuary practices.

The comment is frequently heard about the chief's burial which does not reflect his superior position in life. To date, coffins and fanciful outfits for the deceased are disallowed. The burial specialists, it has been said, are in the habit of removing superfluous items from corpses before burial.

9. **Wɔ'm gara; n na gara, pa bi**
    Who is better; if you are, donate a penny
Commentary: This is a call associated with a certain drunk who was wont to shout as he returned home on market days in his drunken mood. The crux of the statement is that this is an egalitarian society where everybody is more or less in the same economic situation. The initiator makes his point by challenging those who deny his statement to come over and prove him wrong by making a monetary exhibition of their affluence. Here, *bi* means penny, a unit of British currency, and at the time that this statement was first uttered in the 1950s a penny had value. As a currency term, *bi* derived its meaning from the numeral 'hundred' which refers to the exchange value of a hundred cowrie shells against the West Africa British penny, a considerable sum of money in former times.

Kasena retained the currency term *bi* which came to represent the pesewa coin, which has since been demonetized as an effective currency unit in Ghana. *Bi* still remains in the minds of Kasena as a measure of worth. A poor person is described as one who does not have *bi*.

10. **Feila kam ta wo tage wolɔŋɔ**
    The Whiteman is yet to speak an unpleasant word
Commentary: The term *feila* may once have referred to a person of *fulani* extraction. The Fulani or Peul are a nomadic people found through the West African Sahel, they are noted for physical features that look somewhat Caucasian. The prevalence of the term *feila* would suggest that Kasena familiarity with the *fulani* predates the era of colonisation.

In this saying, *feila* may describe the whiteman or his agent. To date there is a distinction between the 'black whiteman' and the European or the 'white whiteman'. A person holding a position of high authority in the civil service or parastatals who is not known to be a member of any of the ethnic groups in the Upper regions may still be referred to as a 'Black *feila*" by local Kasena, even today.

This statement takes us back down memory lane to the early days of the encounter with colonial authority. The joke in this statement concerns a man who did not understand sufficient English but nevertheless came forward as an interpreter for a work master who did not understand Kasem. The latter communicated with the Kasena workers engaged for the job through the volunteer interpreter who could not and did not relay the message to the workers. When he was asked what the master wished done, he had replied thus: *Feila kam ta wo tage wolɔŋɔ* (Whiteman has not spoken an unpleasant word). As the work master had failed to get his instructions through to the workers he vented his frustration by slapping the poor interpreter, who then turned to the workers and remarked: *feila kam laam tage wolɔŋɔ* (now, you see, the Whiteman has said an unpleasant word).

11. **Didwonkwogo yage ne, a yage a nɔne dem; nam done se-a si, a done nanjoa kam**
    Let me go, Spider! How can I let go of my meat. Then get on with it, eat me! How can I eat a fly!
Commentary: The statement is certainly based on an observation of the hunting style of the spider. It takes hold of a fly trapped in its web by the limb and holds tight till the struggling fly dies. Kasena who practiced traditionally mixed agriculture, which combined crop farming and animal husbandry also engaged in hunting, especially in the dry season. They used clubs, bows and arrows, catapults and occasionally spears. They also set traps for wild game. Often their dogs helped to run down wounded game which they would kill instantly. They did not keep wild game as pets and there was no interest in preserving game, although it was not every wild animal that could be killed since some were protected by ritual and totemic beliefs.

Outside this category were the animals that people considered as too despicable to eat, such as the hyena and the vulture. These were not hunted unless they were perceived, as in the case of the hyena, to be a nuisance. Though the winged termites (*kwonnu* in Kasem) are desirable to eat, the house fly remains the archetypal despicable creature. Food could be considered inedible if a fly happens to drop into it. This is because of its unhealthy habits, the same reasons why the scavenging hyena and the vulture are not considered as food.

The spider is remarkable for eating flies. However, its failure to eat up its victim instantly suggests that it is faced with a dilemma: To eat the inedible or to let go of a meal.

12. **"Tɛgɛɔ koro mo tigi tento puu"; konkompwoŋo de ko keira**
Here lies the pile of feathers once belonging to I-take-no-advice
Commentary: Although the dove is in no way comparable to the parrot in
its articulatory abilities, it was credited with pseudo-speech qualities. Its
cry is believed to indicate the time of day. Traditional Kasena believed
that its cry at mid day indicated that it was noon. The articulatory potential
of the dove is further suggested by the following. In an encounter between
the "white" dove and the "red" dove, the Red which is more difficult to
kill boasts: "I am more clever than White dove" and White dove,
counters: "How about your theft of "dawadawa" cheese".

This statement of the saying we are discussing here is presented as
mimicry of the cry of the white dove as it supposedly mourns the fate of
it slain young ones. The white dove is hunted by children in the month of
June when their numbers seem to increase, with the increase in food
supply. Children also like to rob dove nests of eggs and their young
dovelings. In the lament, mother dove is depicted in this statement as
saying she had warned her young against predators by telling them to keep
a low profile. The young would however draw attention to themselves
thus leading to their being killed. When will the young ever learn, the
dove seems to say. Unlike the spider which appears to hang on to an
unsavoury meal, the feathers of the slain bird are plucked there and then,
to its mother's anguish. The mother dove on its return sees the
unmistakable signs and laments the unwillingness of young to heed the
advice of their elders.
This saying has obvious proverb quality.

13. **Feila chulu gwaleyara jeŋa swɛ**
The Whiteman's taboo, the Slave raider's bracelet
Commentary: The source of this staying is obscure but it appears to date
back to the last decade of the nineteenth century, the days of conflict and
instability precipitated by the slave raids. The *gwaleyara*, is definitely a
slaver. The *yarse*, are a people of Mande origin whose communities since
colonial times have been dispersed all over the Upper East Region and
perhaps in the Upper West. They are better known as traders and today
many of them have more or less been absorbed into local communities,
although their adherence to Islam often sets them apart from local people.
Some of the *yarse* seem to have teamed up with the Zamberma slave
raiders to capture slaves from among the local acephalous communities.
The *swɛ* is an ornament made out of ivory which was worn on the arm.
The *swɛ* and the *gungwolo* which was a broad rectangular shaped piece
with a hole in the middle for the wearer's arm is not only bigger but more
expensive. The two items are known collectively as *tuu yeili* (elephant

tusk). The swɛ had a cheaper equivalent (*piu*) hewn from a granite rock. Either sex could wear these ornaments but they were more often found on women. Kasena estimations suggested that an ivory bangle could in the past have cost the equivalent of a cow and in former times a person exhibited his wealth by buying such ornaments for his wives.

It is possible that while for women ivory and stone bracelets were worn for their aesthetic value men might have fortified them for magical use. The statement cited above suggests that the colonialists associated the wearing of these armlets with magical malpractice on the part of the wearer and therefore resented such people, especially where the wearer was noted for slave dealing.

14. Tɔn-zwona mo ba daare se tio wo di
The skin may not remain but the treetop will be attained

Commentary: These are the words of an inexperienced climber determined to reach the tree top regardless of what it takes.

The human skin, regardless of skin colour pigmentation, is referred to as *tɔn-zwona*, the black skin, perhaps because it is felt that the skin imparts to people of African descent or the black person (*nabin-zwona*) the dark pigmentation. When that skin is removed, the flesh is not dark.

Tree climbing is a favourite past-time with children here, as in other many cultures, but adults do climb trees too when it becomes necessary to do so. The technique usually employed involves putting the arms around the trunk of the tree; care is taken not to lacerate the skin in the process. The climber pulls himself or herself up the tree with the help of the arms and the feet as they secure a firm hold on the trunk. For the inexperienced climber, tree climbing is not without tears. The skin on the abdomen may be bruised in the course of climbing a tree with a rough trunk when the abdomen rubs against it. It may pain the climber but a determined child persists.

It is accepted that children say things that make adults laugh, however, these are not the stock from which sayings of the types (*sinseiri*) discussed here are made. The above saying thus becomes interesting coming from an adult who should know better. An adult would not be expected to exhibit such determination where a trivial pursuit such as tree climbing is concerned.

15. N ná jege wiiru bokɔ n da-n ba kua kua
Does it mean that if you are the hyena's son-in-law you should not touch a bone?

Commentary: In many African cultures people enjoy eating bones, if not as much as they do the flesh. Bones sometimes contain marrow and that is nice to eat. Softer bones are chewed. In any case, the bits of flesh that remain stuck to the bone are extracted before the hard bone is discarded The phrase *ku kua* refers to the attempts at removing these bits of flesh from bones.

The hyena is noted for its voracious appetite for food in general and meat in particular. This stereotype of the scavenger is most clearly depicted in Kasena folktales featuring the hyena.

The wife's parents are often viewed as making direct or covert demands on their son-in-law, some of which are not justified. Many a son-in-law and his family are inclined to accede to these demands for fear that the wife's parents might withdraw their daughter. In the context of a meager bridewealth, a rapacious father-in-law had nothing to lose by withdrawing his daughter while a husband had everything to lose if the father-in-law should take such action. For one thing, the domestic economy of the couple which rested on a division of labour on the basis of age and sex, as Naden and Naden (1991) demonstrate for the Mamprusi of the Northern Region of Ghana, would collapse. The demands of the wife's parents come in the form of a request for labour on their farms for which the son-in-law mobilises his village mates and friends to go over and spend a couple of days hoeing up the farms. Kasena expectation is that for the duration of their stay at the affinal community, the visitors should be well entertained and on their departure a gift-making ceremony should be held at which members of the affinal village might renew friendly ties and establish new friendships with the visitors, thereby, cementing inter-village relations.

These services and extra demands can be described as contingent marriage prestations, in the light of Mayer Fortes (1961) classification of marriage prestations. They are contingent in that they not strictly compulsory. They are not like the *gwoŋna* rites where some livestock would be slaughtered for the visiting wife-giver group. In the case of the latter, the wife's family or their representatives are usually invited down for the prestatory performances, although in some sections of the Kasena group, a newly taken wife's "brothers" might descend unannounced on the husband's family and demand a roasted fowl.

Clearly, these sundry demands made by wife-givers, especially for meat, would suggest a comparison to the greedy attitude of the hyena. Kasena can at times be heard to comment that wife-givers are greedy by nature. There is thus concern about the lack of reasonable limits to these affinal demands and the consequent debasement of wife-givers. It is expected that the circumstances of the sons-in-law should be taken into account when making demands on them. The ideal norms regulating Kasena marriage practice do allow for concessions which put a human face to the demands and exactions of wife-givers and in-laws.

What we have here is a statement that may well have been derived from a folktale but which would pass also for a proverb. It is saying that although the hyena may love bones, it cannot decree that its son- in-law should turn over every bone. In the same vein, the proverb's point is that our cravings, no matter how strong, should not make us unreasonable and unjust to others who may happen to be in our power.

16. **Ka kare ka di, ka kare ka di zem da-n di**
   It roves about searching for food, it roves about searching for food, serves you right, let's see you eat today

Commentary: This is a verbalisation of the drumbeat performed by a deceased woman's kin as they return from her preliminary funeral rites held at her husband's village. Kasena funeral rites which are held customarily in the latter part of the dry season are very often delayed for a period ranging from a year to an indefinite period. The celebrations are organised in at least two sequences, the *yibeeila zworim* (lit. the blackening of the graves) and the *lua fulim* (lit. the burning of the funeral). It is customary that the deceased woman's kin pay a formal visit to mourn her demise before the funeral rites can begin. This visit involves a turn out of her agnatic village people who come with drummers to do their "sister" honour. The drum music in question is heard as the affinal party returns home in the evening after they have been received and regaled by the deceased woman's husband's people. The beat is characteristic and unmistakable.

The drumbeat in question may not have been intended originally to utter the statement now attributed to it. In any case, drum language was not developed among the Kasena to the extent that we find among the Ashanti. A drum beat might serve to arrest attention in preparation for an announcement but rarely is the beat itself a surrogate language with extensive communicative value. It can therefore be concluded that the words that are attributed to this beat have been put together by listeners in much the same way that the cry of a dove has words matched to it, as we saw above in Saying # 12. This is particularly so given that the words are not in praise of the deceased but a critical comment on exogamous marriage and its unstable character which compels a woman because of her sex to hop from community to community, trying to make a living and a home with strangers.

The drum music may be in honour of the lost woman but the words associated describe her as one who, like a rolling stone must seek her livelihood away from home. It furthermore calls into question the behaviour of women who cannot stay with one husband for life but must break off one marriage only to enter another. Though this representation of the unstable behaviour of women is not necessarily the norm, nevertheless most men and women enter into trial marriages early in life before they eventually settle down with one spouse. There is the extreme case of the woman who rarely remains with one husband for long and its is perhaps this type of wife who is foremost in the mind of the originator of the saying whose identity remains a question. The unstable woman who throughout life has tantalized men is being tauntingly told that death has put all that gambolling to an end.

17. **Wɔ mo go ye o wo pwoni?**
Who killed but failed to skin the game?
Commentary: The saying has no author, which suggests its antiquity. However, it seems more like a saying than a proverb and for that reason belongs more in this chapter. It is the kind of utterance for which it would be out of question to assign authorship to the ancestors collectively, as one would in the case of a true Kasena proverb. Put differently, this item is saying that nobody kills game and then walks away without bothering to skin the game in preparation for the pot.

The saying is merely pointing out a fact: i.e. that it is hard to kill but easier to skin the slain animal for the pot. Hunting with very simple instruments like bows and arrows or throwing sticks, game animals were hard to kill. However, by the age of ten most traditional Kasena boys would have learnt how to skin an animal using a razor or failing that with a sharp-edge stone flint (*kandɔ-fela*), a useful tool in the past. Women did not engage in hunting neither did they learn to skin a slaughtered animal. As one Kasena proverb has it, a woman does not kill a python and cut its head. It is assumed that if a man had the courage to slaughter one of his livestock he would not be disinclined to having its meat prepared for consumption.

The point of the saying is that it is easier in life to reap or harvest than to plant and sow , just as investments are generally difficult and hard to make although rewards are sweet. This is illustrated by the fact that it would be surprising to find a case where an animal has been killed but where the killer lacked the means or the will to skin the animal for cooking. There are however, unusual cases where the victim used in a sacrificial offering cannot be taken as food by the sacrificers. Generally, consumption of value is easy than production of value.

18. **Nifa nifa naanye. A nakɔ wo Pendaa ne.**
Right is right. My sister is wedded to a Pendaa man.
Commentary: This saying whose authorship is unknown originated in

around 1974 when the Supreme Military Council regime had decided that the country should go metric. Drivers were to drive on the right-hand side of the road as opposed to driving on the left as had been the case previously. The educational messages that were broadcast over Radio and TV in those days carried this message. *Nifa nifa naanye*, in the Twi language, meant "Right is right". Twi is the most widely spoken Ghanaian language however, it is not understood by every Ghanaian, especially those in the northern parts of the country where the local languages belong to a different family (Gur family of languages) which is in no way intelligible with Twi. Kasena listeners to radio who kept hearing this phrase reinterpreted it in their own language by assigning meanings to it which were far fetched from the original message. The Kasem phrase *A nakɔ wo Pendaa ne* is made to stand side by side with the radio message because it rhymes tonally with the Twi message. Pendaa is a Kasena chiefdom now in Burkina Faso.

19. Boŋo ba di sabare, Wagadogo chɔge logo

A goat does not eat thorns, Ouagadougou has spoilt the world.
Commentary: We have in this utterance lexical items that can be found in any Kasena dictionary but which when strung together in the above utterance seem not to have much meaning to the casual observer. Above we have two clauses standing side by side but apparently, not relating semantically.

Item # 19 above like item # 18 is a set of words that are attached to an utterance that is in a different language. 19 is based on a song with a catchy tune by the Ivorian musician, Alpha Blonde. Nonsense it may seem but the question still has to be asked why this particular set of words and the juxtaposition of the two clauses.

To illiterate Ghanaian Kasena, Ouagadougou represents Franco-phone West Africa and Alpha Blonde singing in his indigenous Ivorian tongue would seem like a Burkina Faso or a Ouagadougou person, the two being synonymous. Goats, like all other local domestic animals, feed on grass and the leaves of plants and this includes the leaves of the acacia Albida tree common in the Sudan savannah of the Upper East. This is a thorny plant which is in leaf in the dry season when grass is nonexistent. Domestic livestock are nevertheless able to remove the leaves from its thorny boughs and in this respect, domestic livestock are both like and unlike human beings, whom Kasena say do not eat grass just as livestock do not feed on thorns. The staements *Nabiinu ba di gaao* (A person does not eat grass) and *Nabiinu baa di gaao* (A person will not eat grass) are common statements that will be heard in times of adversity and famine. Implied here is the view that no matter how low the food reserves get humans will yet find the means to subsist on something other than grass. By the same token, a goat will always finds something to eat and will not have to depend on sharp thorns.

Ouagadougou has spoilt the world! This is a theme that is current on the Ghanaian side of the international border. It relates to the attraction of that city and Burkina Faso which it symbolises to poor girls from the Ghanaian side who find it lucrative to do prostitution in Burkina Faso to survive the economic hardships of the times. However, Ouagadougou means not only unstable marriages for people like the Kasena but also death from HIV infection for wives, daughters, mothers and sisters who are compelled by circumstances to leave for Ouagadougou. In this respect "Ouagadougou" threatens the Kasena world order.

20. **Paga ya Paga, paga ya wobre.**
Paga is indeed Paga, it has swallowed.
Commentary: These are words attributed to a Moshie man who lost his money in Paga market. Relations between Kasena and Moshie have not always been cordial perhaps due to the slave raiding perpetrated by Moshie princes in pre-colonial days. As we remarked above, in the early days of the colonial encounter, before the British exercised effective control of the erstwhile Northern Territories of the Gold Coast which later became Northern Ghana and later still was segmented into the three Northern Regions, local groups waylaid and robbed Moshie traders of their merchandise. These hostilities, though sporadic rarely conducted on community basis, occasionally manifested in the form of individual acts of theft visited on unwary Moshie who attended the border market of the Paga chiefdom. To this investigator, Paga market is as safe as any other, nevertheless it has in the past received bad publicity in Navrongo too. In fact, there is a feeling that it is not safe to lower one's guard in the market place. To say to a person, *a wó bere-m Paga yaga tetare zega* (I shall teach you how to stand in the middle of Paga market) is to threaten to teach that individual some sense.

The remark in question is a lament in which a hapless Moshie man complains of the petty acts of thievery found in the Paga market. The originator of the comment is baffled by the ease with which his purse was stolen from him in broad daylight. This is the Kasena rendition of the victim's remark in the Moore language. It can be paraphrased thus, 'truly, Paga market is what they say it is, it has eaten my wealth'.

21. **Kalwoa bam laam gwori da sia mo**
The monkeys are now plucking each other's Bambara beans.
Commentary: This is meant to be a sarcastic remark and one that has wide

currency. Monkeys are notorious for the destruction they cause to bush farms, one of the reasons for the reluctance to cultivate farms outside the immediate precincts of the settlements.

Kasena have several types of farms. The *kaduga* or main farm, is the compound farm which is cultivated on permanent basis. To restore its fertility, manure from the cattle yard and the kitchen midden are used in addition to the ashes of the stubble which is burnt annually before the onset of the farming season. The *didwoɲo*, another farm, is located within the village settlement though some distance from the compound. It may have once been a compound farm. The *bwolo* is lowland that may be within the village settlement or, in any case, only a short distance from it. The bush farm may be located a couple of kilometres away from settled areas and effectively in the bushland while the *buni* is usually still further off. The *kaporo* is most likely the kind of farm that the monkeys would visit most frequently because on these farms are cultivated secondary crops like bambara beans and groundnuts which monkeys love to harvest. It is outside the settlement.

So destructive are wild animals like monkeys and elephants that Kasena have traditionally found it a bother to do farming in the bushlands. Bambara beans are much easier to lay waste because their seeds grow in a bunch close to the surface of the ground. When monkeys move they do so in troupes, which explains their potential to devastate farms. The thoroughness with which they execute their purpose would suggest to the farmer or the on-looker a degree of insensitivity that can only be associated with creatures that have no appreciation of the amount of labour and resources that have been expended on the farm. Monkeys, to Kasena may be humanlike but they are not perceived to share kinship with human beings. This is evidenced by the fact that they are eaten as meat. There is no reason therefore for any expectation that monkeys would share are sympathy with their farmers, or spare farms.

The saying in question seems to suggest that even if monkeys were capable of owning property they would not respect individual property rights and the same level of destruction that is wrought on human farms would be visited on monkey farms. Thus monkeys might look like humans but they are still wild animals.

Human beings themselves however sink occasionally to the level of monkeys or animals when they attack one another causing the kind of wanton damage which human beings are wont to attribute to wild animals like monkeys.

In many respects this saying approaches a proverb and is sometimes used as a cynical comment to point out the failure of kinship sentiment to restore solidarity or regulate behaviour of kin and associates, people who should stick by each other and who may yet occasionally be at loggerheads.

22. Kura mage lia, kura mage lia, lia de zem daa mage kura
Dog beat monkey, dog beat monkey, today may the monkey beat dog
Commentary: This saying is taken from a Kasena folktale in which the dog is for once at the monkey's mercy. The supposed speaker in this saying is the monkey which, out of satisfaction, is telling the dog that the tables have turned and the victim has become the pursuer and the pursuer the victim. During the hunt, it is customary for the hunters to call out to their dogs to chase up game and this includes the monkey troupe. The phrase *Kura mage lia* is one such call.

The saying is used in circumstances that show that the status quo has changed and roles have been reversed. It illustrates the view that no condition is permanent in life and it reflects the satisfaction that the underdog feels when there is a reversal of conditions.

23. Serekwɛ gwɛ ye kalwoŋo ni mo
The hedgehog struts while the hawk watches
Commentary: The hawk is a predatory bird that will snatch chicken, smaller birds and reptiles. A chicken requires speed to escape the hawk as it swoops down on its prey. When people observe its swoop they try to drive it away and save the chicken by making loud noises. The hedgehog would seem the ideal prey; it is solitary and does not have the benefit of the group protection unlike chicken that by their collective quacking help to protect their young. Not only does the hedgehog lack the ability to make loud noise that would deter predators it does not have the agility of movement. Nevertheless it can afford to strut along oblivious of danger. Its sharp spikes, which are a potential danger to predators, serve as its protection. Much as the hawk would love to pick such a meal, it cannot. It can only watch as a potential meal 'walks' away.

There is a comparison that could be made between the hedgehog and the tortoise. The proverb says that the sight of the latter amounts to its capture. In some respects the sight of the hedgehog is tantamount to its capture too. Since the hedgehog is not a tabooed animal children are wont to catch it and roast it for meat.

The saying captures the sense of powerlessness that can sometimes be felt when opportunities go begging because the means to exploit them does not exist or conditions prevent their exploitation.

24. Manlaa tan vei mɛmɛ se tega wó puri
Chameleon, please walk slowly so that the earth does not break

Commentary: The chameleon is one reptile that is dreaded and respected at the same time. It is considered by many to be ugly and sight of it can induces extraordinary fright in some people. Its emaciated appearance and the difficulty with which it moves recall the senility of old age and the aged ancestors. Mature or responsible people do not kill it and forbid children to kill or harm it. For some lineages it has totemic significance, while the magic of the chameleon is used to secure and protect crops, as is evidenced by its symbol on the side of granaries.

The above saying is heard used by children as they observe the reptile's unsteady movement. It seems to choose the spot on which to place its step, a manner suggesting the kind of caution which remind the observers of the fragility of an earth which could open if care were not taken. The saying is hyperbolical, as if to say, why does this creature take so much care in choosing its steps; did it suppose that a frail creature like itself could damage the tough earth if it did not walk so carefully! It is possible that the source of this saying is the common explanation that parents give to the enquiring child who wishes to know why most other small reptiles would scamper out of harm's way while the chameleon appears to strut and saunter on oblivious of danger.

25 Kukura tontoŋno
A dog for a messenger

Commentary: This saying is derived from the folktale in which God sent His two messengers, dog and goat, to mankind and the moon with two messages. One message was about life while the other concerned death. The dog was to tell mankind that the moon would suffer permanent death but man would resurrect on dying. The dog in its greed was detained by an old woman who was doing her evening's cooking. The goat brought the message that proclaimed that the moon would not die permanently but would die and resurrect, thus subjecting man to a life that would be cut short permanently by death. A similar folktale accounts for the taboo against the keeping of goats in Tano basin communities of southern Ghana, see Busia (1954).

While the goat for its crime to man became a tabooed object not to be kept in Tano basin communities, the dog earned a reputation for being an unreliable messenger, one to put his own petty interest first. As the morphology of the term *tontoŋno* suggests, a messenger is like a servant, 'one who works' for another. A message, it is expected, would be delivered in person by the dutiful messenger before any personal affairs can be attended to. Thus, anyone who consents to act as another's messenger but subsequently sees fit to place personal interests before the mission becomes an unreliable messenger, a *kukura tontoŋno*.

26. **Yera ba lage bɛɛsem, Patoyoro.**
The body does not like rough treatment
Commentary: The man, Patoyoro, used to make his rounds to places where people gathered to drink millet beer. He was willing to accept the butt of jokes cracked by merrymakers at his expense in the expectation that they would buy him a drink or give him money for a meal. Though this man was not obese, he did look like somebody who could do with some physical exercise. His physical appearance suggested one who enjoyed leisure by reason of exposure to wealth. The lot of an illiterate person in Kasena society is farming which is not only physically demanding and energy sapping but stressful due to the precariousness of agricultural work in this ecological zone. Patoyoro was a pitiable sight however. He had no wife, no real home, no job and he seemed to depend on charity and whatever menial chores market women might ask him to do for a pittance. He was an enigma in many people's eyes and people did not fail to ask why he could not find more reputable work than to hang around local beer drinking spots. His invariable reply was that "the body resented hard physical work", by which he meant traditional farming chores. This sounded ridiculous to people who at the same time pitied his condition.

27. **Wɛ taa cho Gween**
May God protect Gween
Commentary: This is a statement attributed to a midget who used to live off the Navrongo market in the 1970s; as he has since ceased to come to the market it can be assumed that he is no longer alive. He grew up in one of the clan-settlements of the Paga chiefdom and came to Navrongo in the 1970s where his diminutive stature attracted public interest. He was known to market attendants to have a good nature. The name Gween is unusual and probably began as a nickname which describes his small stature. Midgets are not a common sight among Kasena, perhaps due to the traditional practices that eliminated children with congenital deformities earlier in infancy. Such infants were regarded as *chuchuru* in status, that is to say, masquerading diminutive spirits, *chichiri,* who posed a danger to humans. A person such as Gween would not only be a sight to people who were unfamiliar with such persons but a feared individual as well, since *chuchuru* are believed to have spiritual powers and are deemed to be dangerous. It must have come as a relief for the public to see Gween interact and comport himself in a harmless way. Most people came to see him as good natured *chuchuru,* (*chuchur-ywoŋo* **or** *chuchur-bɔŋɔ*) nonetheless.

Gween was known to repeat this statement on several occasions and it soon became his pet phrase. The context of his remarks are unknown to this writer, nor is it possible to recover the context, now that Gween himself is no more. We can guess that people would proposition a jovial midget as a way of teasing him and getting him to say anything funny. Gween would have brushed aside these suggestions by a phrase like the above which could be paraphrased as "God forbid this eventuality ever happening to Gween". It is not unusual for Kasena people to attribute a reprieve of any kind to God's doing by citing the phrase *Wɛ taa cho* (May God save me). We find this phrase even in personal names as in the name *Awechega* (my God has protected me).

28.   **Yaga dɛ ba jege chega**
       There is no truth on market day
Commentary: This is a saying which comes close to being a proverb but must be excluded because it seems to lack the semblance of antiquity that Kasena associate with proverbs. It would also seem awkward to restate this proverb as, "The men of old in their wisdom remarked that there is no truth on market day". This is so because market culture has changed considerably since pre-colonial times. Not only have some present day markets grown in size, they now are able to attract marketeers from all over the country. Navrongo and Paga markets attract traders from southern Ghana and the Republic of Burkina Faso. This cosmopolitan character has inevitably made marketing more formal and given to it an anonymity unknown prior to the colonial era.

   The market day in the Kasena-Nankana area falls due every three days. In former times the market might have been a small local affair lasting from about 5 p.m to 6 p.m. This suited the local catchment communities of the market. The hours enabled the villagers to do their farming and other chores before going to the market place in the late afternoon. This characteristic of the traditional market is amply suggested by the evidence of the minor rural markets that continue to be held in a similar fashion, like Kajeilo market located some five kilometers from Navrongo town. Today, a big market like Navrongo or Paga market is a far from leisurely affair. It draws crowds from far and near and every marketeer is busy going about his or her business. This includes not only buying and selling but even more importantly, socialising. Whatever the purpose for going to the market, people take the opportunity to drink and to get drunk on millet beer. There is the belief that the best millet beer is brewed on market day. In comparison with everyday routine conduct, marketing has made marketeers unpredictable and unreliable on market days.

   The saying in question is referring specifically to the fact that most people would be likely to be under some influence of alcohol and might take decisions that they did not intend to keep, or they might not recollect having taken those decisions or engaged in those discussions the particular market day.

29. Kukula jene ba di
It is not wise to be indebted to Kukula

Commentary: Kukula is the name of a river god located in the small chiefdom of Kayoro which lies to the west of the other Kasena-Nankana chiefdoms. The home or shrine of this god is on a tributary of the Sisila river which is itself one of the tributaries of the White Volta. This god is widely known in the Kasena-Nankana district and beyond, and its reputation attracts visitors and supplicants from southern Ghana who seem to believe that Kukula is capable of providing its supplicants with untold wealth. The supplicant makes a pact with the god, such as the one described by Dittmer (1961) to have taken place between Wusiga and Goli. To get the river god to carry out its end of the bargain the supplicant makes an outrageous promise. Kasena believe that Kukula sticks to its promises and where supplicants fail to settle their end of the bargain the god is not slow to exact full vengeance. In more than one case, rumours circulating within communities attributed deaths through drowning to pacts with river gods initiated by the kin of the deceased. The rumours suggest that either supplicants involved actually pledged the lives of the deceased kin or failing to carry out their side of the bargain, the river which felt it has been crossed did not fail to exact the ultimate price for the failure to repay the debts owed to the river gods.

30. N ná nɛ swa n nɛ ndwoŋ tei ne
If you are wise in the ways of the world, you learnt your lesson from another.

Commentary: Wisdom from the Kasena point of view may be put to negative or selfish uses or for the benefit of the individual and others. The latter is *swa-goa* (lit. 'Wisdom that kills') and its synonym is *woporo* (lit. the clearing of the inside) and *yeporo* (lit. the opening of the eyes). *Swa* as a concept is thus ambivalent and ambiguous. The man of "wisdom" is distinguished from the thoughtful person who considers the consequences of his actions on himself and on others.

Wisdom in a general sense is not the preserve of one individual and Kasena illustrate this in the play song entitled *Chakana Pɛ Yeilu Goo* in which they sing:: **swa yam do do** (wisdom surpasses wisdom). People learn from each other.

In this saying, *swa* refers to wisdom used solely for the benefit of the individual. The saying maintains that such wisdom derives from negative experiences. It is negative encounters at which an individual has been taken for a ride that open the eyes and make a person to look out for his personal interest at the expense of others.

31. Yiru we o lane wo o ba ne mo
The Genet cat says its beauty is in its neck

Commentary: The Genet cat is commonly referred to as a fox by some educated Kasena, perhaps because the early British administrators saw a resemblance between the fox and the Genet cat. This cat, which lives in the bushlands in the immediate precincts of the settlements, is dreaded as a predator of poultry. It is bigger that the domestic cat which it resembles. The perceived difference between it and the domestic cat lies in the longer neck of the former. A long neck is seen sometimes as appealing aesthetically and in this case a mark of beauty. The saying maintains that the Genet cat takes pride its neck.

32. Ko wó nwoɲi san-yiga naa birakɔga!
Where will it come from, west or east!

This is a saying that is no longer attributable to a named individual, perhaps because of its antiquity. It dates back to the time when ethnic, inter-chiefdom and clan warfare was rampant and slave raiders were about. Life then, for the male especially, was precarious, as a man has to bear arms when called upon to defend his people.

The comment is believed to have been uttered by to a woman who felt that, unlike her co-wife who did not have sons, her future security was assured. She taunted her co-wife whenever she felt like it. She would climb onto her mud-thatched roof and as she relaxed sitting on the perimeter wall, she would repeat this remark to the hearing of her colleague. Her self-assurance stemmed from the fact that she had several strong sons, whereas her colleague had only married daughters living with their husbands in the latter's clan-settlements. The married daughters would pay the occasional visit but they were not always on hand when their mother needed assistance. For the mother of sons, her every wish was seen to by her able sons.

The above saying's statement of contempt for the mother of daughters can be paraphrased thus: 'poverty and insecurity are alien; how could I ever feel insecurity; where would misfortune come from, east or west, given that I have sons to protect me from adversity!'

As fortune would have it, it is recounted, one day there was a call to arms as the village was being attacked. The able-bodied men rushed to arms. At the end of the day the sons of the proud co-wife lay dead, leaving her childless. Thereafter, there was no one to farm for her or see to her needs. By a stroke of irony she became dependent on her co-wife, whose daughters and sons-in-law came over occasionally to assist the widows.

The saying has the quality of a proverb, since it is cited not to induce laughter and merriment but to advice against those who in their complacency laugh at their unfortunate neighbours because they have not been able to have sons or because fortune has not smiled on them.

For some individuals, failure to have at least one son is tragic and husbands have remarried or taken additional wives in the hope that a son would eventually be born. Though mothers themselves like to have daughters, they prefer sons since sons guarantee their rights and privileges in their husband's settlement, especially after the death of the husband.

Specifically, it counsels that although kinship and marriage norms may favour the woman who had given birth to sons in this patrilineal society where 'father-right' counts for much, nevertheless, a person who has been lucky to have sons should not ridicule those who have not been favoured with sons. Sons may seem more valuable to a parent but there are also those conditions where it would seem more beneficial to have daughters rather than sons.

33. **Woro ná ye woro, ko wó yi Awoŋa ba de**
    If the shade is our ancestral shade, it should reach Awonga and company

Commentary: this is a quotation from the folktale. In the folktale in question, one of the characters, Awoŋa, the duiker, sat in the sun and had to be invited into the shade. This he declined saying that if indeed his ancestors wished him to enjoy the shade, they would make the shade come his way. As if by some magic wrought by the ancestors, the shade accordingly moved to where he sat to everybody's consternation.

The statement is quoted mostly in jokes to suggest that what is a person's due will sure come to him or her even if the person did not actively pursue the benefit. The statement corresponds with a view that destiny has a hand in human affairs and brings to pass the good things that happen to individuals. This is enshrined in the concept of *ni wudiu* (mouth food).

34. **N go n nɛ n fwɛ n wo go n nɛ n fwɛ**
    Kill and you suffer for it but if you don't kill, you pay all the same

Commentary: This saying describes a certain wild animal, *namalesiga*, that some Kasena say it is taboo to kill and for this reason the animal is said to be a nuisance to hunters. It is said be to found in the company of game, although it is not itself regarded as fair game. Comments suggest that this animal shields the other game in the sense that it is all over the place running around and mingling with the other animals and therefore making it risky to fire at the safe animals. Should it be killed accidentally the unfortunate hunter responsible for its death must undergo expensive rituals to cleanse himself and his kin.

To add to the myth surrounding the *namalesiga*, it is described as having four pairs of legs, i.e. eight legs in all. It is said to run on one set of four but when tired it would lift the tired legs and bring down the fresh set as a replacement. Some accounts relate the saying above to this animal.

The saying in question is cited in jokes to describe the quandary in which a person finds himself when action and inaction have both negative results for the individual.

35. Naao maa zoore puuri
   The cow is entering into the midden

Commentary: This is another quotation from a folktale. Here, the trickster, Nase has deceived his friend and adversary the hyena to kill his livestock for both to feast. When it came to his turn, Nase who did not wish to share his cow with hyena cut the cow's tail and stuck it in the kitchen midden. He then sent for hyena and told him the cow had disappeared into the kitchen midden leaving only its tail which he Nase had managed to hang on to. Naturally, hyena pushed away Nase, the weaker party and tugged at the tail pulling it out. He took away the tail satisfied that Nase may have lost a cow but he had at least retrieve its tail.

People quote this saying at each other as a jocular way of telling an associate that hurry is necessary if one is not to lose one's share to others who might be only too eager to claim that share.

36. Wudiiru wɛ boŋi n nakɔ, kana wɛ ye boŋi n nakɔ
   In times of plenty invite your sister, in famine times don't invite your sister

Commentary: these are the words that are matched to a popular tune played on the *kaako*, a flute hollowed out of the guinea corn millet stalk by shepherd boys for their entertainment. The flute is special in the sense that it is made and used around October and November when the guinea corn has produced sturdy stalks that can be hollowed for this purpose. This is also the time of plenty, *faao ni*, as Kasena call it, when most crops would have reached the stage where they can be harvested[18].

The tune is an ironical comment on kinship and brother-sister relations. It suggests that sibling love is conditional. People profess their love for their sisters when they have the means to maintain them. In times of plenty, they do not mind having a married sister and her children come to stay and might not see the need to persuade a sister who has returned home because of marital problems to leave for her conjugal home. However, when food reserves are low a brother's primary loyalty is to his own immediate family i.e. wife and children, and then brothers are not enthusiastic to share the little that there is with their married sisters. Then they see the need to persuade an estranged wife to reconcile with her husband and stay with him.

37. **Baleiga we twio diinim mo chamma se ko tuum ba chamm, n ná tu tu n ga n para n to tega ne mu!**
The lizard says it the climbing that is the problem and no the descent, if you have difficulty coming down you simply drop to the ground, mu!

Commentary: The lizard is ubiquitous in Kasena compounds. Unlike the house mouse it does not live inside the dwelling units, nor is it a nuisance to anyone. Children may hunt it but adults ignore it. It is one reptile whose habits are easily observed.

Kasena observe the ease with which the lizard scales the walls and the trees. Easier still is its descent from the heights. It either runs down or jumps down. In jumping down it seems to say why bother to take your time or waste time when you can just jump it. The logic of this saying seems to be that the ascent may be difficult as weight must be lifted. The effort demands bravery, skill and determination, not to mention the pain involved as in the case of the one who maintains that the top will be reached if it means that the laceration of the skin on the belly, see proverb # 246 above. In the case of descent, gravity beckons to the dropping object; it requires no exertion on a person's part, only the pain of the fall and perhaps a fractured limb to nurse.

This saying has not been observed applied in a proverbial context; its use is limited to the skills of the lizard.

38. **Baleiga we nabiina ná baa tei omo, o wó tei otete**
The lizard maintains that if humans will not praise him he will praise himself

Commentary: this saying is related to the previous one, # 37 which remarks on the behaviour of the lizard and its acrobatics. The stunts of the lizard should deserve recognition and praise from observers, especially as man is only too aware of the energy and determination is takes to scale heights and to fall from heights. Such stunts are praiseworthy, if they were performed by humans. They fail to impress because humans do not care for reptiles that they do not breed. As humans would not congratulate the lizard, the lizard my blow its own horn.

This saying is based again on an observation of the behaviour of the lizard. It drops from an elevated position and lying where it fell, it nods its head as though in self congratulation for a wonderful feat. The saying can have general application as a proverb. It is used to justify the need for the individual whose feats have not been duly recognised by society to seek glory. Society is not always fair to all in its allocation of merit and praises. Who you are does determine how much recognition and acclaim society will heap on the individual.

39. **Siseira we omo wó fo fea o yage Wɛ yibia ne, o maa jwoori o fo fea o yage otete yibia ne.**
The house bat says it will urinate onto God's face but it only managed to urinate on its own face.

Commentary: the term *siseira* refers to both the wall gecko and a species of small bat that lives inside the inner chamber of the Kasena huts. The is usually active at night Unlike other species of bat this type is not eaten by Kasena. Like the mouse, there does not seem to be a taboo that forbids the eating of the *siseira* bat. Nevertheless, the bat is a nuisance and its nuisance value is based on the fact that it urinates on people causing blisters and swellings on the parts of the body the urine has touched.

The source of the saying is not known but it might as well have been derived from one of the Kasena folktales. The saying is aimed at portraying the irreverent and the ridiculous. It is deemed arrogant and futile for any creature of God to attempt to fight God and inflict harm on God. The bat seems to attempt the impossible hanging head down and bottom up. Its urine cannot defy the laws of nature. Therefore the urine that it passes cannot be directed at God and the sky above but must descent and soil bat's own face.

End Notes

1. The etymology of this place name does not seem to confirm that Butu, its founder, spoke Nankani. While Navrongo is clearly an Anglicisation of the Nankani name /navɔrʊŋɔ/ which is itself possibly the Nankani version for the Kasem /navɔrɔ/, the explanation and associated etymology suggested by St John Parsons informants viz [naga vɔrɔ], comprises a Kasem word for leg plus a Kasem ideophone that captures the sound made when the dry crunchy soil breaks under the weight of the human foot.

2. Formal divorce is a rare phenomena among the Kasena. Women may return to their parents and subsequently remarry but they are rarely divorced formally, even where the husband has lost interest in his wife. This is because a formal divorce has wider repercussions and can damage relations between the affinal lineages involved. Where the marriage has produced issues these can be claimed by the woman's family in the event of a formal divorce accompanied by return of bridewealth goods.

3. Bowill refers to groundnuts in West Africa as, "... a plant of Latin American origin, its cultivation was first actively encouraged by the French in Senegal in the 1840s, and by the 1920s it had been introduced to all the countries of the Western Soudan". Kasena have varieties of the crop that seem indigenous and they certain have cultivated the crop long before the British arrived. Its place in the domestic economy seems well established though it does not enjoy the measure of importance associated with the traditional grains.

4. The Zegna are the migrants from Zekko country which is believed to be across the international boundary in what is now Burkina Faso today.

5. Legend has it that in the case of Navrongo, there was a time when three brothers claimed the office when it became vacant with the death of their father, the previous incumbent. Rather than initiate an active contest for the office, with its potential disruptive consequences, the two powerful senior brothers decided that they should ask their younger brother to take the office since he stood to benefit most from the income that the office would generate, being poorer than his siblings. This is a

legend which is echoed in other Kasena traditions and is sometimes used to illustrate the view that the people of old allowed an altruism rather than personal ambition, to influence their behaviours.

6. In times of drought when all ancestral intercessions have failed to induce rain Kasena have been known to accept the prayerful interventions of the White Fathers. The comments that are being referred to here do not in anyway assign the credit for rainfall at this time to the prayers of the White Fathers. On the contrary, the impression is that rains were more regular in the past, especially where the first rains were concerned. One does not get the impression that the miraculous achievements of the White fathers, reported by Rev Fr McCoy (1988) in the early days of their mission in the Upper West, were replicated in the Upper East.

7. In ancestral invocations it is customary to call one's ancestors by name, taunt them and exhibit skepticism about their powers, all this as a means of provoking the ancestors and coercing them to respond to a demand. A man may say something like this: "My father Adoa, if indeed you exist let me see evidence. Do this... for me and I shall reward you with a goat".

8. This has been observed from some young girls. Children born and bred outside the Kasem speaking areas have difficulty matching the correct determiners to their nominals. For example, "*chworo kom*" (the hen) can become "*chworo kam*". Five year olds do not make these kinds of errors and when a person who ought to be fully competent in the mother tongue makes such mistakes the audience can only conclude that a person might be a second language speaker.

9. When this researcher was young it used to be believed that palm trees grew on the heads of elephants, a fiction that goes back to the portrayal of an elephant standing by a palm tree in a West African Currency Board shilling coin.

10. In the folktale Ayiying, the prince, who rejected all the women his father found him to wed was claimed forcibly by a half-bodied spirit agent for a husband. It pursued the hero who sought shelter with kin and friends alike but all abandoned him as none would confront the spirit on his behalf. In the end he returned to his father and would not be bothered by the wailing of the spirit. His father responded to the situation by preparing a bon-fire to incinerate the spirit at a public event with all his subjects watching. Having found that the half-bodied creature had not only transformed into a beautiful maid but had also endowed his son with incredible wealth, the chief ordered that this son be burnt instead. This having been carried out the spirit wife revived her husband by ululating three times and calling her truly beloved husband by name resurrected him to the amazement of all. Then the chief's beloved wife, in imitation of the

spirit, ordered that her husband too be thrown into the fire to burn. It was done but her ululations yielded no dividend and so she lost a husband.

11. The exact date for the opening of the Post Office in Navrongo is not known to this researcher but it is not too far fetched to suggest the 1940s or even earlier.

12. Interestingly, the concept of *ni wonnu* implies good things that are destined to come one's way.

13. Pɛ Kwara was chief at the time of the setting up of a British colonial station in Navrongo in 1905. He died about 1917 and was succeeded by Pɛ Awe. Colonial Records in the National Archives of Ghana (NA-G) ADM 63/4/1 which discuss some appeals from the Native Courts show Chinatera making a claim that Awe had inherited 130 cattle on Kwara's death. Pɛ Koratia [sic] but pronounced as /kədətwə/, Kwara's predecessor left no family cattle, according to the testimony of Pɛ Adda, Kwara's grandson, on account of the predatory activities of the Zambarma slave raiders. Kwara on the other hand, "sold hoes .. and bought cattle again for the family. He also bought private cattle".

14. What all this has to do with the *luga* bird is not clear to me.

15. The *pepara* hunt can be in two forms - the informal, non-ritual type whose objective is to hunt for game. True *pepara* is however a ritual that is regulated and takes place occasionally under the authority of the master of the *pepara*. It is dictated by the outcome of a seance.

16. This author was once rebuked for holding a calabash with *sana* (millet beer) in his left hand while drinking from it. In some contexts this could be interpreted as a show of arrogance or an assertion of power to withstand sorcery attacks, a dangerous thing to do indeed.

17. The word *gwoɲina* (the herders) derives from the verb *gwoɲi*, "to drive" or "to herd cattle or other livestock". It may be that in former times this was also the occasion when the wife's brothers claimed the cattle due and drove them home. Today it is the occasion when the affines made their formal request for bridewealth. Once the groom's family accepts to present the items requested the visiting affines are content to received gifts of cooked and fresh meat and various other gifts.

18. *Fani* (lit. mouth of *faao*) or *faawɛ* (lit. time of *faao*) is the harvest season and lasts from about early October to mid November when most crops growing on the compound farms, including the guinea corn, would have been gathered in and active farming would be considered over. The harvest feast, *faao*, known to the Bulsa as *fiok*, could be celebrated anytime between November and January, depending on the head of each individual minor lineage whose members dwell in a compound. In the past, *Faao* was not celebrated jointly by members of a chiefdom, unlike today, nor did every family hold it every year. Its celebration was

contingent upon several factors, including whether the harvest met the family's expectations and whether family members have enjoyed good health in the course of the year. This is because *faao* was regarded as essentially a thanksgiving rite.

Bibiography

Abrahams R D.   1972, "Proverbs and Proverbial Expressions" in Dorson R M ed, **Folklore and Folklife**, An Introduction, Chicago, Univ of Chicago Press

Achebe Chinua 1958, **Things Fall Apart** Heinemann Educational Books Ltd

Adonadaga C. 1972, **Sensole Kukui**, Bureau of Ghana Languages, Accra

Adongo P B, J F Phillips, and F N Binka 1998, "The Influence of Traditional Religion on Fertility Regulation among the Kasena-Nankana of Northern Ghana" **Studies in Family Planning**, vol. 29, no. 1 Pp. 23-40

Agalic J. 1983, **Buli Yam Saka Wamagisima: Proverbs of the Bulsa** Inst of African Studies, University of Ghana

Atadana J. 1987, **Kasena Funeral Rites**

Awedoba A K. 1979, Nominal Classes and Nominal Concord in Kasem M.A Thesis submitted to the Inst of African Studies of the University of Ghana, Legon

1980, 'Borrowed Nouns in Kasem Nominal Classes' **Anthropological Linguistics** vol.22 no.6 pp 247-53

1985 **Aspects of Wealth and Exchange Among the Kasena-Nankana of Ghana**, D. Phil Thesis submitted to University of Oxford, Britain

1989a, 'Notes on Matrimonial Goods Among the Atoende Kusasi' in **Research Review** Vol.5 No.1

1989b, 'Matrimonial Goods Among the Atoende Kusasi: Contingent Prestations' in **Research Review** Vol.5 no.2 pp 1-17

1993, *The Phonetics and Phonology of Kasem as Research Review Supplement* 7: 109 pages: Institute of African Studies, Univ of Ghana, Legon

1996, 'Kasem Nominal Genders and Names', **Research Review** new series, vol 12, nos. 1 and 2 p.8-24

Barker P. 1986, **Peoples, Languages and Religion in Northern Ghana** Asempa Publ, Accra

Bendor-Samuel J T. 1970 'Niger-Congo, Gur' in **Current Trends in Linguistics** vol. 7, 141-178

Bloch M. 1973, The Long Term and the Short Term: the Economic and Political Significance of the Morality of Kinship **The Character of Kinship** (ed) J Goody pp 75-87

Bohannan L. 1970, 'Political Aspects of Tiv Social Organization' in **Tribes Without Rulers** eds Middleton J and Tait D pp 33-66

Bohannan P. 1955, 'Some Principles of Exchange and Investment among the Tiv' **Amer Anthr** 57 pp. 60-70

Bonvini Emilio 1987, 'La bouche entre la parale et l'insulte. L'exemple du Kasem (Burkina Faso)' pp. 149-159, **Journal des africanistes** vol. 57 no. 1-2

Bradbury R E. 1957, The Benin Kingdom and the Edo-speaking Peoples of Southwestern Nigeria, **Ethnographic Survey of Africa** W. A Part xiii, IAI

Brookman-Amissah J. 1986, "Akan Proverbs about Death" **Anthropos** 81, p. 75-85

Busia K A. 1954, 'The Ashanti' in **African Worlds**(ed) D. Forde I.A.I p.190-209.

Cardinall A.W. 1921, **The Natives of the Northern Territories of the Gold Coast.** (Their Customs, Religion and Folklore) London, Routledge and Son.

Dalfovo A T. 1991, "Lugbara Proverbs and Ethics" in **Anthropos** 86 Pp. 45-58

n.d **Lugbara Proverbs**, Bibliotheca Comboniana, IAL Rome

De Carbo E.A. 1977, **Artistry among the Kasem Speaking Peoples of Northern Ghana.** Unpubl Ph.D. dissertation, Indiana University, Ann Arbor, Michigan.

Der G B. 1980, 'God and Sacrifice in the Traditional Religion of the Kasena and Dagaba of Northern Ghana' **Journal of Religion in Africa** XI, 3 (Leiden), 172-187

Dittmer K. 1961, **Die sakralen Hauptlinge der Gurunsi im Obervolta-Gebiet. Westafrika.** Mitteilungen aus dem Museum fur Volker-kunde in Hamburg, vol. XXVII. Hamburg: Cram de Gruyter.

Domowitz Susan 1992, "Wearing Proverbs: Anyi Names for Printed Factory Cloth" in **African Arts**, vol. xxv, no. 3 Pp. 82-87 + 104

Durkheim, E. 1947, **Division of Labour in Society**, Glencoe Free Press

Eyre-Smith St J. 1933, A Brief Review of the History and Social

Organisation of the Peoples of the Northern Territories of the Gold Coast, Accra

Ferguson P. 1972, **Islamization in Dagbon: A Study of the Alfanema of Yendi** Unpubl Ph D thesis (Microfilm), Cambridge University, Cambridge

Finnegan, Ruth 1970, **Oral Literature in Africa**, Oxford University Press, London

Fortes M. 1940, 'The Political System of the Tallensi of Northern Territories of the Gold Coast' in **African Political Systems** (eds) M. Fortes and E.E. Evans-Pritchard, OUP/IAI.

1969, **The Dynamics of Clanship Among the Tallensi** Anthropological Publications, Oosterbort N.B. The Netherlands, and O.U.P.

1969, **Kinship and the Social Order** Chicago, Aldine

1987,'The Concept of Person' in M. Fortes, **Religion Morality and the Person** pp 218-28: ed J Goody

1987b, 'Coping with Destiny' in M. Fortes, **Religion Morality and the Person** p144-174: ed J Goody

Fortes M and E. E. Evans-Pritchard eds.1940, **African Political Systems**, OUP Oxford

Gagnon C.1945a, 'Les Kassenes: Croyance sur Dieu' Missions d'Afrique 41, 4

1945a, 'Les Kassenes: Culte des ancetres' Missions d'Afrique 41, 9

1956, **Moeurs et Coutumes Indigenes** Mission du Navrongo. Navrongo Catholic Mission, Unpubl. Typescript.

Gelb I J. 1952, **A Study of Writing**, University of Chicago Press, Chicago

Goody E N. 1972, '"Greeting", "begging", and the presentation of respect' in **The Interpretation of Ritual** ed. J.S. LaFontaine, Tavistock Publ.

Goody J. 1977, 'Population and Polity in the Voltaic Region' in Friedman J and Rowlands M **The Evolution of Social Systems** (Research Seminar in Archaeology and related subjects)

(ed) 1958, **The Developmental Cycle in the Domestic Group** Cambridge Papers in Social Anthropology, No1. Cambridge, CUP

Gyekye Kwame 1995, **An Essay on African Philosophical Thought**, The Akan conceptual scheme. Revised edition, Temple University Press, Philadelphia

Hart, Keith 1971, Migration and Tribal Identity Among the Frafras of Ghana' **Journal of Asian and African Studies** vol vi pp 21-36

1978, 'The Economic Basis of Tallensi Social History' in Dalton ed **Research in Economic Anthropology** pp 186-216

Harris Grace 1962, 'Taita Bridewealth and Affinal Relationship' in **Marriage in Tribal Societies** ed M Fortes Cambridge Papers in Social Anthropology no. 3

Harruna K. n.d., **Child Training in Nogesinia (Navrongo)** Diss. Inst of Ed, Univ Coll of Ghana, 195 pages, mss

Hertz, Robert 1960, **Death and the Right Hand**, transl by Rodney and Claudia Needham, Cohen and West

Hinds J H. 1947, 'Cowries v Cash. A Currency Problem' The West African Review

Holden J J. 1965, 'The Zabarima Conquest of N-W Ghana' Part I **Transactions of the Historical Society of Ghana** vol. VIII, pp 60-86

Howell, Allison 1987, 'Marriage Practices Among the Kasena of Northern Ghana' unpublished typescript

1996, **The Religious Itinerary of a Ghanaian People** Peter Lang, Frankfurtam Main

Kaba, A R A. 1958, **Six Studies of Children in two Sections of Navrongo town.** Diss. Inst of Ed, Univ Coll of Ghana, 113 pages, typescript

Kazaresam A.E. 1975,**The Kasena of Ghana and Pastoral Approach** Dissertation presented to Lumen Vitae International Institute of Catechetics and Pastoral, Catholic University of Louvain, Bruxelles

Kröger F. 1980, The Friend of the Family or the Pok Nong Relation of the Bulsa in Northern Ghana, **Sociologus**, 30,2, pp 153-165

1984, 'The Notion of the Moon in the calendar and religion of the Bulsa (Ghana)' **Systemes de penseé cahier** 7 pp 149-151

1992, **Buli-English Dictionary** Research on African Languages and Cultures vol 1, Lit verlag, Munster

Kropp-Dakubu M E. ed. 1988, **The Languages of Ghana** Kegan Paul International for IAI

Kumedzro, R U. 1972, 'The Influence of Disease on Population Growth and Distribution in the Kasena-Nankani District - Upper Region, **The Geographer** 1, 1 pp 38-52

Lewis I M. 1975, 'The Nation, State, and Politics in Somalia' in **The Search for National Integration in Africa** eds Smock and Bentsi-Enchill, The Free Press, New York

Liberski D. 1984, "Note sur le calendrier Kasena" **Systemes de Pensee en Afrique Noire**, Cahier 7 p. 100 -120

1991, Les Dieux du territoire. Unité et morcellement de l'espace en pays Kasena (Burkina Faso), These du 3eme cycle, Paris

1994, Le Lin Défait: le deuil et ses rites III **Systemes de penseé en**

Afrique noire, 13 ed D Liberski

Liberski-Bagnoud D. 1996, La Lame du Couteau et la mort Amere: Violence funéraire, initiation et homicide en pays kasena (Burkina Faso). destins de meurtriers, **Systemes de pensee en Afrique noire** 14

Lombard C. 1984, La place des femmes dans la société traditionelle, l'expérience de la société Kasena de la Haute-Volta. Diplome des Hautes Etudes des Pratiques Sociales, Université Lyon II, Lyon

Lynn C W. 1937, **Agriculture in North Mamprusi** Bulletin No 34, Accra

Manessy G. 1969, **Les Langues gurunsi** (2 vols.) Bibliothèque de la SELAF, nos. 12-13. Paris: Klincksiek

    1975, **Les langues oti-volta**. Langues et civilisations à tradition orale, no. 15. Paris: Société d'Études Linguistiques et Anthropologiques de France (SELAF).

Mauss M. 1970, **The Gift: Forms and Functions of Exchange in Archaic Societies** Routledge and Kegan Paul (Routledge Paperback)

McCoy R F. 1988, **Great Things Happen**, A personal memoir of the first Christian missionary among the Dagaabas and Sissalas of northwest Ghana, Society of Missionaries of Africa, Montreal

Mendonsa E L. 1978, "Etiology and Divination Among the Sisala of Northern Ghana" **Journal of Religion in Africa** vol. IX, fasc. 1 Pp. 33-50

Mission de Notre Dame De Sept Douleurs 1906 **Diari de Navarro 1906-1946** 2 Vols.

Naden A T. 1988, 'The Gur Languages' **The Languages of Ghana** ed. M E Kropp Dakubu, Kegan Paul International IAI pp 12-49

Naden, Dianne and Tony Naden, 1991,'Polygyny: Further Factors from Mamprusi' **Amer Anthrop** vol. 93 no. 4 Pp. 948-950

Needham R. 1967, 'Right and Left in Nyoro Symbolic Classification' in **Africa** 37 pp 425-51

    198? **Right and Left: Essays on Dual Symbolic Classification** Chicago: University of Chicago Press

    1975, 'Polythetic Classification', MAN vol 10, No. 3

Nwachukwu-Agbada J O J. 1994, "The Proverb in the Igbo Milieu" Anthropos 89, Pp. 194-200

Obeng, S G. 1996, The Proverb as Mitigating and Politeness Strategy in Akan Discourse" **Anthropological Linguistics** vol. 38, no. 3 p. 521-549

Olson H S. 1981, "The Place of Traditional Proverbs in Pedagogy", **African Theological Journal** vol 10 no. 2 Pp. 26-35

Parsons St John D. 1958, **Legends of Northern Ghan**a Longmans Green
    1960, **More Legends of Northern Ghana**, Longmans Green
Plissart X P B. 1983, **Mamprusi Proverbs** Museé Royal de l'Afrique
    Centrale-Tervuren, Belgique, Archives d'Anthropologie no 111
Radcliffe-Brown A R. 1950, "Introduction", **African Systems of
    Kinship and Marriage** eds Radcliffe-Brown and Forde D
Rattray R S. 1914, **Ashanti Proverbs** Clarendon Press, Oxford
    1932 **The Tribes of the Ashanti Hinterland** Clarendon Press,
    Oxford 2 vols
Rigby P. 1968, 'Joking Relationships, Kin Categories and Clanship
    Among the Gogo' in **Africa** 38 No.2 pp.133-155
Sahlins M. 1972, **Stone Age Economics**, Tavistock Publications
Siran, Jean-Louis, 1993, "Rhetoric, Tradition and Communication: The
    Dialectics of meaning in Proverb use" in **MAN** (ns) vol. 28, no.2,
    Pp225-242
Tamakloe A F. 1931, **A Brief History of the Dagomba People**, Accra
Tauxier L 1912, **Le noir du Sudan** Paris Larose
Tengan E. 1990, "The Sisala Universe: Its Composition and Structure",
    Journal of Religion in Africa XX, no. 1, Pp. 2-19
Turner Victor, 1969, **The Ritual Process; Structure and Anti-structure**
    Routledge and Kegan Paul, London
Teviu C B A. 1963, 'Courtship and Marriage Among the Kasem People
    of Upper Region' **Legonite** 17-19
Van der Geest, Sjaak, 1996, "The elder and his elbow: twelve
    interpretations of an Akan proverb", **Research in African
    Literatures**, vol. 27, no. 3
Vansina J. 1962, "A Comparison of African Kingdoms", **Africa** 32, p.
    324-335
Veblen T. 1970, **The Theory of the Leisure Class** (An Economic Study
    of Institutions) London Unwin Books
Wedjong S P. 1969, **Kasena Sinseri,** Bureau of Ghana Languages,
    ACCRA
    1969, **Kasena Nabaara Le**, Bureau of Ghana Languages, ACCRA
    1970, **Kasena Lui De Lusei**, Bureau of Ghana Languages, ACCRA
    1970, **Kem Laaro Tӡoŋa**, Bureau of Ghana Languages, ACCRA
    1975, **Kwɛɛra Tɔnɔ**, Bureau of Ghana Languages, ACCRA
Welsch R L. 1992, "Dueling Proverbs" **Natural History**, 4 p. 68
Yaguibou T. 1967, 'Le lévirat en pays Kasséna et lobi' Rev jurid et polit
    21, 1 pp 64-75
Yankah K. 1986, "Proverb Rhetoric and African Judicial Processes: The
    Untold Story" **Journal of American Folklore** vol.99, no. 393 p.

280-303
Zajaczkowski, Andrzej, 1967, "Dagomba, Kassena-nankani and Kusasi of Northern Ghana" **Africana Bulletin**
Zwernemann J. 1958, "Shall we use Gurunsi" **Africa** 28 pp 123-125
1963, "Remarques preliminaires sur le verbe du Kasem et du Nuna" **Actes du Second Colloque International de linguistique Negro-Africaine,** Dakar pp 191-199
1964, 'Divination chez les Kasena en Haute-Volta' l.F.A.N 102 pp 58-61
1967, 'Kasem Dialects in the Polyglotta Africana' **African Language Review** 6 pp 128-152
1990, 'Ancestors, Earth and Fertility in the belief of some Voltaic Peoples', **The Creative Communion: African Folk Models of Fertility and the Regeneration of Life,** eds. Anita Jacobson-Widding and Walter van Beek, Pp. 93-109

Index